MW01087644

Criminal Justice
Recent Scholarship

Edited by
Nicholas P. Lovrich

A Series from LFB Scholarly

Intelligence-Led Policing
A Policing Innovation

Jeremy G. Carter

LFB Scholarly Publishing LLC
El Paso 2013

Library of Congress Cataloging-in-Publication Data

Library of Congress Cataloging-in-Publication Data

Carter, Jeremy G., 1982-
  Intelligence-led policing : a policing innovation / Jeremy G. Carter.
    pages cm. -- (Criminal justice: recent scholarship)
  Includes bibliographical references and index.
  ISBN 978-1-59332-627-2 (hardcover : alk. paper)
  1. Law enforcement--United States. 2. Intelligence service--United
States. 3. Crime prevention--United States. I. Title.
  HV8139.C37 2013
  363.2'3--dc23
                                          2013014115

ISBN 978-1-59332-627-2

Dedication

To my parents,
who instilled the importance of higher education,
both in the classroom and in life…I love you both

to my wife Robyn,
who gave me unwavering support and compassion,
my best friend…to say that I love you is an understatement of the truth

Table of Contents

Acknowledgements

I would like to thank Edmund McGarrell, Steve Chermak, John Hudzik, and Michael Rip for their professional and personal support in the preparation of this book. Your insights were truly invaluable.

To my mother Karen, father David, and sisters Hilary and Lauren, words cannot fully convey how thankful I am to have you all and everything you have done for me - I love you all. My parents instilled in me an honest work ethic, personal pride, and respect for everyone - principles that guide me every day. Special thanks go out to my father for not only being the best in that role, but for also walking the fine line between parent and friend. I would never be where I am today without the love, guidance, and knowledge you have given me.

Finally, to my loving and patient wife Robyn... I do not even know where to begin. At times you were a widow to my doctoral degree, sacrificing in order to give me the best chance of success and making life easier for me, but not necessarily for yourself. You took on extra responsibilities so that I could focus on my work. You settled for some not-so-fun Friday and Saturday nights, all with a smile on your face. I look forward to spending the next many years making up for those lost nights together. I cannot say "thank you" or "I love you" enough to begin to convey how sincerely I mean them both.

To everyone... thank you.

CHAPTER 1

Introduction

In order for organizations to be successful they must adapt to their environment. The ways things have always been done must give way to the way things should be done. American law enforcement agencies are not immune to environmental demands, and are perhaps more susceptible to them than other social service agencies. The external environment of policing has evolved over time and in reaction to events. Traditional policing methods that were reactive to, and distant from, the community have given way to proactive methods that require routine police-community interaction. Crime has evolved from local drug trafficking and robbery to complex criminality such as displayed in inter-jurisdictional organized crime, identity theft, and threats of terrorism and radicalization. These external pressures, coupled with changes to the internal environment, require law enforcement administrators to incorporate a higher percentage of non-sworn employees and respond to increasing criminal, community and government demands with overall decreasing resources; these developments are forcing administrators to rely on analytic products more than ever.

Given the infancy of intelligence-led policing post-9/11, there is somewhat of a paucity of conceptual and empirical research to guide a study on its adoption. As will be discussed in detail, community policing and intelligence-led policing have conceptual commonalities that allow for the present study to be guided to a considerable degree by community policing research. Introduced approximately four decades ago, community policing became the new philosophical paradigm to which American law enforcement began to subscribe, gaining significant momentum in the 1980s. This philosophy integrated problem-solving, community partnerships and the flow of informal information to meet community demands as well as reduce actual and perceived crime. Along with the adoption of community policing came the challenge of successful implementation. Some police agencies labeled themselves as community policing agencies, but did so less to adopt to change than to secure external funding allotted for community policing initiatives. Consistent with institutional theory, other agencies adopted community policing in theory, but not in practice - it was simply a form of *window dressing* while operations continued largely as usual. This is not to give the impression that police agencies did not sincerely try to adopt community policing, but many found it difficult given the ambiguity associated with what it really means to be a community policing agency.

Law enforcement now finds itself once again in the midst of a philosophical shift in practice. Intelligence-led policing has emerged as the new policing paradigm that requires varying degrees of organizational shifts in culture and practice. This philosophy is designed to meet the demands of an increasingly complex internal and external environment for post-9/11 American law enforcement. Just as community policing faced implementation challenges of ambiguity and varying degrees of implementation, intelligence-led policing will undoubtedly share the same fate. However, given key similarities between community and intelligence-led policing, many of these obstacles will be informed by past research to guide the present study. Moreover, research on community policing as adopting innovation provides a theoretical and empirical foundation for exploring the adoption of intelligence-led policing. Research on policing innovation in general, and community policing specifically, explains the "how" and "why" of police agencies and their decisions and processes to adopt innovations. Also salient to this discussion are the influences of organizational characteristics, such as structure and context, on an agency's likelihood to either facilitate or inhibit change.

The intent of this study is not to produce another assessment of why community policing was or was not implemented successfully, but rather to demonstrate the applicability of what we have learned from community policing research as a means to identify successful implementation practices for intelligence-led policing. Furthermore, the constructs and concepts gained from the innovation literature further enhance the present study. This study seeks to identify innovation and organizational factors contributing to the successes and failures of state and local law enforcement in their attempts to adopt an intelligence-led policing capability.

STATEMENT OF THE PROBLEM

Law enforcement organizations are experiencing a philosophical paradigm shift in the aftermath of September 11, 2001. As noted by the

9/11 Commission, law enforcement (and the intelligence community) had significant information sharing gaps that contributed to the events leading up to the terrorist attacks on the World Trade Center and the Pentagon (National Commission, 2004). As a result, a new philosophy referred to as intelligence-led policing (ILP) designed to address prior shortcomings in law enforcement practices is gaining momentum among state, local, and tribal law enforcement agencies. The International Association of Chiefs of Police (IACP) intelligence summit in 2002 recommended the adoption of ILP by America's state, local and tribal law enforcement agencies in the post-9/11 era (IACP, 2002). Intelligence-led policing was envisioned as a tool for information sharing to aid law enforcement agencies in identifying threats and developing responses to prevent those threats from reaching fruition in America's communities.

This initiative was reinforced by a recommendation in the National Criminal Intelligence Sharing Plan (NCISP) to adopt ILP and has been echoed broadly by law enforcement leaders as well as reflected in new programming by the U.S. Department of Justice (DOJ) and the U. S. Department of Homeland Security (DHS) (Carter, 2009). It should not be assumed that ILP is solely an "anti-terrorism" concept; it applies directly to policing operations as a whole. The demand for intelligence-led policing has come from a variety of government recommendations, reports, and mandates. Moreover, government funding agencies have required intelligence-led policing to be incorporated into proposals for research and assistance - such as can be witnessed in the Bureau of Justice Assistance's "Targeting Violent Crime Initiative[1]". In the post-9/11 era information sharing is both paramount and a somewhat "slippery slope" to negotiate. Police agencies are required to implement this philosophy, and in attempting to do so may shift resources and practices in a manner that may be neither effective nor efficient. Moreover, most likely as a result of uninformed practices, information sharing practices may also come dangerously close to depriving individuals of their constitutionally protected civil rights[2].

---

[1] For more information visit http://www.ojp.usdoj.gov/BJA/grant/tvc.html

[2] Such was the case in Denver, CO in 2004 where the Denver Police Department disclosed having retained information on non-criminal civilians.

As will be discussed, intelligence-led policing and community policing (COP) share common conceptual foundations that allow COP research to provide a useful guide to research on ILP. A litany of empirical studies exists that assess the level of community policing adoption across American law enforcement agencies. The present study is cut from a similar mold and will incorporate many of the same methods and frameworks already established in the community policing literature. Furthermore, intelligence-led policing will be examined as an innovation among police agencies. As ILP emerges as a "state-of-the-art" philosophy it lends itself to the constructs discussed within the organizational, policing, and community policing innovation literatures. More specifically, the diffusion of this new policing philosophy will be examined as a multidimensional construct.

This approach is not to mislead researchers and practitioners into thinking examining intelligence-led policing is as easy as simply substituting intelligence-led policing variables for those of community policing. Despite many common similarities, community policing and intelligence-led policing are quite different philosophies designed to achieve different results. Community policing draws from established relationships between a law enforcement agency and that agency's given community - or patrol areas - to reduce crime and the fear of crime. As such, community policing is primarily an externally-oriented practice in that community members and COP officers are determining priorities. Conversely, intelligence-led policing is designed to influence operations across the entire law enforcement organization - both internally and externally - and priorities are identified from within the organization to not only target threats and crime, but also allocate resources internally. The relationship between the two philosophies is based on the use of community policing as a mechanism that enhances intelligence-led policing via two-way information flow between police and the community.

The problem facing academics and practitioners is a lack of understanding as to what intelligence-led policing actually is and how it should be tailored to different police agencies in order to achieve successful implementation. Success is determined by individual

---

Case: *American Friends Service Committee, et al v. City and County of Denver*, 2004 U.S. Dist. LEXIS 18474.

agencies - their needs and the demands of those they serve. As such, what successful intelligence-led policing is for one particular agency will be different than for another agency. Organizational, political and even geographical differences will influence implementation. At the outset of this study it is important to recognize, and expect, acceptable degrees of variance across agencies' mode of adoption of ILP.

In short, there is a significant gap with respect to research on law enforcement intelligence practices. Exploratory research on these practices is necessary to begin establishing a starting point for empirical research on these issues. More specifically, exploring characteristics of agencies that influence the adoption of intelligence-led policing will not only aid in the foundation of an ILP literature, but also provide baseline recommendations for public policy.

PURPOSE OF THIS RESEARCH
The study seeks to explore factors that facilitate or inhibit the adoption of intelligence-led policing as an innovation. Specifically, the study seeks to: 1) Explore innovation diffusion constructs that facilitate intelligence-led policing adoption; 2) Explore organizational structure and context characteristics that influence the adoption of intelligence-led policing; 3) Explore the effects of analyst performance evaluation methods on the adoption of intelligence-led policing; 4) Explore if differences exist among agencies that self-report to have adopted intelligence-led policing and agencies that have adopted intelligence-led policing as operationalized in an index for the present study; and, 5) Employ case studies to provide context for quantitative findings in an intelligence-specific environment.

Explore Innovation Diffusion Constructs that Facilitate Intelligence-Led Policing Adoption
Simply put, policing innovations are practices, programs, or technologies that are "state of the art" within the field. What constitutes the threshold of "state of the art" is somewhat ambiguous and will be discussed at more length to follow. Briefly, intelligence-led policing can be examined as an innovation since it is widely regarded to be the new policing philosophy as recognized by both professionals and the few academics currently familiar with the concept. Conceptual literature on policing innovation (and innovation in general) focuses on diffusion - or the "how" and "why" agencies decide to adopt the

innovation. Empirical literature on policing innovation has determined the diffusion of innovation is not a one-dimensional construct, but that it is clearly multidimensional. Of the four diffusion of innovation constructs used in this study, three are from the community policing innovation research - familiarity, peer emulation, and risk mediation. The fourth construct is derived from emerging homeland security innovation research and it is risk of threats. These four construct variables are each indexes created from a survey instrument to be discussed below.

Explore Organizational Structure and Context Characteristics that Influence the Adoption of Intelligence-Led Policing
The influence of an organization's structure on adoption and change has been examined to great lengths across several academic disciplines. Findings in the literature have been mixed with respect to structural variables. Salient structural variables are discussed here and included in the present study. Organizational structure is typically categorized into constructs of organizational complexity and control. With respect to organizational complexity, the current study examines formalization and occupational differentiation. The degree to which an organization adheres to formal policies and procedures has been found to both inhibit adoption - since these formal policies increase bureaucracy and red tape, as well as facilitate adoption - since formal policies provide guidance and reduce ambiguity among those assigned the task of carrying out the adoption. Occupational differentiation (also referred to as civilianization) is the proportion of sworn personnel to non-sworn personnel. This structural factor has been found to increase community policing adoption (Wilson, 2006) in as much as this philosophy relies heavily on non-sworn personnel to carry out significant portions of the community policing mission. Other research (Maguire, 1997) has found no relationship between civilianization and police agencies adoptions of innovations.

With respect to organizational control, the present study examines both functional differentiation and performance evaluation. Functional differentiation focuses on different units within the agency to carry out different tasks. Generally, findings have suggested that the more functional units an agency has, the more likely they are to adopt new innovations (Greene, 1989; Zhao, 1996; Maguire, 1997) as they have the multitask-oriented infrastructure in place to do so. Civilianization is measured as the proportion of sworn personnel to non-sworn personnel. Each of the remaining three structural variables is an index created from items featured in the survey instrument developed for this study. As with organizational structure, the influence of organizational context on adoption and change has been examined to great lengths within policing (Zhao, 1996; Maguire *et al.*, 1997; King, 2000). Findings in the literature have been mixed with respect to context variables as well. Salient context variables are discussed here and included in the present study. Perhaps the most commonly included measure of context in organizational research is that of agency size. In terms of policing innovation, size has yielded rather evenly mixed results. Some scholars argue size positively effects adoption as larger agencies have more resources - whether it be in the form of capital assets or personnel - to incorporate change (King, 2000; Wilson, 2006). Others argue that size inhibits change (Zhao, 1996; Maguire *et al.*, 1997) due to bureaucracy and the inability of large organizations to react quickly to change.

Organizational commitment to an innovation - in the form of administrative support - has overall found positive results. Studies within policing (Brown, 1989; Yates & Pillai, 1996; Morabito, 2010) and in the private sector (Collins & Porras, 2002) have found a positive relationship between administrative level commitment to an innovation and the organization's adoption of that innovation. Training for new innovations has also been found to have a consistent positive influence on the adoption of a new innovation in policing (Schafer *et al.*, 2009; Morabito, 2010). As commonsense would suggest, as knowledge about and expertise with an innovation increases so too would the degree of organizational adoption of that innovation. Another strong indicator of innovation adoption is a police agency's task scope - that is, the ability of that agency's personnel to carry out multiple responsibilities. Consistent with functional differentiation, the more tasks personnel can carry out the more apt they are to meet the additional responsibilities of innovative change. Given the political and historical culture of varying regions within the U.S., the geographic region within which an organization is located has been found to affect impact innovation adoption - specifically, police agencies located within the Western region of the United States have been the most open to innovation (Wilson, 1968; Wycoff, 1994; Maguire *et al.*, 1997).

Agency size will be measured as the sum of sworn and non-sworn personnel from each agency. An agency's region is determined given their location within one of the five common U.S. census designated regions - Northeast, Southeast, Midwest, Southwest, and West. Each of the remaining three context variables represents an index created from items featured in the survey instrument to be described at a later point.

Explore the Effects of Analyst Performance Evaluation Methods on the Adoption of Intelligence-Led Policing
Performance evaluation has predominantly been a focus of studies in private sector business and industrial-organizational psychology examining quality-based metrics for employee performance. As intelligence-led policing relies on the quality of analysts' products, in theory a more comprehensive performance measurement system should yield a more quality intelligence-led approach to policing - and thus facilitate its adoption. The survey instrument used in this study asked respondents to indicate the methods they viewed critical for evaluating an analyst's performance.

Explore if Differences Exist among Agencies that Self-Report to have Adopted ILP and Agencies that have Adopted ILP as Operationalized in an Index Developed for the Present Study
Consistent with institutional systems theory and organizational learning - specifically the notion of turning knowledge into action (Pfeffer & Sutton, 2000) - is the haziness of what ILP adoption actually requires. Institutional theory posits that police agencies will tend to label themselves as being innovative and consistent with emerging practices when the opposite is actually true. This phenomenon was consistently documented in the community policing literature (Wilson & Kelling, 1982; Crank, 1994; Wilson, 2006). Many agencies indicate they have adopted community policing and are actively engaged in the appropriate practices. However, when their practices and programs are examined more closely it becomes apparent that community policing in the agency is largely "window dressing" rather than reflective of an organization culture featuring productive engagement with the community Ambiguous definitions and inconsistent practices also contribute to what may be seen as failed, or stalled, community policing adoption. Intelligence-led policing is expected to follow a

similar path to that of community policing with respect to ambiguous adoptions, varying implementation, and "window dressing" applications.

Similarly, organizational learning theorists posit that organizations often mistake "talking about action" as "action actually occurring" with respect to innovation. While there is obviously a slight lag with respect to causal order in that organizations must talk about adopting innovations before they actually put the innovation into action, some organizations are inclined to maintain a constant level of "talk" and therefore never achieve expected outcomes. In the context of policing innovation, agencies will often have meetings, develop focus groups and task forces, and even write mission statements that display the idea of an agency adopting an innovation. However, these actions fall under the scope of "talking about action" rather than actually engaging in new innovative practices.

Employ Case Studies to Provide Context for Quantitative Findings in an Intelligence-Specific Environment
Given the general lack of knowledge with respect to law enforcement intelligence practices, a contextual component to the present study helps to support quantitative findings and establish validity. The role *fusion centers* play in intelligence-led policing is paramount as they serve as the lynchpin for multiple jurisdictions of law enforcement, private sector business, and public sector organizations. Detailed narratives discussing the administration and operation of the Florida Fusion Center and Southern Nevada Counter-Terrorism Center are featured in this book. These narratives are informative in their own right, and are also rich with context to give life to the analytical constructs examined in this study.

The study will utilize secondary data analysis from an on-going National Institute of Justice study on law enforcement intelligence programs and practices. This study utilizes a "key informants" survey method that serves as a purposive sample from a population of persons who have attended the Law Enforcement Intelligence Toolbox[3] training

---

[3] The Intelligence Toolbox is a Department of Homeland Security, Office of Grants and Training (GT-T4-K005, 2006-GT-T6-K011 and 2006-GT-T6-K005)-funded training program developed and delivered by the School of

program. This population represents the core group of practitioners attempting to establish an intelligence-led policing philosophy at the state and local level. These persons are responsible for developing and sustaining the intelligence capability for their respective agencies. Additionally, a qualitative approach will be taken in the form of case studies. This approach will be used to validate the intelligence-led policing constructs identified through theory and derived from the author's professional experience. This mixed methods approach also provides necessary context for such constructs as the current literature on intelligence-led policing is not even sparse at best. The case studies were conducted in state fusion centers determined to be representative of diverse geography and threat responsibility, as well as operating at different stages of operational maturity.

DEFINITIONS OF TERMS
In the interest of clarity the following terms are operationally defined as they apply to the current study.

Adoption / Implementation: The extent to which a philosophy of practice is integrated into the operations of an organization. Adoption and implementation are used interchangeably in this study.

Community Policing: Community policing is a philosophy that promotes organizational strategies which support the systematic use of partnerships and problem-solving techniques to proactively address the immediate conditions that give rise to public safety issues such as crime, social disorder, and fear of crime (COPS, 2009).

Complex Criminality: Crimes requiring longitudinal planning and extensive operations. Examples include organized crime, terrorism, and financial crimes (e.g., ponzi scheme).

Fusion Center: A fusion center is a mechanism to exchange information and intelligence, maximize resources, streamline operations, and improve the ability to fight crime and terrorism by merging data from a variety of sources (GIWG, 2003).

Criminal Justice at Michigan State University to provide state, local and tribal law enforcement with the knowledge and resources necessary to develop and sustain an intelligence capability.

Innovation: A process which brings a new method into an organization or a discrete product or program that an organization adopts (Kimberly, 1981:85).

Intelligence-Led Policing: The collection and analysis of information related to crime and conditions that contribute to crime, resulting in an actionable intelligence product intended to assist law enforcement in developing tactical responses to threats and/or strategic planning related to emerging or changing threats (Carter & Carter, 2009a:317).

Organizational Complexity: Differentiation in accomplishing organizational tasks (Wilson, 2006).

Organizational Control: The coordination of mechanisms needed to manage organizational complexity (Wilson, 2006).

Suspicious Activity Report: A report and process wherein criminal indicators and behaviors that appear to have a criminal nexus are documented and processed through a law enforcement organization to determine if a crime is being planned, in the process of being committed, or has been committed (Carter, 2009:451).

CHAPTER 2

Law Enforcement Intelligence

The intelligence-led policing literature has yet to be established. While academics and professionals have shared the workload in producing the few works that are available, a consistent understanding and conceptualization remains somewhat lacking. This is not to discount the works authors have done to this point as a great deal of progress has occurred. Current conceptual works specific to intelligence-led policing have generally focused on the role of intelligence analysts (Cope, 2004), intelligence and crime analysis (Ratcliffe, 2008b), counter-terrorism (McGarrell *et al.*, 2007), police management (Ratcliffe, 2005, 2008a; Ratcliffe & Guidetti, 2008), and operational concepts (Carter & Carter, 2009a). However, from an empirical standpoint, there has been little advancement in as much as the only empirical studies in the United States at the time of this study have come from the fusion center perspective[4] (Forsyth, 2005; Simeone, 2007; Nenneman, 2008; Ratcliffe & Walden, 2010; Graphia-Joyal, 2010: Saari, 2010).

There has yet to be an empirical examination of intelligence-led policing specifically at the state and local level of law enforcement. In order to undertake such a study appropriately, it is necessary to develop a multi-disciplinary theoretical framework to best examine effectiveness of law enforcement intelligence practices in the United States. Utilizing literature on organizational behavior, relevant constructs are presented along with traditional community policing perspectives to best establish a theoretical foundation for an assessment of intelligence-led policing adoption.

---

[4] Ratcliffe (2005) examined intelligence-led policing as an approach to police managerial perspectives in a New Zealand case study. Moonen *et al* (2008) also provide a quantitative assessment of "information-led policing" and community policing in Belgium; however, the authors operationalize "information-led policing" as a mathematical, data-driven formula for police management that is not consistent with the conception of "intelligence-led policing" used in the present study.

A BRIEF NOTE: NATIONAL SECURITY VS. LAW ENFORCEMENT INTELLIGENCE

For the purpose of avoiding confusion from the outset, it is important to briefly note the difference between national security intelligence and law enforcement intelligence. A common misconception is that they are one in the same, when in fact they are actually quite different. While a comprehensive discussion discerning the two is neither necessary nor appropriate for the current study, identifying fundamental differences as applied in practice is useful to establish context for the constructs to be discussed.

To begin with, national security intelligence is primarily concerned with "protecting the homeland". That is to say, national security is responsible for preventing threats to the United States and its interests as a country. Such threats include international and domestic terrorism and cyber-attacks on the U.S. defense network and financial markets. The primary concern of law enforcement intelligence is focused on threats to state and local government jurisdictions as well as to the "homeland". These threats range from armed robbery and burglary to domestic extremism and terrorism. These different responsibilities result in different operational products. Many national security intelligence products are created with the intent to inform policy decisions by the federal government. A significant component of national security intelligence involves the integration of products from the Central Intelligence Agency (CIA) and military, or Department of Defense, intelligence. Conversely, law enforcement intelligence products are intended to be "pieces of the threat puzzle" and integrated into both operational and tactical responses to threats and crimes.

There is certainly overlap between these two different types of intelligence - particularly in terms of terrorism as state and local law enforcement serve as the force multiplier for prevention. In this regard, national security intelligence and law enforcement intelligence supplement one another quite well. From a legal perspective, national security intelligence agencies are not liable under Section 1983 civil rights lawsuits[5] as they are not as constitutionally constrained as are

---

[5] Federal law enforcement agencies are subject to a Bivens lawsuit. For more information reference the following Supreme Court decision: *Bivens v. Six Unknown Federal Narcotics Agents, 403 U.S. 388 (1971).*

state and local law enforcement - primarily due to their responsibilities being in line with the protection of the United States as a country.

Lastly, it should also be noted that "law enforcement intelligence" and "intelligence-led policing" are not synonymous. Law enforcement intelligence is a broad, over-arching concept that encompasses all components of intelligence at the state, local and tribal levels. For example, the concept of fusion centers is different than intelligence-led policing, and both fall under the umbrella of law enforcement intelligence. Conversely, intelligence-led policing is the application of utilizing analyzed information to inform decisions, identify trends, and ultimately prevent threats.

CONTEXT OF INTELLIGENCE-LED POLICING
Intelligence-Led Policing in the United Kingdom
In order to examine the organizational, theoretical, and practical contexts of ILP it is important to understand its origins and the characteristics which have remained consistent over the years. Traditionally, the British have a long and somewhat more sophisticated legacy in criminal intelligence than does U.S. law enforcement. All 43 provincial British constabularies, as well as the London Metropolitan Police, have had some form of intelligence function to deal with complex criminality within their jurisdictions dating back to the early 1980s with the National Drugs Intelligence Unit, the early 1990s with the National Criminal Intelligence Service, and more specifically 1993 when ILP originated in the 1993 Audit Commission.

The acceptance and encouragement of ILP was not only driven by increased criminality - both in volume and complexity - but by a decrease in resources. The first documented rise of this issue was in a 1993 report by the Audit Commission proclaiming an ineffective and inefficient use of public resources by law enforcement in the U.K. (Heaton, 2000). One of the solutions posited in this report was to shift law enforcement's focus from general crime to specific offenders. As a result of this new focus, Her Majesty's Inspectorate of Constabulary (HMIC) released a report titled "Policing With Intelligence" which began to outline the practice of intelligence-led policing (Ratcliffe, 2003). The British government began developing a business-oriented philosophy for all elements of government service. This approach had two fundamental initiatives intended to address the resource issues illustrated in the 1993 Audit Commission report: 1) either outsource with the private sector to provide portions of government service; or, 2) apply a business model to remaining government services.

The National Criminal Intelligence Service (NCIS) was created (previously the National Drugs Intelligence Unit) to address varying forms of organized crime. Specifically, the NCIS evolved in response to the changing political environment associated with the European Union (EU). Member countries of the EU eliminated immigration and customs checkpoints for persons traveling between the EU countries and as a result made it easier for criminal enterprises to operate in Western Europe (Carter & Carter, 2009a).

Consistent with this movement, the NCIS and HMIC developed the British National Intelligence Model (NIM), which was formally adopted as policy 2002 by the British Association of Chief Police Officers (ACPO). The NIM followed government recommendations and public demand for a business process model to deal with crime control and thus employed the ILP philosophy to introduce intelligence into virtually all aspects of the policing business plan[6]. The NIM identified four tactical priorities for intelligence-led policing; 1) targeting of offenders; 2) management of crime and disorder hotspots; 3) investigation of related series of crimes; and, 4) application of preventative measures to reduce crime and disorder (Ratcliffe, 2003).

The adoption of the NIM by ACPO represented the transition between traditional policing to intelligence-led policing. Adoption of ILP by British law enforcement, consistent with the NIM, was not easy. Many local agencies did not understand the concept; ILP required a reallocation of resources and added a significant analytic component to each police force (Carter & Carter, 2009a). The NIM was criticized as being an esoteric model that created a surplus of data and new processes that were not providing a return on the investment of resources (ACPO, 2005) - a contradiction to one of the driving forces behind a more lean, intelligence-driven organization. Despite varying problems, the NIM provided some clearly positive outcomes. Many lessons were learned from the British experience that can be applied to ILP efforts in the United States, and there is a unique set of model

---

[6] These recommendations included the UK's 2005-2008 Policing Plan that called for all British law enforcement agencies to integrate intelligence across all levels of the organization (Home Office, 2004).

practices, such as analytic models, derived from the HMIC. However, American law enforcement agencies have a significantly different experience in law enforcement intelligence that prohibits wholesale adoption of British ILP, with some notable exceptions in the predominantly larger U.S. cities.

The smallest of Britain's 43 constabularies has approximately 900 sworn constables who police large geographic areas with both urban and rural characteristics. The majority of these agencies employ 1,200 to 1,600 sworn personnel (Carter & Carter, 2009a). While not a national police force, there are national standards that apply to all of the local agencies for training, promotion, operations, and salary (Bayley, 1992). Given the size of these police forces and their budgets, all have the resources to hire analysts and the flexibility to reassign personnel to operate an ILP philosophy. Crescenzo (2007) echoed this sentiment in a qualitative study with intelligence professionals in the U.K. and U.S., noting specifically the inability of the NIM to be implemented successfully in the U.S. without the imposition of uniform standards across levels of law enforcement. This is not meant to imply that the constabularies had an easy road for implementing ILP; rather, significantly more flexibility, resources, and greater diversity of expertise can be found in large agencies than in small departments - as is the case in the United States. Having an intricate foundation for law enforcement intelligence, British law enforcement was able to implement the NIM and, consequently ILP, with greater ease than agencies in the United States.

When compared to the British police structure, the majority of approximately 17,876 U.S. law enforcement agencies (BJS, 2003), many of which have fewer than ten sworn officers, have varied policing standards between and within states. The budgets of most of these agencies are small compared to those in the U.K. and typically come from local funds supplemented by short-term federal grants. New policing philosophies, emerging initiatives, and federal standards and recommendations are largely unenforceable unless explicitly stated in special conditions of a grant. In light of these differences and the significantly different history of law enforcement intelligence, when comparisons are drawn between U.S. and U.K. policing it is a leap of faith to assume that the basic practices of the NIM, and thus ILP, can be implemented effectively in the United States on a short-term wholesale basis. In the United States, law enforcement agencies need to start at a more foundational level to establish an intelligence-led approach that is appropriate for their specific agency - a facet of intelligence adoption that will be discussed further.

A functional model of ILP must be developed that has both the flexibility and applicability to U.S. law enforcement.   From the beginning, ILP should be viewed as a philosophy, not a process. American law enforcement agencies should rely on ILP to develop new intelligence-based processes that functionally balance each agency's jurisdictions, characteristics, and resources (Carter & Carter, 2009a). The lessons learned from community policing can be a valuable guide. Developing intelligence-led policing in a law enforcement agency requires two developmental activities: 1) devising an information collection framework to manage threats within a jurisdiction; and, 2) develop the organizational infrastructure to support the ILP initiative.

Intelligence-Led Policing Before 9/11
Police Informants, Surveillance and Resource Management
The most glaring difference between ILP before and after 9/11 is how raw information is utilized.   Prior to 9/11, information received from police informants and surveillance was used interchangeably with the term intelligence. Law enforcement would tap informants for information and use this information to guide tactical operations. This is not intelligence per-se unless this information is analyzed or validated. Rather than being an intelligence-led policing approach, this method more closely resembled tipped-off interception of crime events. Law enforcement would use informant information to learn of where and when specific crimes were likely to occur and then direct resources to intercept persons in the act of committing these crimes - such as burglary, robbery or drug trafficking.

An early example of the emergence of a law enforcement "intelligence" capacity occurred when the Kansas City Police Department's (KCPD) Special Operations division created the Criminal Information Center (CIC) which, at the time, they considered to be an information-clearing house (Heaton, 2000). This center was driven by information provided via the use of police informants, covert operations, and surveillance. The KCPD used this information for what they called "Location Oriented Patrol" (LOP) and "Perpetrator Oriented Patrol" (PerOP). The CIC would gather and organize information they received and disseminate it back out to the LOP and

PerOP police units on the streets. These units would go to the location of anticipated crime and intercept the persons involved. An examination of these programs determined that LOP and PerOP units had a significant influence on targeted crime reduction (Pate *et al*, 1976). This approach is crime-driven with a focus on serious offenders. While studies have shown the approach of intelligence-led policing as practiced in the form of apprehending repeat offenders is both promising (Eck, 1983; Martin, 1986; Martin & Sherman, 1986) and an ethical slippery slope (Sheptycki, 2000), this version of information-led policing is not consistent with that practiced currently.

Targeting repeat offenders through the use of informants and surveillance has also been referred to as intelligence-led policing in Australia and the United Kingdom. Ratcliffe (2002)[7] illustrates that the use of surveillance devices, closed-circuit television, undercover officers, and informants were the mechanisms by which law enforcement gathered intelligence in order to apprehend repeat offenders. These methods were similar to those of the KCPD's LOP and PerOP units. However, a key distinction is important between these two approaches. The information gathered via informants and other means was put through an analysis process in order to produce intelligence - not just raw information, as was the case in Kansas City. By putting information through the intelligence cycle[8], law enforcement was able to respond more effectively and efficiently. Effectiveness and efficiency are important components of this approach since the driving force behind a repeat offender initiative was the result of a demand for more cost-effective policing in the "Helping With Enquiries - Tackling Crime Effectively" report issued by the U.K. government (Ratcliffe, 2002). The idea was simple and based on the theory of crime proportionality - a small percentage of criminals account for a large percentage of crime (the "80/20 rule"). As a result, the police would invest in efforts focused on repeat offenders rather than all offenders in order to have the most significant impact on crime

---

[7] The publication year of this article is 2002; however, the article was written and accepted into the journal prior to September 11, 2001.

[8] The intelligence cycle includes five processes; Planning and Direction, Collection, Evaluation, Collation, Analysis and Dissemination.

compared to resources invested - with the goal of a more efficient return on investment for policing.

Investigations and Resource Management
Before state and local, and especially federal, law enforcement became hypersensitive to threats - whether they are terrorist, biological, natural or criminal - the concern was crime control and fear of crime. It should be no surprise then to find intelligence-led policing literature and practices before 9/11 as having a focus on reducing crime and the community's perception of crime. A clear distinction of crime types must be made at this point. Prior to 9/11, ILP research and practice mostly targeted street and violent crime. Post 9/11 the ILP emphasis shifted towards complex criminality, organized crime, terrorism, and street crimes - all with the underpinning of prevention.

It is important to acknowledge from the beginning that prior to 9/11, federal, state and local law enforcement began to put the pieces in place for an intelligence-led philosophy. However, the key difference between ILP before and after 9/11 was the integration of analyzed information (e.g., intelligence) into each step in the policing process. Prior to 9/11, information was a supplement to decision that had already been made by those within the police organization. After 9/11, intelligence began to influence police decision making across all levels and operations. It is more accurate to refer to intelligence-led policing prior to 9/11 as information-supplemented investigation and resource management.

As a result of the 1988 *Anti Drug Abuse Act* - which created the Office of National Drug Control Policy (ODNCP) - the 1998 *ODNCP Reauthorization Act*, and as a result of growing political pressure to govern resources and accountability for program effectiveness under the Clinton Administration, High Intensity Drug Trafficking Areas (HIDTA)[9] across the United States were created. HIDTA centers were seen as a response to the demand for increased effectiveness of anti-drug initiatives and increased resource efficiency by allowing for HIDTA centers to absorb existing effective anti-drug initiatives and cutting those determined ineffective. Law enforcement personnel from

---

[9] For more information on the 28 HIDTAs in the United States, visit: http://www.whitehousedrugpolicy.gov/hidta/index.html

multiple levels of jurisdiction are assigned to HIDTA centers, each with the responsibility of analyzing and disseminating intelligence from their respective agencies (Martinez, 1997). HIDTA centers generally mirror what are currently referred to as fusion centers - which will discussed at length later on - in that they have multi-level and multi-jurisdictional representation from law enforcement for the specific purpose of sharing information. However, the focus of this information sharing was for the purpose of aiding investigations and tactical operations.

> The ultimate goal of the HIDTA Intelligence Division is to be a knowledgeable resource capable of providing critical information in support of criminal investigations, regional planning.....and task for operations (Martinez, 1997:10).

The creation of HIDTA centers was one of the first steps towards an effective intelligence-led approach by embracing personnel from multiple jurisdictions "under the same roof" for purposes of sharing information.

While not domestic, a similar approach was taken in 1991 by the Royal Canadian Mounted Police (RCMP) creating the Criminal Intelligence Directorate (CID) in response to a growing awareness of increased extremist and organized crime activity in Canada while also identifying strategic priorities for resource allocation. The structure of the CID differs from HIDTAs in that multiple agencies and jurisdictions are not represented and invested in the organization; however, it has similar priorities and offers similar products. The CID serves as a "one stop shop" for law enforcement seeking intelligence to inform investigations as well as guide decision making.

> The CID provides RCMP senior management with a wealth of finished, current intelligence, not only on the nature and extent of criminal activity in Canada and abroad, but also on emerging trends and the future of crime...the identification of intelligence priorities, meanwhile, means that planning focuses only on relevant issues, an essential consideration in a time of shrinking financial, human and material resources (Smith, 1997:11).

Once again the conceptual components of a post-9/11 intelligence-led approach are demonstrated by the CID's mission to provide intelligence that influences organizational decisions - whether it be resources or crime - via strategic priorities. As is discussed further on in the book, a successful ILP philosophy guides the overall decision making of law enforcement agencies through the interpretation of a threat environment.

Intelligence-Led Policing After September 11, 2001
In October 2001, approximately six weeks after the 9/11 attacks, at the International Association of Chiefs of Police (IACP) annual meeting in Toronto, Ontario, Canada, the Police Investigative Operations Committee discussed the need for state, local, and tribal law enforcement (SLTLE) organizations to take actions in response to intelligence gaps. This meeting called for agencies with intelligence units to re-engineer their intelligence function and for more law enforcement agencies to develop an intelligence capacity. It also pointed to the need for national leadership to establish standards and set a clear direction for the intelligence process in these agencies (Carter, 2009). Shortly after this initial meeting, the IACP, with funding from the Office of Community Oriented Policing Services (COPS), held an "Intelligence Summit" in March 2002. The summit in question established a number of recommendations, including the development of a criminal intelligence sharing plan and the adoption of ILP (IACP, 2002).

In response to the IACP Intelligence Summit recommendations, the Global Intelligence Working Group (GIWG) was created. The purpose of the GIWG was to move forward with the recommendations from the intelligence summit. The first GIWG product was the National Criminal Intelligence Sharing Plan (NCISP). The intent of the NCISP was to provide SLTLE agencies - particularly those that did not have an established intelligence function - with the necessary resources to develop, gather, access, receive, and share intelligence. This sharing plan essentially served as the first "road map" for law enforcement intelligence.

To this end, the plan established a number of national standards that have been formally recognized by the professional law enforcement community as the proper role and processes for the contemporary application of law enforcement intelligence (Carter, 2009). The NCISP had a significant influence on shifting organizational policies and procedures - even in some cases affecting the physical realignment of units within the agency (Ratcliffe & Guidetti, 2008). One of the most significant recommendations from the NCISP was for American law enforcement agencies to adopt intelligence-led policing. However, this recommendation lacked guidance for evaluating progress and determining benchmarks for success.

This lack of baseline standards for evaluating intelligence effectiveness makes it difficult for practitioners to assess the impact intelligence is having on the operations of their organizations. Moreover, without some basic idea of how intelligence is being integrated into law enforcement agencies and the mechanisms by which these agencies share information inhibits researchers from evaluating intelligence practices. A successful ILP philosophy can be determined through the effectiveness of state, local, and tribal law enforcement agencies' ability to collect, analyze, disseminate, and integrate intelligence into the operations of the organization. Two predominant models of intelligence-led policing are presented in the literature.

Models of Intelligence-Led Policing
Intelligence-led policing is conceptualized in two leading approaches within the literature - the Ratcliffe (2008a) model and the Carter and Carter (2009a) model (C&C hereafter). Both models put forth similar philosophical characteristics, but more importantly they have contrasting operational tenants that are important to distinguish - characteristics that influence how intelligence-led policing is interpreted by law enforcement and thus adopted. Table 1 provides a summary of the key similarities and differences of the Ratcliffe (2008a) and C&C (2009a) models. These similarities and differences are discussed at length below.

From the outset it is important to identify the key distinction between the Ratcliffe (2008a) model and the C&C (2009a) model. Ratcliffe's (2008a) model is developed on a foundation that is incident-driven and focuses on the prevention of street crime and disorder. This approach is consistent with the CompStat paradigm. Ratcliffe (2008a) refers to his model as the *"3-i model"* of ILP[10]. This CompStat

---

[10] Ratcliffe discussed ILP in multiple publications. His "Intelligence-Led Policing" book published in 2008 is a synthesis of his prior works and

foundation is present in that it utilizes crime analysis and crime mapping along with criminal statistics to develop intelligence products.

Table 1: Similarities and Differences of the Carter and Carter Model and Ratcliffe Model

Similarities of Carter & Carter (2009a) and Ratcliffe (2008a)		
✓ Organizational commitment ✓ Prevention-oriented ✓ Analyst's ability to influence decision making ✓ Chief Executive's ability to impact the environment		
Differences of Carter & Carter (2009a) and Ratcliffe (2008a)		
	Carter & Carter (2009a)	Ratcliffe (2008a)
Influence of British Model	Partial Adoption: Best Practices Applied to US	Wholesale Adoption: Applied Directly to US
Conceptual Foundation	NCISP	CompStat
Operational Focus	Threats and Crimes	Crime and Disorder
Geographic Focus	Inter-jurisdictional	Intra-jurisdictional
Analytic Component	Intelligence Analysis*	Crime Analysis / Mapping
Information Push / Pull	Push and Pull	Pull
COP as a Foundation	Yes	No

*Intelligence analysis involves multiple analytic processes which includes crime analysis and mapping.

collective thoughts regarding ILP, and as such will serve as the primary source for the discussion of his approach.

Alone in this approach intelligence analysts more closely resemble crime analysts and would seem to have little, if any, influence on the chief executive as a result of their tasks being investigation-oriented. Lastly, the conceptualization of the criminal environment in the *3-i* model is limited to a single jurisdiction where crime or disorder occurs. Analysts and officers focus their investigative and information sharing efforts with persons in a specific area - such as patrol officers from a specific beat, witnesses, or other persons who may contribute to learned information. While this approach is sound and proven in many policing arenas, the focus is on criminal incidents that have already occurred. Moreover, this model views policing philosophies as operating independent of one another.

In contrast, the C&C (2009a) model is grounded in an all-threats and all-crimes approach that embraces tenants of the National Criminal Intelligence Sharing Plan (NCISP). Rather than focusing on incidents that have occurred, this model emphasizes suspicious behavior, specific threats, complex criminality, and street crimes. As this model asserts, intelligence analysts provide the chief executive with quality intelligence products that allow for strategic and operational priorities to be developed that guide resource allocation, personnel decisions, and all facets of police operations. Intelligence analysts draw from resources of multiple law enforcement agencies, the communities of multiple jurisdictions, open source resources, the private sector, and other organizations such as public health to inform their analytic process.

The key conceptual distinction between these two models is as follows: The Ratcliffe model views different policing philosophies - such as problem-oriented policing, community policing, and CompStat - as operating independent of one another based on their conceptual tenants (how these philosophies are conceptualized, not how they are put in practice by law enforcement). Specifically, Ratcliffe (2008a:80) notes "...intelligence-led policing is significantly different than community policing". As such, intelligence-led policing operates independent of these philosophies. Conversely, the C&C (2009a) model views the different policing philosophies as a foundation for intelligence-led policing. Therefore, intelligence-led policing essentially draws from the best practices of these existing philosophies and incorporates a significant analytic and preventative component to these practices - a position taken by others in the academic community as well (cf. McGarrell *et al.*, 2007; Chappell & Gibson, 2009; Lee, 2010). Moreover, this position is reaffirmed by the Office of Homeland Security in the "National Strategy for Homeland Security":

> Intelligence-Led Policing is a management and resource allocation approach to law enforcement using data collection and intelligence analysis to set specific priorities for all manner of crimes, including those associated with terrorism. ILP is a collaborative approach based on improved intelligence operations and community oriented policing and problems solving, which the field of law enforcement has considered beneficial for many years (HSC, 2007:19).

Given the dynamic nature of law enforcement intelligence and the wide ranging needs of different agencies attempting to grapple with intelligence processes, the interpretation of how intelligence is incorporated into the organization can be difficult. The Ratcliffe (2008a) model simplifies the systematic use of intelligence as it would be applied in the majority of police departments. The name "3-i" is derived from the actions - influence, interpret, and impact - that occur between the agency and its environment.

In this model, the analysts actively interpret the criminal environment in a manner consistent with priorities of their organization (e.g., New York City Police Department will have different priorities for their analysts than a rural agency in Montana). The direction of the arrow for interpretation indicates a pull model of information collection rather than a push model. Ratcliffe (2008a) posits that while a push model - where analysts request information from patrol officers and these requests are fulfilled - is desirable, it is not a reality of how information is exchanged. As a result, a pull model where analysts actively search for desired information is utilized. The interaction between the analyst and the decision-maker is based on the ability of the analyst to influence a decision-maker. A decision-maker is not necessarily the chief executive, but a person who has the ability to affect the criminal environment. The responsibility rests on the analyst to determine who the true decision-makers are in the organization and attempt to influence their actions as a result of their analyses. The ability of analysts to have an influence on decision-makers is difficult given the traditional role of analysts (mostly civilians) in police agencies as publishers of reports and clerical-type personnel that do not carry the administrative weight to influence (Cope, 2004; Ratcliffe, 2008a).

The final interaction of this ILP model is the ability of the decision-maker to impact the criminal environment as a result of deploying responses based on intelligence analysis. As Ratcliffe notes, this is perhaps over-zealous based on the accountability of crime reduction to rest with agency leaders, not an analyst-based recommendation. However, the ILP philosophy draws from available information on specific priorities and thus, that information should be applied in the form of a solution.

There are six premises of Ratcliffe's 3-i model that require elaboration;

1) Crime vs. threat focused
2) Crime analysis vs. intelligence analysis
3) ILP as a top-to-bottom hierarchy
4) Broadening of the "criminal environment"
5) Push vs. Pull of information flow
6) Relationship of community policing and intelligence-led policing

Within the academic literature there are two predominant definitions of ILP - consistent with the two predominant models identified previously. The author of the present study endorses the following definition of ILP as a basis for this research and implementation within law enforcement organizations:

The collection and analysis of information related to crime and conditions that contribute to crime, resulting in an actionable intelligence product intended to aid law enforcement in developing tactical responses to threats and/or strategic planning related to emerging or changing threats (Carter & Carter, 2009a:12).

Ratcliffe proposes a definition of ILP as follows:

... a business model and managerial philosophy where data analysis and crime intelligence are pivotal to an objective, decision making framework that facilitates crime and problem reduction, disruption and prevention through both strategic management and effective enforcement strategies that target prolific and serious offenders (Ratcliffe, 2008a:89).

While both definitions share the commonality of ILP as a "business model" for effective strategic planning, Ratcliffe's definition clearly focuses on "crime" and "serious/prolific offenders". In this approach, ILP is intended to prevent street crimes (e.g., robbery and assault) and target habitual offenders. In the C&C (2009a) model, intelligence-led policing certainly has implications for street crime; however, the underlying philosophy is principally threat-driven. Intelligence-led policing was originally conceptualized as a threat-driven initiative. The IACP Intelligence Summit of 2002 (IACP, 2002), National Criminal Intelligence Sharing Plan (GIWG, 2003), Fusion Center Guidelines (GIWG, 2005), Bureau of Justice Assistance (BJA, 2005; 2009) all conceptualize ILP as being a threat-driven philosophy for preventing complex forms of criminality.

This model of ILP as a means to prevent street crime reinforces the notion that Ratcliffe's (2008a) definition of ILP more closely resembles CompStat with a crime analysis component. A common misconception is that crime analysis and intelligence analysis are the same thing. Crime analysis is *incident-driven* and incorporates specific crime variables (e.g., homicide locations and offender housing) with the intent to prevent future crimes, provide context for past crimes and arrest perpetrators. Conversely, intelligence analysis is *threat-driven* and relies upon the analysis of information from a variety of sources and assessments to determine sources of intelligence, potentially vulnerable targets, and actionable information to mitigate or prevent the threat from occurring. Simply put, intelligence analysis is the "human element" of critical thinking. This is not to imply these two types of analysis are mutually exclusive, because they are both an integral part of intelligence processes. The most salient point to note is that intelligence analysis and crime analysis are driven by different means and intended to produce different ends. Ratcliffe (2008b) explains that crime analysis and crime intelligence contribute to resource allocation; however, there is no distinction between crime analysis and intelligence made by Ratcliffe. This failure to distinguish the two types of analysis runs the risk of creating conceptual confusion. Traditional crime analysis is unlikely to predict threats, and has it limited ability to inform decision-makers on strategic priorities for the long term.

Ratcliffe's (2008a) conceptualization of ILP more closely resembles the Comparative Statistics (CompStat) process. CompStat is a managerial process of accountability by which police organizations attempt to identify ways to reduce street crimes more efficiently and effectively (Silverman, 1999; Henry & Bratton, 2003). First implemented in the New York Police Department, this process utilizes crime analysis to identify "hot spots" of criminal activity where police decision-makers can allocate resources to reduce the amount of crime occurring in the area. This process also involves gathering statistical data that represents (hopefully) a reduction in crime to demonstrate to senior officials and the public that the CompStat process is effective. Given that a large component of CompStat is to ensure community safety from street crimes (Walsh, 2001), the process has to be - and is - intra-jurisdictional, incident-driven, and time-sensitive. While Ratcliffe's (2008a) model of ILP is consistent with these factors, the C&C (2009a) model is not.

The C&C (2009a) model relies on a multi-jurisdictional approach that is threat-driven and relies on a long-term strategic analysis to prevent threats. This does not mean that this model cannot be applied to street-crime. The importance of strategic analysis it to identify threats of all shapes and sizes, whether they be terrorism, organized crime, homicides, or residential and commercial establishment robberies. Through the use of strategic analysis, the needs and priorities of the agency can coincide with resource allocation to mitigate threats. For the NYPD this could involve terrorist threats as well as street crimes. For a rural agency in Montana, in contrast, this could involve burglaries and truancy.

Strategic and operational priorities are established by persons at the top of an organizational hierarchy - the chiefs or command-level officers. From this perspective, it can be argued that ILP is a top-down management style. However, one of the central tenants of ILP is the ability of an intelligence analyst to influence the decision-makers - a difficult feat in a top-down environment. Much like COP, information on threats and crimes flows into the intelligence cycle from the community and street-level patrol officers. This information is then evaluated and interpreted and presented to decision-makers in the form of proposals for mitigation. The very nature of intelligence is that it tends to flow from the bottom to the top, or in some instances from the bottom to the middle just as Ratcliffe (2008b) notes; the decision-maker may not necessarily be the chief executive, but another actor within the organization that has the ability to influence the criminal environment.

Ratcliffe does not provide a definition of what constitutes the criminal environment in his 3-i model of ILP. Based on various discussions within his works, the criminal environment is likely a general reference to a collection of variables associated with crime such as location, perpetrators, housing, development, and racial heterogeneity. Intelligence analysts do not only draw information from a crime environment as described above, but also from a much broader "information environment" - and such an environment is consistent with the C&C model. An information environment is a collection of a criminal environment, private sector organizations, community members, politics, open-source information (Internet) and other law enforcement organizations. Rather than the interpretation of a criminal environment, analysts must interpret the threat potential through the means of an information environment.

Despite acknowledging that community policing provides fundamentals for an intelligence capacity, Ratcliffe proposes that COP does not provide a conceptual foundation for ILP implementation because COP has had very little success in American police agencies. The basis for this position is that ILP is an "...approach that concentrates on prolific offenders and criminal groups...as opposed to specifically working to alleviate community concerns and address issues of public trust" (Ratcliffe, 2008b:269). Moreover, he asserts that "...a community's concerns are not permitted to perpetually trump an objective assessment of the criminal environment" (Ratcliffe, 2008b:269-270). Once again, his arguments focus on a crime-driven ILP philosophy rather than a threat-based environment.

In contrast, the C&C (2009a) model of ILP is a threat-based policing approach in which the input and concerns of the community are paramount. The conceptual foundation of the C&C (2009a) model of ILP incorporates best practices learned from community and problem-oriented policing, crime and intelligence analysis, the NCISP, an all-threats and all-hazards approach, and the utilization of suspicious activity reports (SARs). Community members serve as an important force multiplier of raw information by providing suspicious activity reports as well as tips and leads to law enforcement agencies. This information is vital to intelligence analysis and helps law enforcement better understand the potential threat environment. Moreover, ILP does in fact alleviate community concerns in the form of fear reduction - an outcome consistent with COP goals. Interactions between law enforcement and community members provide a two-way information flow that generally benefits both parties.

The transaction type - the type of information exchange (cf. JIEM, 2006) - in which information is shared within and among law enforcement agencies is an important characteristic when striving to conceptualize ILP. Ratcliffe (2008a) characterizes this process as a "pull" model of information flow between analysts and the criminal environment as opposed to a "push" model. Information pull occurs when a person requests and receives a specific piece of information. If information is sent in anticipation of a person's need, or the person's response includes information not directly solicited, the exchange is characterized as information push (Adama *et al.*, 2007).

In the context of the 3-i model, analysts actively search the criminal environment for information contributing to their priorities. This involves reaching out to officers within their own agency as well as reaching out to other law enforcement officers or other public safety organizations that may have beneficial information. Ratcliffe (2008a) notes this is not the ideal interaction and that a push model - where officers are providing information to the analysts as they receive it - would be more effective. A push model presents challenges in the law enforcement context given poor communication lines in a complex bureaucracy where a culture involves much of the information gathered being stored in the brains of police officers as a type of task resource (Higgins, 2004; Ratcliffe, 2008a). As current practices suggest, Ratcliffe (2008a) is correct in his assumption that the majority of information is the result of being pulled from sources by analysts. However, given the current suspicious activity reporting (SAR) initiatives and narrowing intelligence requirements, a shift towards a push model is likely to occur.

Community policing lies in the core of the C&C (2009a) model of ILP. As a result of increased homeland security responsibilities at the state and local level, police executives have expressed a common concern that the shift toward ILP may require a shift of resources away from community policing (Carter & Carter, 2009a). Rather than distinguishing between the two philosophies, the current practice is to identify and embrace how community policing and ILP are potentially integrated. Intelligence-led policing depends on strong community relationships that, in many state and local agencies, have already been established by a COP component of some consequence. Community support and crime will inevitably be a critical responsibility for law enforcement. These responsibilities, coupled with increased community awareness as a result of homeland security initiatives (Moynihan, 2005), require the need to maintain a close, interactive dialogue between law enforcement and the community they serve.

Problem solving, environmental scanning, effective communications with the public, fear reduction, and community mobilization to deal with problems are among the important attributes community policing has developed in many law enforcement officers; these all directly support new ILP responsibilities (Carter, 2009). The NCISP observed these factors, noting:

> Over the past decade, simultaneous to federally led initiatives to improve intelligence gathering, thousands of community-policing officers have been building close and productive relationships with the citizens they serve. The benefits of these relationships are directly related to information and intelligence sharing: COP officers have immediate and unfettered access to local, neighborhood information as it develops. Citizens are aware of, and seek out COP officers to provide them with new information that may be useful to criminal interdiction or long-term problem solving. The positive nature of COP/citizen relationships promotes a continuous and reliable transfer of information from one to the other. It is time to maximize the potential for community-policing efforts to serve as a gateway of locally based information to prevent terrorism, and all other crimes (GIWG, 2003:4).

These factors facilitated the implementation of ILP as an underlying philosophy of how intelligence fits into the everyday operations of a law enforcement organization. As mentioned, ILP draws on community policing principles, building on tactics and methodologies developed during years of community policing experimentation.

Information management plays a critical role in both the COP and ILP approaches. Community policing utilizes information gained from community members to help establish the parameters of community problems while ILP relies on raw information put into the intelligence process as the essential ingredient for intelligence analysis. Two-way communication with the public is essential for COP since information is sought from the community about problems and offenders while disseminating information to the public aids in crime prevention and fear reduction. With respect to ILP, when threats are defined with specific information, communicating critical information to citizens may help prevent a terrorist attack and, as in the case with community policing, will reduce fear among citizens (Moore, 1992).

Scientific data analysis provides a critical crime analysis component in the CompStat process (Shane, 2004; Ratcliffe, 2008a) and also serves as a key component for intelligence-based threat management. Problem solving skills allow community policing officers to reconcile community conditions that are precursors to crime and disorder (Mastrofski *et al.*, 1995; Weisburd & Eck, 2004). Within ILP, this same process is used for intelligence to identify trends in factors related to vulnerable targets of criminality. Like community policing, ILP requires commitment of effort on the part of all members of the organization as well as on the part of the community (Maguire, 1997; Wilson, 2006). Based on the principles of the ILP philosophy and the standards of the NCISP, law enforcement intelligence is an organization-wide responsibility that relies on a symbiotic relationship with the community.

Lastly, and perhaps most importantly, the C&C (2009a) model embodies the definition of strategic priorities by the chief executive. It is a pragmatic recognition that priorities vary significantly throughout jurisdictions as they determine what threats and crimes are most pertinent. Just as ILP was first conceptualized before 9/11 as a risk model for cost-efficient policing, the chief executive must establish priorities to allocate limited resources in police agencies. Information management, analysis, and evaluation allow for these priorities to be accurately defined and resources applied in a manner that will most effectively mitigate threats and crime. The ability of this study to identify indicators related to successful adoption of intelligence-led policing will provide practitioners with information on common barriers and impediments to guide intelligence-led policing as it best fits their respective agencies.

A Brief Note on the Adoption of Intelligence-Led Policing
Law enforcement and criminal justice scholars find themselves in a familiar position with intelligence-led policing - namely drawing flashbacks to when community policing became the "default philosophy of policing" in the U.S. There was such a high degree of ambiguity as to what COP actually was that agencies were not sure how to integrate or revert to it within the existing policing function. While the argument can be made that ILP is more easily defined than COP (Ratcliffe, 2008b), there is still no clear guideline as to how ILP can be adopted within a policing organization. This is largely a result of such a wide variance with respect to the needs and priorities of American law enforcement agencies. With minimal guidance and an increased demand for ILP, there are likely to be agencies that refer to themselves as "intelligence-led" but lack the functional capabilities to actually practice ILP.

This phenomenon was found with community policing where agencies were being labeled as COP organizations, but in reality were unable to practice COP and used the COP label to retain legitimacy in the eyes of the public (Moore, 1992; Crank, 1994; Reisig & Giacomazzi, 1998; Greene, 2000; Sunshine & Taylor, 2003). This is certainly not to imply that agencies which are practicing ILP in theory are simply doing so to mask themselves against criticism or to obtain federal funds tied to ILP. Having a theoretical ILP philosophy is critical to effective practice of ILP. As such, agencies that have yet to make the transition from theoretical ILP are in the infant stages and perhaps just a few steps behind in the learning curve.

The concept of implementation fidelity is consistent with the adoption of intelligence-led policing. Implementation fidelity aids the explanation that new innovations will be adopted differently across organizations with acceptable degrees of variance (Blakely *et al.*, 1987; Durlak, 1998; Greenberg *et al.*, 2001). Simply put, organizations are variously structured, have different responsibilities, and face different demands; consequently, the manner in which they adopt new programs should vary somewhat due to these differences.

While the NCISP states all agencies, regardless of size, must have an intelligence-led policing capability, there is no common understanding as to what an intelligence-led policing capability for agencies of different size and responsibility should look like. Intuition is correct in assuming that a larger police agency will have a more comprehensive intelligence capacity than a smaller agency. While this is an appropriate assumption, it is not appropriate to automatically consider a small police agency's "basic" intelligence capacity as being insufficient. An agency's intelligence-led policing capability need only be as advanced as the responsibilities that agency requires. The New York Police Department (NYPD) will have a significantly different intelligence-led policing capability than that of a rural department with fewer than five sworn officers. While this is a crude example, it serves to point out the foundational difference. Rather than being fixated on the label "intelligence-led policing", both practitioners and academics alike need to be concerned with identifying an appropriate level of intelligence practices that allow an agency to fulfill its role in the greater law enforcement intelligence landscape. For example, a small rural agency will not need to employ an intelligence analyst and won't need connectivity with the most secure information sharing systems - they simply need to be aware of intelligence practices, have a process in place to send and receive information, and be able to identify and collect information consistent with the collection requirements identified in their jurisdiction.

The difficulty for interpreting levels of adoption is that academics and practitioners alike struggle to identify characteristics of an appropriate intelligence-led policing function for an agency that has certain size and responsibility characteristics. As such, it becomes difficult to discern if an agency is either in the process of adopting intelligence-led policing or they have already adopted an appropriate level of intelligence-led policing for their specific agency type.

CHAPTER 3

Organizational Influences on Police Change and Intelligence

ORGANIZATIONAL FRAMEWORKS FOR POLICING

A variety of organizational theories have been applied to policing environments. For purposes of this study only the most salient theoretical frameworks featured in the research literature will be discussed in the context of law enforcement intelligence practices.

Systems Perspectives and Policing

Traditional law enforcement perspectives deal with stabilizing immediate problems rather than attempting to analyze comprehensively each situation and determine the best course of action so that problems resulting from the "quick fix" attitude do not arise anew (Carter, 2002). In contrast, a systems thinking organization would stabilize the immediate problem and call upon support organizations to aid in the permanent solution to the problem. In the current context of intelligence-led policing, the solution of problems pertains to the ability of intelligence-driven operations to prevent or mitigate threats and crime. Systems theories offer new philosophies for analysis and actions which can be implemented within any existing community policing-practicing organization given the aforementioned similarities between ILP and COP.

Systems perspectives emphasize the importance of cohesiveness and interdependency within organizational structures and communities (Aldrich & Ruef, 2006; Boland & Tenkasi, 1995). When members of a team share common visions and goals, they work together as a part of a process to achieve positive results through commitment rather than compliance. Often this co-active process can require a difficult transition for individuals adverse to change - as is the case with "old school" police executives who have yet to accept ILP or refuse to do so. Systems perspectives encourage members to examine how one's own actions influence others, and include learning to recognize the ramifications and tradeoffs of chosen actions.

A number of researchers have begun to frame police organizations as open - or complex - systems (Langworthy, 1986; Zhao, 1996; Maguire, 1997; Mastrofski, 1998; Crank, 2003; Wilson, 2006). This position is based on the perception of police agencies as organizations that must be dynamic and sufficiently nimble to meet the changing needs and demands of the environment in which they operate. This perspective is reaffirmed by those researchers (Cordner, 1978; Kuykendall & Roberg, 1982) who noted police organizations provide non-routine tasks within unstable environments and thus cannot be viewed as a closed-system organization. Law enforcement organizations operating as open systems are most commonly framed in two dominant system theories; contingency theory and institutional theory. Contingency theory has a significant shortcoming in that it is undermined by the notion of an endless amount of contingencies (Wilson, 2006); nonetheless, it provides an appropriate context within which law enforcement intelligence must operate. Institutional theory is favored within the policing literature (Crank, 2003), largely as a result of efforts to evaluate community policing (Crank, 1994; Mastrofski, 1998), and will provide a valuable perspective for the adoption of ILP.

Briefly, contingency theory explains the interactions between an organization and its environment. The success of an organization to meet the demands of its environment is referred to as "fit" (Aldrich & Pfeffer, 1976). Contingencies are results from reactions to change and are assessed through effectiveness. When an organization's environment changes, the organization must adopt new methods by which the interactions with the changing environment yield effective outputs. In terms of COP, some of the ways in which police agencies achieved this were by assigning officers to consistent foot patrols and participating in meetings with community members to identify community problems (Skogan, 1998). With respect to ILP, a variety of changes occurred as a result of government recommendations[11] to

---

[11] Examples include the National Criminal Intelligence Sharing Plan, Global Justice Information Sharing Initiative, Global Intelligence Working Group, and the Law Enforcement Intelligence Unit – all of which put forth recommendations and standards for changing and improving law enforcement information sharing.

change the practices of law enforcement information sharing. Most recently, the Program Manager's Information Sharing Environment (PMISE) has outlined a detailed plan for law enforcement agencies across all levels to adopt and participate in a seamless information sharing environment. As a result of these various recommendations and initiatives, police agencies are re-allocating resources and changing existing policies to meet emerging demands. The effectiveness of these new initiatives and policies - in the form of ILP - is difficult to determine given a variety of organizational and evaluation issues at play. These several issues will be discussed in the following section.

The predominant view of police open systems is that of institutional theory. The underlying assumption of this perspective is that organizations conform to the social expectations of the environments in which they operate. This theory emerges from Parsons' (1951) work in which he identified three core components of an organization: technical, managerial and institutional. The institutional component consists of an organization's perceived legitimacy. This legitimacy aspect of an organization was later argued to be determined externally (Thompson, 1967) by the norms, myths and social beliefs (Meyer & Rowan, 1977) of its environment.

This theory is consistent with Ratcliffe's (2008a) view that COP was more along the lines of a label police agencies attached to themselves in order to gain public trust, legitimacy and external funding rather than an operational policing philosophy. Other authors (Wilson & Kelling, 1982; Crank, 1994; Wilson, 2006) support the position of COP as institutionalized by social expectations of police to serve as "watchman" of a community. Wilson (1978) demonstrated the influence the external environment can have on the type of policing taking place in differing communities; specifically, his findings illustrated the significant impact social perception can have on police behavior as he observed during the height of the civil rights movement and the protest movement against the war in Vietnam. As a result of heightened scrutiny - in the form of social events - police behavior became rather polarized. This same premise applies in the intelligence arena in the form of civil rights violations - often brought into the public eye by organizations such as the American Civil Liberties Union (ACLU)[12].

Institutional theory also has significant implications for ILP given potential geographical sensitivity to law enforcement intelligence. The social expectations of law enforcement intelligence vary greatly depending on political environment and intelligence-related history (e.g., lawsuits and publicized events) in a given geographic location. More specifically, if a community, or city, has existing political beliefs or has experienced events directly related to law enforcement intelligence, their expectations of their police agency's adoption of ILP will be influenced. Three examples will illustrate this point. First, the city council of Ann Arbor, MI has put into writing its objection to having an intelligence capacity within the city. Consequently, the Ann Arbor Police Department cannot have a formal intelligence capacity. Given the traditional political views of the Ann Arbor community, this does not come as a surprise. Many members of this community are likely to adhere to myths of law enforcement intelligence that more resemble those of the 1960s and 1970s, a time in which police agencies were keeping dossiers on persons they should not have been, thus perpetuating the notion of "big brother is watching".

Second, the Denver, CO Police Department was found legally liable under a Section 1983 deprivation of civil rights lawsuit for collecting and retaining information on a group of nuns who were not doing anything illegal. The lawsuit resulted in a multi-million dollar settlement and the scrapping of the department's intelligence unit. The members of the Denver community are well aware of the implications of a law enforcement intelligence capacity, and thus their expectations of that capacity have been altered. Lastly, on the other end of the intelligence continuum from these previous two examples is the New York Police Department (NYPD). Given the enormity of the attacks of 9/11 and previous terrorism attacks and attempts, the NYPD has adopted a core intelligence-led policing philosophy. This is not only to better meet the needs of their community, but also because it is

---

[12] For more information on the ACLU and law enforcement intelligence visit: http://www.aclu.org/national-security/aclu-weighs-attempt-expand-law-enforcement-intelligence-systems

expected by their community members as appropriate to promoting a secure environment.

Organizational Knowledge and Policing

Generally speaking, law enforcement practices have evolved from the professional model of policing to community policing, and presently to intelligence-led policing. An effective intelligence capability can enhance law enforcement's ability to adapt to their ever-changing environment. Parsons (1937) outlined four prerequisite functions carried about by organizations that allow them to evolve and meet the demands of their environment. These four functions, described and applied to law enforcement intelligence (LEI), are as follows:

1) *Adaption*; the actions of establishing relationships between the system and its external environment. This consists of an exchange mechanism required to bring necessary resources into the system, and an explanation of how those resources are used to alter organization and the environment within which it operates.
   a. LEI; relationships between the police and their environment (e.g., community, private sector) are established in the form of partnerships and educational awareness programs. The necessary resource brought in via these relationships is raw information to feed the intelligence cycle, which in turn yields an interpretation of the threat/crime environment through intelligence analysis.

2) *Goal attainment*; the intent of the system to manage resources necessary to achieve goals.
   a. LEI; information management and collection strategies are critical to the success of intelligence and information sharing. Information management includes adhering the laws and regulations regarding the collection, retention and dissemination of intelligence as well as responding to requests for information. Disseminating intelligence to persons who need to know, when they need to know it is at the crux of an effective intelligence capability.

3) *Integration*; the process of actions to establish control, inhibit deviant tendencies, and coordinate between parts.

   a. LEI; the integration of intelligence into everyday police operations represents the implementation of intelligence-led policing to influence resource decisions, identify preventative strategies for threats and crime, and provide information and support for other law enforcement agencies.

4) *Pattern maintenance*; the actions that accumulate and distribute energy in the form of motivation - the success of adaptation.

   a. LEI; successful implementation of intelligence-led policing could result in a decrease in crime, threats and public fear of crime as well as increase police agency effectiveness and efficiency of operations.

Public service organizations, especially police agencies, utilize emerging technology and information sharing practices in an effort to become more effective and efficient when responding to their environment (Brown & Brudney, 2003). More specifically, the analysis of raw information to provide actionable intelligence to guide law enforcement operations is an example of police agencies turning knowledge into action in order to respond to a complex environment (Osborne, 2006). Intelligence-led policing has been conceptualized as a business-model for police agencies to guide, among other things, resource decisions (Ratcliffe, 2008a; McGarrell *et al.*, 2007). As such, perspectives that lend themselves to both public and private sector organizations to achieve more effective and efficient processes can be explored. Specifically, by what means do organizations adapt to the evolving environments in which they do business? Schwandt and Marquardt (2000) put forth the Organizational Learning Systems Model (OLSM) to provide a road map for private sector organizations to design methods for information analysis and communication in an attempt to become more responsive to environmental/market demands.

This model is described as having "linear-sequential functions" by which organizations gather, retain and apply information derived from their environmental scanning. The OLSM mirrors the intelligence cycle used by law enforcement to analyze information in that it posits an organization that scans its environment for relevant information that may influence the organization's operations, and then puts this information through a filter to determine if it is worth retaining. If this information is consistent with the organization's operations, it is placed into schemas - a predetermined area of interest that it will influence (such as a police investigation of organized crime) - and then distributed to persons who will utilize the information most effectively. The distribution of this relevant information is referred to as the distribution of knowledge within the OLSM framework.

The present author has expanded this framework to include two distinct types of knowledge for distribution - those being operational knowledge and functional knowledge. Operational knowledge is the "know how" of an organization - an understanding of what processes need to be completed for desired tasks to be accomplished. Functional knowledge relies on the processes in place within the organization to carry out tasks effectively. In the context of law enforcement intelligence, operational knowledge pertains to the commitment to the ILP philosophy through the training of personnel while functional knowledge is having an analytic capability to produce accurate actionable intelligence products as well as a means by which these products can be disseminated and integrated into the decision making process.

The difference between operational and functional knowledge is critical when examining the effectiveness of policies and procedures. Pfeffer and Sutton (2000:1) paraphrase this dilemma quite well when they say "knowing what to do is simply not enough." Public organizations are handicapped by their inability to turn knowledge into action (Friedmann, 1987; O'Toole, 1997) given their tendency to have large vertical hierarchies and to be highly bureaucratic in nature (Grant, 1996; Pfeffer & Sutton, 2000). These structural limitations are examined as organizational complexity. A large body of literature exists with respect to complexity and organizational learning (Dodgson, 1993; McElroy, 2000; Schwandt & Marquardt, 2000), complexity and organizational change (Hannan & Freeman, 1984; Pettigrew *et al.*, 200), and complexity within law enforcement agencies attempting to implement new initiatives (Zhao, 1996; King, 1999, 2000; Maguire, 2003; Wilson, 2006).

Within complex organizations, talking about and studying options for new policies and procedures is often substituted for actually putting new initiatives into action. This is commonly a result of two predominant shortcomings of actors within organizations. First, people make the mistake of considering the process of talking about action taking place as the functional equivalent of purposive action (Pfeffer & Sutton, 2000). When people sit through meetings and produce reports that talk about the desired actions the organization needs to take, and even integrate these changes into the mission statement of the organization, this is not actual action occurring. As Ratcliffe (2008a:236) notes "...holding meetings is insufficient to warrant the label *intelligence-led...* intelligence is inherently actionable."

The second shortcoming is a lack of evaluation and follow-up to assess the consequences of the actions taken within organizations (Pfeffer & Sutton, 2000). If no benchmarks for progress or success exist, there can be no determination of action taking place. This is especially true when dealing with law enforcement intelligence given "a widespread paucity of evaluation of police tactics and the intelligence process...without feedback there is no evidence and without evidence there is no learning and improvement" (Ratcliffe, 2008a:113). Moreover, a common mistake made by organizations attempting to adapt to their environment via learning and knowledge is that complex language, ideas, processes and structures are more effective than simple ones (Pfeffer & Sutton, 2000). These shortcomings have profound implications for the assessment of law enforcement intelligence effectiveness. As it has been established, law enforcement agencies are complex organizations, governed by bureaucratic policies while strictly observing hierarchical lines of communication.

Organizational Communication and Policing
Complexity continues to inhibit effective intelligence-led policing through its impact on communication. In order for action to occur within organizations, the intended change or implementation must be understood by those involved. As complexity increases, the likelihood of everyone involved understanding what needs to be done is significantly decreased (Pfeffer & Sutton, 2000; Culnan, 2007). This is especially true when the agents for change are scattered throughout a large geographic area - as is typically the case with state, local and tribal law enforcement agencies, especially in the context of effective information sharing. Complexity compounds the ineffectiveness

commonly associated with establishing lines of communication for information sharing since as the level of complexity in communication increases the likelihood of information transmitting slowly and being altered also increases (DuBrin, 1978). The policy and/or practitioner implications are rather straightforward. As the complexity of the organizational structure increases, the likelihood that decision making will be effective and efficient decreases. Complexity often results in poor planning, empty meetings, and the likelihood that a mission statement will be created that is either incomplete or falsely asserts the organization's objectives and goals. The lesson learned is that simplicity in structure as well as informed and acute decision making will provide proper planning and strategies to produce desired goals and objectives.

The infrastructure and relationships necessary for communication are paramount for effective intelligence practices. From an infrastructure perspective, agencies must have access to formal electronic information sharing systems, such as the Regional Information Sharing System (RISSnet) or Law Enforcement Online (LEO). Moreover, processes for sharing information with other law enforcement and public organizations must be in place. These connections are typically established informally as officers develop professional relationships with persons from other organizations. Information is often shared informally through these networked relationships - typically as easy as over the telephone (Weiss, 1997, 1998). While formal lines of communication are desired to share intelligence and safeguard against civil rights issues, informal methods serve as the "bread and butter" of raw information input into the intelligence process. Information gathered via suspicious activity reports (SARs) and "tips and leads" are typically the result of informal communications.

As is usually the case, SARs and tips and leads are simply field interview reports, street-level officers' observations, instincts, and experiences that focus on suspicious behaviors (Martinelli, 2009). Opportutnies for SARs are more a reality than would be expected since it is likely law enforcement and the community will come into contact with potential terrorists and criminals during the planning phases of an event (Manhattan Institute, 2006). Lastly, relationships for communication and the sharing of information can be built on feedback. Providing feedback during the communication process allows parties involved to rely on the resources resulting from the relationship (Jorgenson & Papciak, 1981). Moreover, feedback has also been shown to facilitate organizational cultural attachment and commitment within law enforcement organizations (Beck & Wilson, 1997) - a necessary ingredient for successful policy implementation (Matland, 1995).

Organizational Innovation
The literature on organizational and policing innovation provides a framework by which appropriate factors contributing to the adoption of intelligence-led policing can be identified. Innovation research slowly made its way into the policing literature in the late 1970s and early 1980s as a vehicle for scholars to best explore and explain how and why new practices, programs, and technologies present themselves in law enforcement agencies. For decades scholars from a wide range of disciplines have examined the concept of innovation within organizations, and as a result if anything can be said for certain it is the consistent difficulty of defining (or operationalizing in the case of empirical evaluation of innovation) what is "innovative".

Some scholars have defined innovation as the adoption of an idea or behavior - whether in the form of a system, policy, program, or process - that is new to the adopting organization (Rogers and Shoemaker, 1971; Daft, 1982; Damanpour & Evan, 1984). Other scholars focus on significant change to how organizations accomplish tasks (Kimberly, 1981; Wilson, 1966) and innovation as "state-of-the-art" practice in the field of the organization (Baldridge & Burnham, 1975; Kimberly, 1981; Kimberly & Evanisko, 1981). A challenge to the latter approach is establishing what constitutes "state-of-the-art" in the field. With respect to research in policing, scholars have reviewed contemporary academic journals to establish what is "state-of-the-art" (Zhao, 1996), while others have conducted interviews with professionals in the field (Moore *et al.*, 1997; Spelman *et al.*, 1992).

Types of Innovation
In the 1960s and 1970s, innovation research was challenged by a lack of appropriate methods to gather information and interpret this information accurately. The unit of analysis evolved from individual perceptions of identifying innovative leadership to using these individual perceptions in an attempt to measure adoption of innovations

within an organization (Rogers, 2003) - that is, a clear switch was made from a micro to macro-level analysis. As Downs and Mohr (1976) acknowledge, this method creates inadequate measures of how an organization is actually adopting or implementing innovation as it relies solely on the perceptions of one individual. Moreover, this method does not account for organizational characteristics - the internal, or determinant, factors that may either facilitate or inhibit innovation.

In an effort to remedy these methodological shortcomings, King (2000) explains three general types of innovation research upon which scholars have relied: *diffusion studies, innovativeness studies,* and *process studies.* Diffusion research is perhaps the most commonly applied approach to examining innovation within organizations (cf. Wenjert, 2002). In the most general sense, diffusion is a process by which an innovation is communicated through certain channels over time among the members of a social system (Rogers, 2003). Simply put, organizations are influenced to adopt innovations that are also adopted by neighboring organizations of similar industry as a result of learning about, or being exposed to, the innovation. Diffusion can occur as a result of being geographically contiguous to an innovative organization or through formal and/or informal communication channels.

Another view of innovation is that it is influenced by certain determinant factors present in the social system's environment - such determinants range from political and economic to geographic and social (Downs, 1976). Generally speaking, factors associated with the diffusion of innovation are external to an organization while factors associated with the determinant approach are internal. These two approaches are not necessarily competing views, but have been consistently examined in contexts independent of one another (cf. Weiss, 1997). Distinguishing between factors attributed to the diffusion approach from the determinant approach is a grey area at best. It is difficult to conceptualize factors that can influence innovation from an environmental perspective (diffusion/external to the organization) that in some form or fashion have no influences on internal organizational factors. For example, restricted state budgets - an external factor - affect the budgets of state agencies - an internal factor - that provide public services. Such an example is pertinent to the current discussion given innovation research that suggests organizations with more resources are more likely to be innovative

(Wenjert, 2002). It is more intuitive to examine innovation as dependent on the intersection of factors that are both external and internal to the organization - or the determinants of the diffusion process (Klinger, 2003).

Organizational innovativeness is another prominent type of innovation research. The intent of innovativeness research, also referred to as variance research in the literature (Van de Ven & Rogers, 1988), is to identify the determinants of an organization's capacity to be innovative. This type of research adopts a variance model - such as a regression model - to explain the variance in a dependent variable using strictly quantitative analysis where the unit of analysis is the organization (Mohr, 1982). This dependent variable, which is an organization's capacity to be innovative, has generally been operationalized as a composite score based on the number and/or scale of innovations adopted by an organization (Wolfe, 1994). This type of research also allows scholars to focus on the impact of organizational structure as it has been argued by many to consist of the primary determinants of organizational innovation in both the organizational innovation literature (Damanpour, 1991; Kimberly and Evanisko, 1981) and the policing innovation literature (King, 2000; Wilson, 2005; Schafer *et al.*, 2009).

However, this research approach is not without its shortcomings. Perhaps the most significant shortcoming associated with this research type is a consistent lack of characteristics that differentiate innovative organizations from those that are not (Rogers, 2003). This lack of consistency with respect to the factors that either facilitate or inhibit innovation has provided a platform for scholars to put forth improvements to guide innovativeness research. Most salient among these recommendations for improvement is the need to focus on the process of implementing innovation as opposed to deciding whether or not to adopt an innovation (Wolfe, 1994). Even more specific to this recommended direction for research is the recognition of organization-specific attributes that predispose certain organizations to successful innovation implementation (e.g., access to resources) and to conceptualize the dependent variable consistent with characteristics of the actual innovations within an organization (Downs & Mohr, 1976; Wolfe, 1994; King, 2000) rather than the characteristics of the organization itself. Van de Ven and Rogers (1988) posit that research focusing on these two temporal stages of innovation represent a shift in innovation methodology from a variance method to a process method that utilizes a longitudinal approach to capture sequence of events related to the adoption of innovation.

Process research is focused on the time-ordered sequence of innovation events utilizing both quantitative and qualitative analysis. Process approaches explore how innovation evolves within an organization over time and has multiple temporal stages. The literature reveals a variety of temporal stages[13]. In short, these stages range from the point at which an innovation is conceptualized or initiated within an organization, then progresses through stages where the innovation is formalized, evaluated, rejected, confirmed, expanded, routinized, and/or infused. These stages, regardless of the number of them or how they are labeled, represent the temporal process of implementation innovation (cf. Rogers, 2003). Utilizing this process method requires more qualitative data collection to provide context for the quantitative data analysis. Scholars acknowledge the attractive utility of a hybrid process-innovativeness methodology that draws on the strengths of the contextual process method and the quantitative analytical innovativeness method. A similar hybrid - or mixed methods - approach is utilized in this study, and is discussed in greater detail in the methods section to follow.

INNOVATION RESEARCH IN POLICING
Innovation research in policing draws from two inter-related perspectives. The first is the extent to which police agencies are innovative as organizations. This approach examines a multitude of agency characteristics that can influence how innovative, or resistant to change, an agency will likely be. Such factors include size, longevity, urban versus rural, geographic proximity to metropolitan areas and other policing agencies, and the amount of external funding an agency receives. The other perspective is one that examines what technologies, programs, or practices adopted (or in the process of) are themselves innovative. For example, the progression of use-of-force policies/technologies and community policing are examples of innovations adopted by law enforcement. These perspectives are inter-

---

[13] Wolfe (1994:410) provides an excellent summary table of the literature related to these stages of the innovation implementation process.

related in that they have common intersections with respect to adoption or implementation of new philosophies or change within the agency. For instance, a study examining the adoption of community policing would utilize the research on what type of policing agencies are most innovative as to aid in the determination of which agencies are more or less likely to adopt community policing. Conversely, scholars who examine how innovative police agencies are often operationalize this innovation by measuring the existence of programs such as community policing. A comprehensive discussion of the policing innovation literature is beyond the scope of this study; however it is appropriate to identify the primary research studies that have been conducted thus far to establish the fundamental baseline premise that intelligence-led policing constitutes an innovation in policing.

As with many constructs in the policing literature, scholars of diffusion of police innovation have provided mixed findings on how and why some agencies learn about new innovations (cf. Lingamneni, 1979; Weisburd & Braga, 2006). Moreover, the literature is generally divided on what types of factors facilitate or inhibit the adoption of innovations. Zhao *et al.* (1995) concluded that police departments adopt community policing largely in response to external political pressures, such as police chiefs wanting to leave their mark on a department (Skogan & Hartnett, 1997). Weiss (1997) included measures of risk mediation and peer emulation in his model of innovativeness to represent actions made to reduce risk of civil liability and outreach to other agencies to learn of local innovations. Other researchers have found evidence of internal factors as facilitators of diffusion of innovation. Mullen (1996) concluded that police innovations are adopted due to internal factors - such as availability of computers and technology. These results are consistent, and somewhat similar, to Wejnert (2002) who identified familiarity with an innovation as one of the factors facilitating its acceptance - such as previous experience with computers and adopting new computer-aided technologies.

Policing scholars have examined a wide-range of innovations. Some of the first policing innovation studies looked at agencies adopting new managerial changes (Guyot, 1979, 1991; Kuykendall & Roberg, 1981). Policing innovation research gathered momentum as scholars began to frame advancements in technology and enforcement equipment as "state-of-the-art". Such innovations have included computerized information management (Mullen, 1996; Skogan &

Hartnett, 2005), integration of crime analysis (Manning, 2001) and crime mapping (Weisburd & Lum, 2005), and fingerprinting identification systems (Klug *et al.*, 1992). More relevant to the current study is policing programmatic innovation research.

A litany of research has examined the adoption of community policing. Most scholars look at the influence of organization factors such as structure and context (cf. Maguire *et al.*, 1997; Zhao, 1996; King, 1998, 1999; Maguire *et al.*, 2003) - consistent with the approach taken in the present study. Others have looked at specific external influences of adoption, such as funding (Helms & Guiterrez, 2007), while others have concentrated on agencies as a whole and both the internal and external influences of adoption (Skolnick & Bayley, 1986; Weisburd & Uchida, 1993; Moore *et al.*, 1997; Oliver, 2000). More specific to the present study is the examination of community policing as an innovation. While a variety of authors have conceptually visited this approach (cf. Skogan & Harntett,, 2005), only two have empirically tested the concept thus far - King (2000) and Morabito (2010). King (2000) concluded that police innovation is a multi-dimensional construct that cannot be explained by a single method of diffusion. Morabito (2010) found strong relationships between organizational commitment and also organizational context and community policing adoption in the form of innovation. Both studies posited community policing as an innovation due to the philosophy as being "start-of-the-art" to policing. More specifically, community policing has been regarded as an innovation due to its influence on the change of police structure and procedures (Pierce & Delbecq, 1977; Skogan, 2004; Morabito, 2010).

Only in the past six years have scholars began to frame homeland security as an innovation in policing - or perhaps more appropriately so, an accepted shift in policing. Such studies have broadly conceptualized homeland security as the next era in policing (Oliver, 2006: Morreale & Lambert, 2009; Stewart & Morris, 2009), a challenge to law enforcement organizational structures (Berber *et al.*, 2005), its role coupled with community policing (Brown, 2007; Friedmann & Cannon, 2007), a law enforcement response to terrorism (Eisinger, 2004; Foster & Cordner, 2005), and also law enforcement preparedness (Schafer *et al.*, 2009; Giblin *et al*, 2009; Burress *et al.*, 2010). Thus far, the only innovation-specific study of homeland security was conducted by Schafer *et al.* (2009) who found that large agencies and agencies located within a close proximity to a large metropolitan city[14] were most likely to adopt homeland security.

Most pertinent to the present study are the constructs which are thought to primarily explain the innovation of intelligence-led policing. In this sense, the notion of "why" police agencies determine they need to innovate and "how" they go about innovating is of importance. Why police departments have decided to adopt innovations in the past - such as new technologies or programs - has varied widely. Weiss (1997) found police agencies determine the need to innovate in order to mediate the risk of civil liability. Schafer *et al.* (2009) concluded that agencies which determine threats exist within their jurisdiction are likely to adopt homeland security innovations. How police departments have proceeded to adopt innovations is slightly less varied.

Damanpour (1991:562) described what he refers to as the "initiation stage" of adopting innovation as consisting of all activities pertaining to problem perception, information gathering, and attitude formation...leading to the decision to adopt". A key component to this initiation stage is establishing familiarity with the proposed innovation. Similar to agencies being familiar with innovations was Weiss' (1997) concept of "innovativeness" that contributed to adoption. This process is furthered by conclusions from Weiss (1997) that agencies learn about and achieve innovation as a result of reaching out to similar agencies that are also in the process of adopting the new innovation.

Intelligence-Led Policing as Innovation

To this point the literature of police innovation has leaned on the standard requirement that an innovation must be "state-of-the-art" - simply put, a new program or technology that was not present in the past. How policing scholars have gone about ascertaining if a program or technology was "state-of-the-art" is somewhat ambiguous and inconsistent. Some of the methods taken by scholars thus far include reviews of scholarly literature (Zhao, 1995) and law enforcement panel interviews and surveys (Spelman *et al.*, 1992; Moore *et al.*, 1996; King, 1998). Other scholars have broadly labeled innovation as something

---

[14] The authors defined a small agency as having nine or fewer sworn officers. Proximity to a metropolitan area was measured as agencies located within the same county as Chicago, IL.

new for the policing agency, but did not explain how or why the particularly new innovations were actually "new" (Mullen, 1996; Weiss, 1997). Intelligence-led policing can be categorized as an innovation by following similar steps. It is important to make a key distinction at the beginning of this section. This study considers intelligence-led policing as an innovation in its *post-9/11 form.* As discussed earlier, ILP was present in law enforcement agencies - both in the U.S. and in the U.K. - prior to the events of September 11th, 2001; however, as a result of these events ILP has gone through a dramatic philosophical and practical evolution into a substantively different concept. This post-9/11 ILP concept as it has been conceptualized in this study is the context by which ILP is considered "new" in policing agencies.

A portion of the literature related to the emergence of intelligence-led policing is found in the homeland security field. Authors typically merge the two concepts, taking the position that ILP is a function of homeland security (Oliver, 2006; Carter & Carter, 2009b; Schafer *et al.*, 2009). Such a position is correct, but this is true for many facets of law enforcement and preparedness with the litany of homeland security responsibilities as tasked by the federal government. As such, it is more appropriate to focus on literature and recommendations specific to intelligence-led policing to solidify the "newness" of the concept. Intelligence-led policing, as it is known post-9/11, has come to be defined and applied in somewhat of a piecemeal fashion. This is to say that academics and professionals alike have been developing different components since 9/11 that are now interwoven with one another to create an overarching philosophy. Such components include crime and intelligence analysis, fusion centers, and public-private partnerships (to name but a few).

In March 2002, more than 120 criminal intelligence experts from across the U.S. gathered for an "Intelligence Summit" hosted by the International Association of Chiefs of Police (IACP). At this summit law enforcement professionals expressed frustration in the lack of guidance from the federal government as to how ILP should be defined and put into practice. Specifically, one of the core recommendations was to "promote intelligence-led policing through a common understanding of criminal intelligence and its usefulness" (IACP, 2002:v). Ratcliffe (2005) reaffirmed this frustration among police practitioners in New Zealand, noting that while very excited about the potential benefits of the ILP philosophy, New Zealanders found it difficult to adopt as a result of a lack of consistent understanding of the new concept. As a result, the Global Intelligence Working Group was created and their first product was the National Criminal Intelligence Sharing Plan (NCISP) that stated "all agencies, regardless of size, must have a minimal criminal intelligence sharing capability" (GIWG, 2003:iii). The NCISP also served as the "road map" for state, local, and tribal law enforcement agencies to develop and engage in intelligence-led policing. Law enforcement currently relies heavily on the "Law Enforcement Intelligence Guide" (Carter, 2009) as the "manual" for engaging in law enforcement intelligence practices. This guide has gained popularity because it serves as a comprehensive resource for the multitude of issues arising in contemporary law enforcement intelligence as a result of the practices being so new that few persons in the field tasked with the responsibility of carrying out the intelligence function have a good understanding of such practices.

Enhancing the utility of ILP was the purpose of "fusion centers". Many states have developed or are in the process of developing fusion centers to increase the exchange of information and data across government and private sectors to enhance law enforcement's ability to fight crime and terrorism and prevent threats (GIWG, 2005; McGarrell *et al.*, 2007). The relationship between intelligence-led policing and fusion centers is reinforced by the Office of Homeland Security's "National Strategy for Homeland Security" that identifies ILP as one of the primary tools available to combat terrorism and threats to the U.S (HSC, 2007). Fusion centers increase the production and sharing of crime and intelligence analysis products. Manning (2001) suggested that crime analysis is a step in the right direction for policing, but that it lacks the actual analytic component to inform decision making. As discussed previously, ILP serves as the vehicle by which informed decision making can result from the utilization of analytic products. Ratcliffe (2002) noted that ILP is a new tactic relying on crime analysis that can rapidly improve police processes and management, while Cope (2004) discussed emerging cultural differences between traditional law enforcement personnel and analysts as a result of the new role and professional presence of intelligence analysts within law enforcement agencies.

Lastly, academics (Ratcliffe, 2008a; Ratcliffe & Guidetti, 2008; Carter & Carter, 2009a; Scheider *et al.*, 2009) and practitioners (BJA,

2005; Fuentes, 2006; Guidetti & Martinelli, 2009) alike agree that ILP is not only new to policing, but so new in fact that it requires a shift in police management, organizational structure, and even day-to-day operations. It has already been discussed, but should be mentioned again, intelligence-led policing relies on the central tenants of previous police philosophies - such as problem-oriented policing and community policing - to be successfully adopted. Furthermore, Scheider *et al* (2009) identified ILP specifically as a policing innovation, and noted that while it is new to law enforcement the lessons learned from previous policing innovations are critical to successful adoption of ILP.

ORGANIZATIONAL CHARACTERISTICS AND POLICING

Organizational communication, performance evaluation, and policy adoption are grounded in organizational characteristics. Some of these characteristics are not easily assessed, and include structure - in the form of complexity and control - and context, while others are more straightforward dimensions such as size - and location. As such, the influence of organizational variables on COP must be reviewed and taken into consideration when examining ILP implementation phenomena. In this regard, organizational characteristics are examined in two frameworks that are consistent with the literature – namely, structure and context. The literature discusses structure in two separate, but inter-related components. The first is complexity, meaning the content of differentiation in accomplishing tasks (Wilson, 2006:4). The second component is control, meaning the mechanisms by which the organization manages complexity (Wilson, 2006:4). Context refers to the environment in which the organization operates and the services it is designed to render. Once again, the discussion on organizational variables will be succinct given the intent of this section to focus on research methods and models.

Organizational Structure

Complexity and control provide considerable implications for ILP implementation - as they are both similar to and different from those discussed in the COP literature. While the majority of previous research has found relationships between organizational structure and COP (Zhao, 1997; Maguire, 1997, 2003; Katz, 2001), Wilson (2006) did not - a finding he concluded to be striking given neither occupational nor functional differentiation, the number of police stations and officer ranks were all non-significant. It is important to remain cognizant of the organizational context variables discussed in the previous section when examining the following influences of organizational structure because they are often inter-related.

Civilianization
Langworthy (1986; 65) defines occupational differentiation as the degree to which an organization relies on specially trained and skilled workers for accomplishing agency tasks.   This concept is often measured by the proportion of non-sworn employees to sworn officers (Wilson, 2006; Maguire, 2003; Guyot, 1979). The emerging increase in the proportion of non-sworn personnel within law enforcement agencies is referred to as civilianization (King, 1999; Crank, 1989). Specifically, Guyot (1979) suggests this emerging trend is not only cost-efficient, but also allows agencies to meet needs that are not met by existing sworn personnel. Wilson (2006) found that civilianization increased as COP implementation increased, but this was not a significant finding - similar to the findings of Maguire (1997) on the impact of civilianization's on COP and on organization structure.

As a result of intelligence analysts being predominantly non-sworn personnel as compared to other police personnel, civilianization is likely to have a direct influence on ILP implementation. Once again, size of the agency will influence this construct since smaller agencies are less likely to employ an intelligence analyst or even have access to one. It is anticipated that agencies which are successful in implementing ILP will have a positive relationship with occupational differentiation, and thus civilianization.   The effect of increased occupational differentiation will be discussed more fully when formalization is addressed with respect to the organizational control aspect of structure.

Functional differentiation
Functional differentiation refers to the specialization of tasks, differing from occupational differentiation in that the focus is on tasks rather than personnel (Langworthy, 1986; 66).   Blau (1970) confirmed common sense when his study found a direct relationship between organizational size and functional differentiation - the larger an organization the more separate tasks it will be responsible for maintaining.   With the adoption of COP come additional

responsibilities, such as community-based education and cooperation, thus an increase in functional differentiation, a finding supported by Maguire (1997) and Zhao (1996). This finding is supported by Greene's (1989) suggestion that police agencies having a community relations unit would be more successful in COP implementation since the desired function already exists. Moreover, the presence of an intelligence unit within a police agency is likely to facilitate the effectiveness of intelligence-led policing. These are results similar to those found in research on gang units within police departments (Katz, 2001; Katz *et al.*, 2002).

The influence of functional differentiation on ILP is difficult to anticipate. To begin with, ILP should serve as the core philosophy of police operations - or functions. As a result, ILP should be integrated within each function of the police organization to a certain extent. During the first stages of implementation, ILP will most likely operate separate from existing police operations. More specifically, intelligence analysis and actionable intelligence products will most likely be provided, but produced after decisions have been made and strategic/operational priorities have been identified. Here ILP and the policing function are working separately. Once successful ILP implementation has occurred, actionable intelligence productions will drive decision making to guide strategic/operational priorities as a part of each police agency function - intelligence analysis guiding the operations from the outset. Here ILP and the police functions are working together seamlessly - in theory of course. The relationship between ILP and functional differentiation will have to be teased out as implementation progresses. However, this study does not have a longitudinal component and this anticipated effect will have to be explored in another study.

Here, a more operational determinant of functional differentiation and ILP is examined. Just as Greene (1989) suggested for COP, a police agency already has necessary functions in place for a successful intelligence capacity and can build on these functions to implement ILP. Moreover, since intelligence analysts specialize in providing a function of ILP not found prior to ILP implementation, there will likely be a relationship between civilianization and functional differentiation. Lastly, ILP requires the addition of functions not previously carried out by many police agencies, such as the development of public-private partnerships and operational relationships with fusion centers. These emerging functions are consistent with Maguire's (2003) finding that non-routine tasks and functional differentiation were positively related. The anticipated findings will be consistent with Maguire (1997). As functional differentiation increases, so will ILP implementation.

Formalization
The extent by which an organization is governed by written rules, policies and procedures is referred to as formalization (Hall *et al.*, 1967). The influence of formalization on COP implementation is also contested. Some COP researchers argue formalization impedes the underlying philosophy of COP (Mastrofski, 1998) since the foundation of COP is informal relationships with community members and the utilization of officer discretion. Conversely, others insist written regulations facilitate COP implementation (Zhao, 1996; King, 1999) as a method of control to guide innovation and changes in policy. While not a significant finding, Wilson (2006) found that as formalization increased, so did COP implementation. Maguire (1997) was unable to validate his hypothesis that formalization would decrease as COP was implemented. Formalization is a method organizations use to coordinate complex efforts. As the complexity of an organization increases - such as with occupational and functional differentiation - it becomes more dependent on formalized policies and procedures to control the separate groups. Formalization is opposite of the open systems approach in that written procedures do not allow for organizations to adapt to dynamic environments, do not promote critical thinking, and do not allow for operational-level autonomy.

It is anticipated that ILP will be positively related to formalization. This assumption is consistent and inter-related to three previously discussed constructs - occupational and functional differentiation as well as training (legal liability). Since successful ILP implementation will likely involve high civilianization, increased tasks within the agency and an increased likelihood of legal liability, formalization will be required to coordinate and control implementation. Written policies and procedures are increasingly important with respect to legal liability to safeguard agencies against lawsuits, especially with heightened sensitivity from the American Civil Liberties Union and their views of law enforcement intelligence. The interactions among sworn officers and civilian intelligence analysts also require formalization as a result of misunderstandings on behalf of both sides with regard to how each carries out their respective duties. Officers tend to be unaware of the types of products analysts provide and at times will view them as clerical staff whereas analysts view officers as not being able to interpret their products (Cope, 2004). Lastly, formalization is required to guide the strategic planning component of ILP operations and thus the multiple functions of the police agency.

However, this section should highlight one caveat - the importance of informal interactions and ILP. While many of the day-to-day operations of ILP have written policies, the foundation of ILP is typically informal. This is consistent with the implications organizational structure can have on the ability of its members to share information. A flattened bureaucracy (e.g., less formal) lends itself to a more effective means of sharing information across organizational members (Woods & Shearing, 2007). Many officers must build professional rapport with other officers and intelligence analysts. These relationships are often a result of informal networking and result in the most efficient methods of communication and information sharing. These relationships will most typically serve as the intelligence liaison for small police agencies. Weiss (1998) noted the importance of informal networks and information channels for police organizations to obtain necessary information. While his work does not focus on individual-level networking among officers for the purpose of sharing criminal intelligence, it does provide keen insight into the informal nature of law enforcement organizations.

Organizational Context
Size
The influence of size on COP implementation is a matter of debate. Wilson (2006) and King (2000) have found size has no affect on COP implementation, whereas Maguire *et al.* (1997) and Zhao (1996) found a positive association between the two. Schafer *et al.* (2009) found large agencies (10 or more sworn officers) and small agencies located in a close proximity to metropolitan areas are more likely to adopt homeland security innovations. With respect to both community policing and homeland security, Lee (2010) found that smaller agencies are more likely to assign community policing and homeland security tasks to the same officers, thus integrating the two out of resource necessity. The size of police organizations will have a somewhat different influence on the implementation of ILP. Agency size is less

salient with respect to COP given the types of operations involved. Interaction with the community has been typically achieved through consistent foot patrol beats, officer-citizen community meetings and an increased focus on police-citizen interaction. Whether an agency is large or small, the tasks carried out to support COP are the same, but larger agencies will obviously have to incorporate more of these tasks as compared to smaller agencies.

The NCISP states that all law enforcement agencies, regardless of size, shall adopt a minimum intelligence capacity (GIWG, 2003). The influence of agency size on ILP is much different since the tasks carried out by larger and smaller agencies will differ. Intelligence capacities must be tailored to fit the strategic priorities of each agency as well as the community they serve and their role in the "big intelligence picture". Large municipal agencies will have more complex capacities than their smaller counterparts. Large agencies will - or should - be connected to national information sharing systems (e.g. LEO or RISS.net), employ or have access to multiple intelligence analysts, have developed detailed collection plans, and have a records management system. On the far other end of the continuum, small rural agencies will have no need for an intelligence capacity of this complexity. Rather, these smaller agencies must have established a relationship with a larger agency in the form of an intelligence liaison officer who is responsible for passing the information along and getting it into the intelligence cycle. Other responsibilities for smaller agencies would include training or awareness of legal liability (28 CFR Part 23) as well as suspicious activity reporting (SARs).

Administrative Commitment
Commitment to an emerging philosophy has been shown to be a significant construct of successful strategic planning and change, both in the private sector (Collins & Porras, 2002) as well as in community policing (Brown, 1989; Yates & Pillai, 1996; Morabito, 2010). Perrow (1967) discussed commitment in the form of technical control, the willingness of administration to provide the resources needed for the production of outputs. Schafer *et al.* (2009) found a significant impact of an agency's willingness to commit additional resources towards homeland security preparedness and the agency's ability to achieve such preparedness. Ford *et al.* (2003) found commitment to be positively associated with COP operations, a tenet outlined as a

philosophical "must have" for successful COP implementation (Trojanowicz & Bucqueroux, 1994). Moore and Stephens (1991) refer to chiefs of COP agencies as "executives" in that they are aware of strategic management that will allow for the successful integration of necessary philosophies to meet the needs of their environment. The necessity of commitment from the chief executive for successful ILP implementation has been acknowledged by a variety of scholarly (Ratcliffe, 2008a: 2008b; Carter & Carter, 2009a) and professional publications (IALEIA, 1997; GIWG, 2003; BJA, 2009).

Training
Training is an essential component of any change or policy implementation within any organization. As policy and procedures change, so must the knowledge, skills and abilities of those who are tasked to carry them out. As noted by Franklin (2004), the IACP Intelligence Summit Report (2002) documented several core recommendations specifically related to law enforcement training:

- Training should provide recipients with the skills to provide targeted, evaluative summary data to decision makers.
- Appropriate training must be provided to both current and entering law enforcement personnel on information sharing systems and criminal intelligence concepts.
- Training should promote building trust for intelligence sharing and maintaining civil rights/constitutional protections.
- Training should emphasize that all personnel, regardless of their job, have a role in intelligence and sharing information.
- Training should equip personnel to use new technologies.

While all of these aspects need to be addressed for successful intelligence-led policing, perhaps the issue most pertinent to the effectiveness (and willingness) of police agencies to share information is related to violations of civil rights.

Law enforcement intelligence provides a platform in the public spotlight for police agencies to face legal liability. Since the *Monell vs. New York City Department of Social Services* (1978) decision in which it was determined government organizations could be held liable just as individual persons, law enforcement administrators have been liable under Section 1983 deprivation of civil rights lawsuits for a variety of legitimate and illegitimate reasons. A number of researchers have argued that deficiencies in policies and procedures have resulted in this form of successful legal liability against law enforcement agencies (Ross, 2000; Worrall & Gutierrez, 1999; Vaughn *et al.*, 2001). These deficiencies are typically the result of inadequate training. Deficiencies in policies that guide the legal collection, retention and dissemination of law enforcement intelligence can be costly - such as a civil rights case in Denver, CO that resulted in the police department paying out millions of dollars in damages (Carter, 2009).

For ILP adoption to be successful, agencies should seek out adequate training in the administrative and operational areas of intelligence - specifically in the areas of intelligence-led policing, analytic processes and standards, available resources, and 28 Code of Federal Regulation Part 23[15]. Training focused on COP is widely accepted; 99% of state and local police academies have courses designed for COP operations. In contrast only 11% have courses designed to encompass issues most commonly associated with intelligence, such as terrorism and homeland security (Rojek *et al.*, 2007). Morabito (2010) found a positive relationship between training and COP adoption, while Schafer *et al.* (2009) found a positive relationship between training and local law enforcement agencies in Illinois that are adopting homeland security preparedness. As awareness and standards for law enforcement intelligence continue to increase, so does the need for training - especially with respect to legal guidelines. As the current economic crisis continues to threaten law enforcement resources, agency executives are becoming increasingly conscious of resources and any threats to those resources that could possibly come to fruition in the form of civil rights lawsuits - an emphasis that can been documented as impacting police practice (Archbold & Maguire, 2002).

Task Scope
Organizational technology refers to the tools, techniques, and action used to transform inputs into outputs (Daft, 2001). Intended outputs of

---

[15] 28 CFR Part 23 is a guideline for law enforcement agencies that operate federally funded multijurisdictional criminal intelligence systems.

police organizations are to service the community in a manner that both responds to criminal incidents and protects community members from possible incidents. Perrow (1967) argued that technology is a function of task variety - the frequency of an event occurring that requires a specialized response - and task analyzability - the transformation of inputs into outputs is an analytic process. When an organization frequently requires unique tasks that are based on an analytic process it is thought to be non-routine. Maguire (2003) and Wilson (2006) argue that community policing should be considered non-routine and can be measured by community-based activities conducted by the organization.

While some scholars have argued that the technology of community policing organizations produces outputs that are labor - and knowledge-intensive and immediately consumed since service is used immediately and cannot be stored (Wilson, 2005), the outputs of the intelligence-led policing model can be - and most certainly should be - stored. Within the intelligence-led policing context, the tools, techniques, and actions refer primarily to intelligence analysts and their ability to engage in critical thinking and conduct computer analyses in order to transform raw information into intelligence. These outputs are in the form of intelligence products such as risk assessments, strategic planning reports, and awareness reports. Furthermore, these intelligence products are disseminated to other agencies for the integration of the information as well as being stored in records systems.

Some organizational scholars have conceptualized technology - and thus task scope - as a characteristic of organizational structure (cf: Child & McGrath, 2001; Hsu et al., 1983; Perrow, 1967). However in the policing literature task scope or task variability has not appeared to be related to organizational structure (Maguire, 1997; Wilson, 2006). As such, the present study will examine task scope as a characteristic of an organization's internal environment, and thus as a contextual dimension. Maguire (1997, 2003), King (1998), and Wilson (2006) constructed a scale of task scope by adding the number of functions for which the organization maintained primary responsibility. A similar approach will be applied in the present study by adding the number of different products an intelligence analyst is responsible for creating.

Region
Regional differences in public organizations, including policing, have been frequently examined across the literature. Even though Maguire

et al. (1997:375) note there is a lack of consistency as to why scholars control for regional variation, they point out three important reasons as to why policing scholars do control for this variation: 1) regional differences in policing structures; 2) regional variation among innovation diffusion networks; and, 3) regional differences in the historical development of the police. With respect to community policing and institution theory, geographic region may influence COP adoption to the extent that residents of different regions have different expectations of police activities. Regardless of the reasons for regional variation, prior research on community policing has consistently identified regional differences. Wycoff (1994) and Maguire *et al.* (1997) found that Western state agencies were more likely to be engaged in community policing than were agencies from other regions - followed by the South, Midwest, and lastly the Northeast. Zhao (1996) found no differences by region with respect to change in COP; however, he did find that agencies in the Northeast region implemented COP less than those in the Midwest and South.

PERFORMANCE EVALUATION
Performance evaluation can be targeted either towards behaviors or toward outcomes characteristic of the given task. As Ouchi (1979) posits, these characteristics are: 1) knowledge of the transformation process (or task programmability); and, 2) the ability to measure outcomes. Applied to the present study, knowledge of the transformation process is the ability of an agency to adopt the methods by which intelligence analysts engage in critical thinking and become adept in the use of analytical tools and techniques which yield varying insightful analytic products; simply put, they adopt a qualitative systematic approach to evaluation. The ability to measure outcomes is somewhat more straightforward in that this is the "counting widgets" approach. A police agency utilizing this evaluation method is likely to count the number of analytic products created - the more products analysts produce, the more positive their evaluation.

Performance measurement has been cited as a central tenet to determine the effectiveness of law enforcement intelligence (HMIC, 1997). Being able to evaluate and measure performance accurately within an organization plays a critical role in the organization's ability to assess efficiency, effectiveness and progress of outcomes and outputs. Measurement allows administrators to make accurate decisions for resource allocation, regarding daily operations, and with respect to the performance of individuals and the organization as a whole (de Lancer Julnes & Holzer, 2001; Radin, 2000). Administrators are tasked with the responsibility of turning their knowledge, or the knowledge of their employees, into action. Fundamental to any organization is that "what gets measured gets done" (Osborne & Gaebler, 1992). Performance evaluation poses significant challenges to law enforcement decision makers, but with these challenges comes the potential to best align their agency with the demands of an emerging intelligence environment.

As intelligence-led policing relies on a quality analytic component to achieve optimal results, and intelligence analysts are the source of this analytic component, it follows that the quality of an analyst's product will have an impact on the intelligence-led process. It should be noted that a common concern among practitioners tasked with the responsibility of providing a qualitative assessment of intelligence products find their hands bound by traditional classification systems. For example, if an intelligence product is classified at the "Top Secret" or "Secret" level, it may have to be redacted to such an extent for the evaluation that it transforms what used to be a quality intelligence product into a less effective report. Since analysts and their products serve as the lynchpin for a successful intelligence-led policing capability, hence affecting the overall utility of this policing philosophy, a brief discussion of the organizational-level impacts of analyst evaluations is appropriate at this point.

Consistent with research from the business and economic literature (Griffin *et al.*, 1981; Bommer *et al.*, 1995; Roberts, 2003), intelligence analysts need to be evaluated based upon the quality of their products, as opposed to the quantity of products produced. Quality intelligence products are reports and/or recommendations provided by analysts that influence the decision-making of persons within the organizations for purposes of resource allocation, investigations, and operations. The ability of analysts to achieve this level of performance relies significantly on the evolving professionalization of the analyst position as well as the changing culture of police organizations. A lack of standard criteria for analysts' training and performance (IALEIA, 2004), coupled with a reluctance to recognize analysts as professionals within the law enforcement arena, has inhibited the progress of analysts' ability to provide influential products (Osborne, 2006).

Moreover, law enforcement organizations by nature have been traditionally deductive in reasoning - inhibiting the inductive approach applied in strategic assessments (Quarmby, 2004).

The relationship between individual evaluation and organizational performance has been well documented in the literature (cf: Ahire *et al.*, 1996) and focuses on two critical elements - efficiency and effectiveness. Efficiency involves evaluating the process by which intelligence operations are handled. Public law enforcement agencies focus on policy and operation procedures (i.e., records management, privacy policy). Law enforcement intelligence is prone to a lack of empirical evaluation. This is not to say law enforcement is unique in this regard, because other governmental agencies experience difficulty evaluating organizational performance due to coordination problems within a multi-level system which produces many rules and more regulations, intra-organizational conflicts, clearance points, and misunderstandings (Swiss, 1984). Effectiveness is centered on outputs as well as outcomes. Outputs are the result of processes, or the end product. As discussed, actionable intelligence is the desired output of law enforcement intelligence. Outcomes, for purposes of this discussion, can be defined as the level of performance or accomplishment of a process (London & Smither, 1995). Does actionable intelligence produced by law enforcement intelligence functions serve as a means to prevent or mitigate threats? Does the quality of intelligence analysis influence decisions made within the agency? Does the police executive use intelligence to guide their allocation of resources for strategic goals? These are questions that effective intelligence evaluations will seek to answer.

Much of the literature on organizational effectiveness is focused on organizational goals - commonly referred to as the goal model. However, the goal model, as it is commonly discussed in the literature, operates under the assumption that organizations as a whole can have discernible goals (Perrow, 1968; Warner & Haven 1968). The opposing argument is that organizations are composed of individuals, and thus the goals of these individuals account for organizational goals (Georgiou, 1973; Quinn & Rohrbaugh, 1983) - even if individual goals contradict organizational goals (Latham & Yukl, 1975; Erez *et al.*, 1985). Many of these studies show: 1) that the organization does not realize its goals effectively; and, 2) that the organization has different goals from those it claims to have (Bresser & Bishop, 1983, Lan & Rainey, 1992).

At the organizational level the goal model makes an invalid assumption regarding levels of analysis. Etzioni (1960) gives an example of this occurring when the current position of an organization is compared with the desired position. Some studies of informal organizations commit a similar mistake when they compare the mission statement of an organization with actual organizational practices and suggest that organizational change has taken place. Typically, the organization has created an informal structure and the new mission of the organization never existed in practice (Etzioni, 1960). These concepts will be increasingly important to keep in mind as intelligence-led policing requires a re-structuring of organizations as well as the creation, sustaining and network capacity building for ongoing interaction with state and local fusion centers to further enhance the information sharing environment.

An alternative model that can be adopted for law enforcement intelligence analysis is the system model. The intent of this approach is not the goal itself, but a working model of a social unit which is capable of achieving a goal (Thompson, 1967). This method is based on an assumption that not all means are devoted to the desired outcome of the organization, but that some means are devoted to functions which sustain the organization (e.g., maintenance staff) - therefore increasing effectiveness. As such, an organization that devotes all its efforts to fulfilling one functional requirement including obtaining desired outcomes, will undermine the fulfillment of this functional requirement, because necessary functions of the organization will be neglected (Thompson, 1967).

A study of organizational effectiveness by Georgopoulos and Tannenbaum (1957) is one of the few studies that distinguish explicitly between the goal and system approaches to the study of effectiveness. Instead of using goals, they constructed three indexes, each measuring one basic element of the system; *station productivity* - an organizationally set standard of outputs (e.g., number of intelligence reports produced), *intra-organizational strain* - the incidence of tension and conflict among organizational subgroups, and *organizational flexibility* - defined as the ability to adjust to external or internal change (Georgopoulos & Tannenbaum, 1957). Each state has multiple state, local and tribal law enforcement agencies that are currently in the process of developing an intelligence capability. This approach to measuring effectiveness provides a foundation upon which to build a more applicable model to measure this phenomenon within the intelligence context. A common issue related to intelligence analysts is the production of quantity versus quality intelligence reports. The function of intelligence is not to produce the greatest number of reports, but reports of the highest quality intelligence that can guide law enforcement operations - both tactical and strategic. As such, station productivity should be operationalized as the number of intelligence reports that result in successful operations - such as threats that were mitigated or prevented or strategic priorities identified and allocated resources as a result of analysis reports.

Even though the raw number of intelligence products disseminated is an inappropriate evaluation measure of intelligence until performance it is currently the only objective measure available. These poor measures persist largely because most police agencies do not have the resources to invest in identifying more appropriate measures of intelligence unit accomplishments. Perhaps to a lesser extent, but also contributing to this problem is a lack of understanding of the role intelligence analysis plays in the organization. As Cope (2004) notes, there is a consistent clash of cultures among law enforcement officers (sworn personnel) and intelligence analysts (non-sworn personnel) as a result of each party having a misunderstanding and preconceived notion of what police officers and analysts actually do within a police agency. Analysts are typically viewed as publishers of reports (Osborne, 2006) and traditionally have occupied the role of supplementing police investigations (Ratcliffe, 2008a). These practices have been institutionalized in policing, and when coupled with a lack of understanding of the roles of personnel within the organization result in the persistence of poor evaluation measures (Pfeffer & Sutton, 2000).

Lastly, the possibility exists that if valid empirical measures are identified and evaluated, the results may not be favorable - and as such, cast doubt and negativity on not only the initiative being evaluated, but the chief executive and department as a whole. Ratcliffe (2008a) notes that this is a common challenge within law enforcement intelligence and that senior officials may be more willing to determine the new initiative as a success rather than risk negative implications. This view is consistent with business practices in the private sector (Ingraham *et al.*, 1998) and furthered by administrators in the public sector who fear a lack of forgiveness from constituents (Ruscio, 1996).

Maintaining a standing of good-faith from the community is difficult for all law enforcement agencies. As previously mentioned, some scholars have argued that community policing was in major part designed to promote police agencies as more legitimate social institutions in the eyes of their constituents and that a similar approach could be argued for ILP. As Ratcliffe (2008a) points out, the need to address public perceptions of crime in the United Kingdom began to trump initiatives to address crime itself. This was illustrated by the Home Office's[16] published standards for police evaluation that emphasized community assurance and a citizen outreach focus. This type of police performance evaluation is somewhat at odds with what is necessary to promote an intelligence-led approach. Evaluation based on community assurance relies more on public perception than on the analysis of information and statistics (Ratcliffe, 2008a).

SUMMATION OF ORGANIZATIONAL RESEARCH FOR POLICE CHANGE

In summary, the present study draws upon a diverse set of conceptual studies and the existing empirical literature. Research specifically on intelligence-led policing is sparse to this point and lacks general consistency, both in context and application. The two predominant conceptual approaches to intelligence-led policing are becoming more unified as the philosophy continues to evolve. However, the fundamental differences remain in that the Ratcliffe model views intelligence-led policing as an incident data-driven method that operates independently of previous policing philosophies. The C&C (2009a) model views intelligence-led policing as a melting pot of best practices and lessons learned from community policing, problem-oriented policing, CompStat, and crime analysis, while maintaining an all-hazards, all-crimes, all-threats orientation. Such fundamental differences are pertinent to the adoption of intelligence-led policing. While agencies are not likely to view the adoption of intelligence-led policing as an automatic disregard for community policing, some may

---

[16] The Home Office is the United Kingdom's lead government department for immigration and passports, drugs policy, counter-terrorism and police.

have increased difficulty in translating the rhetoric into practice if there is not familiar ground upon which to build a new foundation for ILP.

Since the intelligence-led policing literature is just emerging, this study draws from the depth of research on community policing adoption. Community policing and intelligence-led policing feature conceptual similarities that enable the current study to adopt similar theoretical and methodological approaches to those used to study COP to inform an exploration of ILP. Furthermore, research on organizational and policing innovation has been greatly informative. The exploration of state-of-the-art policing cannot presently find a better fit than with intelligence-led policing post-9/11. The "how" and the "why" intelligence-led policing gained so much momentum are critical elements in explaining its widespread adoption in American law enforcement circles. Lastly, research on homeland security is highly beneficial as often times any topic which is "intelligence related" seems to get lumped together under the umbrella term of "homeland security" in the post-911 setting. Such research is necessary. however, as law enforcement intelligence does indeed have many intersections with emergency preparedness, response, and counterterrorism. Once again, the National Criminal Intelligence Sharing Plan states "all agencies, regardless of size, must have a minimal law enforcement intelligence capability" (GIWG, 2003:iii)...to this point, no one has empirically given light to exactly how this is to be achieved.

CHAPTER 4

Research Design Exploring ILP Adoption

A review of intelligence-led policing, community policing, innovation, and homeland security literature has demonstrated the need to identify characteristics that influence the adoption of law enforcement intelligence practices. The review indicated a lack of empirical assessments related to law enforcement intelligence. Sources of either quantitative or qualitative data may be difficult to obtain for examination or comparison. Moreover, given the slew of possible adaptations intelligence practices can take within the varying types of law enforcement agencies in the United States, a mixed methods approach (Tashakkori & Teddlie, 1998) is imperative for this study. This section will begin with the identification and discussion of the appropriate source of data for the current study. A discussion of the survey instrument and research questions is also featured in this chapter.

MICHIGAN STATE UNIVERSITY INTELLIGENCE TOOLBOX TRAINING PROGRAM

A foundation for the current study is the interaction with intelligence professionals gained through the Michigan State University "Intelligence Toolbox Training Program" that was launched in 2005. From 2005 until early-2011 this program trained 4,723 law enforcement officers representing 2,102 different agencies across the United States. These experiences have played a pivotal role in the development of the theoretical framework as well as the operationalization of variables included in the models. This approach can be best described as a deductive/inductive hybrid. While theory guides the present study, the application of theory to the intelligence-led policing phenomenon would be difficult at best without practical knowledge. Moreover, given the ambiguity of the ILP concept operationalizing measures to test the theoretical models would be virtually impossible. At the time of the present study, there is simply too little known from the research literature to guide a study on intelligence-led policing without interaction with key persons tasked with the responsibility of adopting this new philosophy in their law enforcement agencies.

THE ORIGINAL EVALUATION PROJECT

The current study will involve secondary analysis of data gleaned from the "Understanding the Intelligence Practices of State, Local, and Tribal Law Enforcement Agencies", a grant to the School of Criminal Justice at Michigan State University funded by the National Institute of Justice[17]. This section will discuss the survey instrument, the data collection process, and the quantitative components of the original evaluation project as this is also the methodology for the current study. A section will follow that discusses how the data for the current study were gleaned from the original evaluation project.

The original project study was designed to examine two facets of law enforcement intelligence and information sharing; 1) identify the major obstacles of effective intelligence gathering and information sharing; and, 2) identify best practices for integrating domestic intelligence into the information sharing environment. The original project relied upon two research approaches; the first approach entailed two national surveys targeting two different populations within the law enforcement intelligence community - state, local, and tribal law enforcement agencies and regional and state fusion centers. The present study conducts a secondary analysis of the data collected from the state, local, and tribal population. The second approach relies on case studies identified by the investigators for having established and demonstrated successful intelligence practices. The data collection strategy of the original evaluation project involved compiling and analyzing open source documents that were supplemented by interviews with key informants. The focus of this qualitative approach is the intelligence practices of state and local law enforcement. More specifically, since these practices are so new to the field of policing they are subject to conceptual interpretation due to consistent ambiguity. A potential increase in systematic error with respect to accurate conceptual interpretations is minimized by contextual

---

[17] Grant number 2008-IJ-CX-0007 awarded to Michigan State University, School of Criminal Justice in 2009.

understanding achieved through a case study approach (Tashakkori & Teddlie, 1998).

Survey Instrument and Data Collection

The quantitative data gathering technique employed was a self-administered questionnaire completed through a web-designed survey provider[18]. As mentioned, the present study utilizes the data gathered from the state, local, and tribal law enforcement population that was sampled using a key informant method of subject identification. The survey was administered to law enforcement personnel who attended the Department of Homeland Security-funded training program, "Developing an Intelligence Capacity in State, Local, and Tribal Law Enforcement Agencies[19]." In June 2009 when the survey was disseminated, the program had provided training to 2,395 law enforcement personnel from 967 agencies; these 967 agencies comprise the purposive sample population.

The project chose to survey this population for two principal reasons. First, this sample included law enforcement personnel who have sufficient understanding of key issues related to building an intelligence capacity, and as a result are the most appropriate to respond to the survey items. Second, their awareness of the intelligence structures, requirements, and formal communication networks increased the likelihood that they will have direct knowledge about the strengths and weaknesses of these issues within their own organizations. Differences in demographic composition, size, jurisdiction[20] of agencies, and the variety of personnel[21] that attended the training program, and thus comprise the survey population, ensures the sample includes personnel that will have operational information

---

[18] www.SnapSurvey.com

[19] This training program was developed and delivered by the School of Criminal Justice at Michigan State University through funding provided by the Department of Homeland Security-FEMA Training Exercises and Integration/Training Office.

[20] Type of jurisdiction refers to agencies that are state, municipal, county, and tribal.

[21] Variety of personnel refers to chiefs of police, command staff, patrol officers, and civilian analysts.

for understanding the factors associated with facilitating and inhibiting successful intelligence-led policing adoption.

The questions posed on the survey included structured, semi-structured, and open-ended items. The survey was developed and administered in four phases. First, the principal investigators developed draft survey instruments. These instruments were reviewed for comment and vetted by the Advisory Board for the Michigan State University, School of Criminal Justice, Intelligence Training Program - a group composed of law enforcement intelligence executives at the local, state, tribal, and federal levels who are broadly considered to be subject matter experts. Second, the survey was pre-tested to a group of line-level law enforcement personnel. These line-level officers represented agencies of a variety of sizes, geographic locations, and functional responsibilities. Each of these line-level officer groups was involved in the pre-test phase to assess the survey instrument for validity.

Interviews were conducted with the persons involved in the pre-test to determine problematic questions, oversights in the questionnaires, and potential problematic response items. Third, after the pre-test had been completed and the survey revised, a letter was sent informing the participants about the evaluation study and requesting their involvement with permission of the principal investigators from the Intelligence Training Program. After the initial contact letter was disseminated seeking participation in the study, an email message was sent asking them to complete the survey. Fourth, every two weeks, hence an email message was sent to personnel who had not yet responded.

The response rate of self-administered surveys is always a methodological issue in self-administered surveys (Yu & Cooper, 1983; Jenkins & Dillman, 1995; Dey, 1997). With this in mind, the project investigators took into account source legitimacy, addressing the letter to specific personnel, and topic salience. Legitimacy was demonstrated through support from the National Institute of Justice as well as having the survey administered by Michigan State University, a known entity to the respondents due to their participation in the

Intelligence Toolbox training program[22]. As noted above, it was possible to send letters to specific personnel since the project had access to a database that included the names, addresses, and emails of all of the law enforcement personnel who had attended the Intelligence Toolbox Program. Third, an increasing level of interest in intelligence and the areas that were the focus of the survey influenced the number of surveys returned. In some instances email addresses were no longer valid - resulting in an automated return message that the survey was undeliverable. In an effort to remedy this problem, a graduate assistant assigned to the original evaluation project contacted agencies over the phone that had faulty emails. Agencies that expressed a willingness to participate in the study were provided the website link to complete the survey. Specific number of agencies and respondents for the current study are provided below during a discussion of the response rate.

Sensitivity was taken with respect to the construction of the survey instrument and the case study interview tool. Such sensitivities are required to improve reliability and validity - both for purposes of testing hypotheses and ensuring accurate and consistent responses (Bernard, 2002). Consistent with principles of survey methodology, safeguards for the construction of the surveys included (Bernard, 2003):

1) Utilize common wording and terminology.
2) Ensuring that the questions remained neutral and did not "lead" respondents.
3) Categorizing and ordering items so that - when needed - questions would seem organic in topic and flow.
4) Maintain simple and straightforward instructions for survey completion and submission.
5) Maintain transparency with respect to the intent of the research.
6) Communicate that the survey was completely optional and at any point participants could cease participation.

---

[22] The MSU Intelligence Program represents a partnership with the Intelligence Divisions of the FBI and DEA, and has been developed through the major DHS-supported intelligence training programs.

A Brief Note on Survey Population
As it has been established, the concept of intelligence-led policing is, at best, in its infancy. Ambiguity and a general lack of knowledge with respect to intelligence practices within law enforcement agencies make it difficult and inappropriate to use traditional random sampling techniques. Thus the present study utilizes a "key informant" sampling method (cf. Phillips, 1981). The key informant method recognizes that specific persons within an organization have specific knowledge pertaining to specific concepts as a result of their role and responsibilities within the organization. For purposes of the present study, rather than randomly selecting individuals from within a police agency to respond to survey items regarding intelligence practices, the key informant method identifies persons assigned to carry out the agency's intelligence function - thus targeting the person(s) who is most likely to provide a valid judgment about the agency's intelligence practices. The intent of such a sampling method is that persons responding to the survey questions will be less likely to have minimal knowledge with respect to the concepts and therefore reducing systematic error. This approach has been utilized in policing when examining issues such as informal information sharing (Weiss, 1997), policing the mentally ill (Borum *et al.*, 1998), and policing sex workers (Simic *et al.*, 2006).

Mixed Methods Research Component
Given the present study will integrate case studies for contextual insights into the constructs that will be examined quantitatively, a discussion of the relevance and application of qualitative methods is appropriate at this point. Mixed methods research in the social sciences first used as a label for the use of multiple methods to measure a single construct (Jick, 1983). The proclaimed legitimation of mixed methods research in the social sciences is attributed to the discussions in methods textbooks, a practice still common currently (Hammersley & Atkinson, 1995). Typologies of mixed methods have increased several times over with respect to data, researchers, theory, and methods (Denzin, 1970). In terms of variable measurement, mixed methods contribute to the researcher's ability to improve convergent validity. In studies that seek to examine highly complex or unclear phenomenon, mixed methods improves to the researcher's ability to achieve a more

accurate and comprehensive understanding of the phenomenon (Gorad & Taylor, 2004).

Even though the use of mixed-methods research has become more prevalent in social science research, a debate still exists between quantitative and qualitative purists and the advantages mixed-methods may have (Johnson & Onwuegbuzie, 2004). Advocates of both perspectives view their methods as the best practices for research, and as a result have advocated the incompatibility theory which insists qualitative and quantitative research methods cannot and should not be mixed (Howe, 1988). Despite the incongruence among these purists, there has been substantial support for mixed methods approaches (Johnson & Onwuegbuzie, 2007; Morgan, 2007; Tashakkori & Creswell, 2008). A discussion on the debate among quantitative and qualitative purists is not pertinent to this discussion; more appropriate is a discussion as to which qualitative approach is most beneficial to examine ILP adoption. A mixed methods approach utilizing quantitative data analysis as well as case study observations will be employed in the current study.

Case study research is an approach that utilizes a variety of data sources (e.g., reports, interviews, and documents) to examine a bounded system (Creswell, 2007). Narrative and phenomenological approaches are not appropriate given these methods are based on stories and personal interpretations of events. An ethnographic approach could possibly provide very insightful results with respect to informal and line-level aspects of law enforcement intelligence, such as the interactions and behaviors among those responsible for intelligence tasks. However, ethnographies are extremely time - consuming and require a broad range of resources, all of which are not logistically reasonable for this study.

Case Study Research
Popularity of case study research gained momentum during the 1960s when researchers became concerned about possible limitations of quantitative methods (Tashakkori & Taddlie, 1998). Much like other qualitative approaches, case studies have potential pitfalls. Case study is known as a mixed methods research strategy. Feagin *et al.* (1991) asserted that mixed methods can occur with data, investigators, theories, and even methodologies. Stake (1995) posited that protocols that are used to ensure accuracy and alternative explanations are called

mixed methods. The need for mixed methods arises from the ethical need to confirm the validity of the processes (Stake, 1995). A frequent criticism of case study is that it typically relies on a single case examination, leaving the method vulnerable to critics of the approach's ability to generalize results (Yin, 1994). This criticism is reinforced by the notion that case studies lack statistical abilities (Kennedy, 1979), objectivity (Johnson *et al.*, 1999) and external validity (Schofield, 2002).

Hamel *et al.* (1993) took the position that regardless of the number of cases examined this approach does not transform a multiple case into a macroscopic study. The goal of the study should establish the parameters, and then should be applied to all research. In this way, even a single case could be considered acceptable, provided it met the established objective (Hamel *et al.*, 1993). Yin (1989) notes that case studies can be seen to satisfy the three tenets of qualitative methodology – namely describing, understanding, and explaining. The applicability of case study research to the current question - and ILP adoption - is the prevalent use of case study techniques in government and evaluative situations (Fitzpatrick & Sanders, 2003). Moreover, this method has been applied effectively to community-based prevention programs in social science research (Holder, 1987; Maton & Salem, 1995). Yin (1994) acknowledges the literature in case study research is limited in comparison to that of experimental or quasi-experimental research. However, he correctly notes the requirements and inflexibility of quantitative methods make case studies the default alternative for the study of certain phenomenon. Since case studies do not need a minimum number of cases or specified sampling methods, it is the responsibility of the researcher to apply appropriate methods for a given situation. Case studies can be single or multiple-case designs.

Single cases are used to confirm or challenge a theory, or to represent a unique or extreme case (Yin, 1994). Single-case studies are also ideal for cases where an observer may have access to a phenomenon that was previously inaccessible. Single-case designs require careful investigation to avoid misrepresentation and to maximize the investigator's access to the evidence. Stake (1995) and Yin (1994) both identified six primary sources of evidence in case studies - documents, archival records, interviews, direct observation, participant-observation, and physical artifacts. Multiple-case studies follow a strict replication logic. Each individual case study consists of a complete study, in which facts are gathered from various sources and conclusions are drawn on those facts (Yin, 1994). When replication is not possible, the researcher has no choice but to apply single-case designs. The present study utilizes a qualitative interview design which makes replication difficult, but is most applicable in exploratory research. Yin (1994) posits the generalization of results, from either single or multiple designs, is made to theory and not to populations. As with any method, multiple cases strengthen reliability through pattern-matching, thus increasing confidence in the theory being tested.

Yin (1994) lists several examples along with the appropriate research design for case studies. These designs included exploratory, explanatory, and descriptive case studies, each of which can be contain single or multiple-case studies. In exploratory case studies, fieldwork and data collection may be occur before research questions are formed. Nonetheless, the framework of the study must be created ahead of time (Yin, 1994). Explanatory cases are applied for causal studies and draw upon complex and multivariate cases as well as pattern-matching techniques. Descriptive cases require the researcher to develop a theoretical framework prior to beginning the case study. However, the selection of cases and unit of analysis is developed similar to exploratory and explanatory studies. The underlying function of case studies is to develop holistic understanding of cultural systems of action. Cultural systems of action refer to sets of interrelated activities engaged in by the actors in a social situation (Feagin *et al.*, 1990). Case study research is not sampling research, and as such must always feature explicit boundaries (Stake, 1995, Creswell, 2007). However, the selection of cases must be done so as to maximize what can be learned in the period of time available for the study. The unit of analysis is a critical factor in the case study, and it is typically a system of actions rather than an individual or group of individuals (Stake, 1995). Case studies typically select one or two issues that are critical to understanding the system being examined.

A case study's questions are typically "how" and "why" questions (Yin, 1994). The research questions developed to guide the study are created from these basic "how" and "why" questions. However, not all studies need to have such testable propositions. An exploratory study, rather than having propositions, would have a stated purpose on which the success of the case should be determined. The unit of analysis defines what the case is, which could be groups, law enforcement organizations, or whole countries. Linking the data to propositions and the criteria for interpreting the findings are the least developed aspects in case studies (Yin, 1994). Construct validity is suspect with respect to case study research as a result of the possible subjectivity of the researcher. Yin (1994) proposed three methods to mitigate these criticisms: 1) using multiple sources of evidence; 2) establishing a replicable chain of evidence; and, 3) having a draft case study report reviewed by multiple key informants. Internal validity is typically only a concern when the explanatory design is used. This is usually a problem of inferences in case studies, and can be dealt with using pattern-matching (Yin, 1994).

External validity is a criticism against case studies in reference to single-case studies. However, this criticism goes back to the discussion on a lack of acceptable generalizability. Reliability is enhanced in many ways in a case study; one of the most important methods in this regard is the development of a detailed case study protocol. As with all other qualitative approaches, or social science research in general, case studies are not without significant challenges. A difficult challenge, with no concise clarification of how to mitigate it, is the task of properly identifying the bounded system of interest (Creswell, 2007). Complicating this task is the decision of using a single- or using a multi-case design. While Creswell (2007) notes multi-case studies normally should not include more than four or five cases, the temptation exists to include more in an attempt to bolster generalizability.

Case Study Interviews
Researchers utilize interviews in a variety of different methodological approaches, thus it is important to discuss how interviews were conducted for this study. King (1994) best describes the approach utilized, and refers to it as the qualitative research interview. This approach differs from the commonly used structured interview in that it relies heavily on open-ended questions that result from persistent probing by the administrator, often times resulting in a free-flowing dialogue between interviewer and interviewee. King (1994) identified a number of situations in which the qualitative research interview is most appropriate and among them are situations where exploratory research is required prior to conducting the interview. More specifically, the qualitative research interview relies upon an

unstructured set of questions which are typically asked in a pre-determined manner. The interviewer has a set of general questions that target issues which might be addressed throughout the interview. As case studies, or additional interviews, are carried out the set of general items may be modified in order to supplement them with questions directed to target areas of interest as they emerge.

Numerous practical issues related to qualitative research interviews arise in every study. Flexibility and adaptability among interviewers is a critical component to this process. Typically, each interview begins with common questions, but each session tends to be unique as the interviewer adapts to the interviewee's preferences and seeks to identify appropriate follow-up questions to probe for further information. It is critical that the content of the questions is consistent with the level of the interviewee, and that the interviewer properly acknowledges and is appreciative of any executive interviewees. The latter is important, especially with respect to this study because many of the persons interviewed were in leadership positions in their respective agencies. These persons are likely to expect treatment and differential forms of interaction that are consistent with their organizational status. If appropriate care is not taken in these respects, an interviewer may offend the interviewee, resulting too often in the restriction of information.

Reliability may be problematic when utilizing the qualitative research interview. As a result of not having a structured questioning format, qualitative research interviews can be particularly weak in terms of their reliability. Since each interviewer has a unique interpretation of issues examined throughout the interview, and also follows-up with different probing questions, it is unlikely that the same interview conducted by different interviewers would yield similar findings. As such, and as the intent of the present study has explained, this interview approach is best utilized for exploratory purposes; the interview data gathered in this way may not be appropriate for theory testing or rigorous qualitative data analysis (Miles & Huberman, 1984).

In quantitative research, validity is a reflection of how well a measurement device actually measures what it claims to measure (Maxfield & Babbie, 2006). While quantitative research validity focuses on method, qualitative research validity focuses on quality of interpretations (King, 1994). For valid qualitative research, a researcher's conclusions and interpretations must accurately reflect the reality of the information relayed from the interviewee. To enhance validity, King (1994) recommends that interviewers engage participants in feedback loops. The researcher communicates his/her interpretations and conclusions to the interviewee to reaffirm they have correctly interpreted the facts of the interviewee's reality. In this study feedback loops are achieved through the interviewee reviewing the narrative of the case study site visit. For purposes of exploratory research, qualitative interviews are a useful tool. Such an approach enables researchers to obtain contextual insights which were previously outside the purview of researchers given a lack of established literature.

Mixed Methods for Intelligence-Led Policing Adoption
The present study employs the previously discussed quantitative and qualitative methods to explore the adoption of intelligence-led policing innovation among American law enforcement agencies. It has been argued that the most appropriate qualitative method to employ is a mixed-methods approach for examining intelligence-led policing adoption via a case study approach. Given the dynamic nature of law enforcement intelligence environments where policies and practices are constantly changing along with periodic personnel turnover, case studies provide a definable environment in which the practices, experience and interpretations of intelligence-led policing can be examined. Moreover, as noted case studies are best applied to instances where further explanation and understanding are needed in an understudied area of research. Much of what law enforcement intelligence personnel do is learned on the job. Police agency personnel are often assigned intelligence responsibility out of necessity rather than qualification, thus they face the challenges of a steep learning curve. There are also specific aspects of law enforcement agencies and intelligence alike that require case study analysis to provide appropriate context for quantitative analyses.

As noted earlier the size of an agency serves as a significant contextual condition for the use of case studies. An agency with 500 sworn police officers and 15 full-time intelligence analysts will have a substantially different ILP capacity than an agency with five sworn officers and no access to an intelligence analyst. Given the focus of ILP adoption, coupled with the fact most law enforcement agencies have fewer than 50 sworn officers, the policies and procedures by which ILP is adopted across these agencies will provide profound insight. The present study utilizes case studies from the fusion center context. While fusion centers are local agencies, the integration of many state and local agencies under the auspice of fusion centers allows for the intelligence practices at the state and local level to be studied effectively. Moreover, not only are these practices demonstrated, but they are done so in the most appropriate law enforcement intelligence environment - thus making facilitators and inhibitors of successful adoption most salient for the researcher to document.

Case Studies and Information Collection
Fusion centers provide a unique intelligence-specific organizational environment where intelligence-led policing practices at the state, local, and tribal levels can be systematically observed. Site visit locations for the fusion center case studies were determined through consultation with subject matter experts who identified fusion centers they believed to be involved in the most innovative and successful intelligence practices. Such an approach to identify agencies with effective and innovative practices has been used successfully in other studies of this general nature (Weiss, 1998; Chermak & Weiss, 2000). These site visit locations were also based on geographic diversity and type of population served. For example, the Florida Fusion Center structure is a multi-tier system with regional fusion centers operating under the guidance of the state fusion center. This structure best serves their geographic and population responsibility as the state of Florida has many large cities with a variety of present and potential crime and terrorism threats. Conversely, the Southern Nevada Counter-Terrorism Center operates independently and its focus is primarily on the City of Las Vegas.

Primary data collection for the case studies was achieved through interviews with members at all levels of the fusion center. At both locations, members from the executive, analytical, and operational level were represented. As noted in Chapter Two, these interviews were conducted in the qualitative, unstructured context. While each interview had standard questions to generally guide the interview, each interaction with the fusion center personnel had its own fluid movement. This approach is necessary as each fusion center has some nonobvious characteristics that allow it to be successful. These best practices are what research strives to identify, learn about, and examine with the intent of translating them for purposes of broader application.

Another step to enhance the validity and reliability of the case studies was the collection of documents provided to the research team by fusion center personnel. These documents often included operational planning, strategic missions, organizational structure, and policies and procedures. All of these documents were carefully vetted for security purposes. Once again, to maximize the validity and reliability of the information obtained at the site visits a supplemental source of data collection was that of open source documents. Open source documents were gathered before and after both site visits. All open source materials were provided to the fusion center executives for purposes of making certain that the information collected was accurate. The intent of the interviews was to provide a detailed overview of the structure, activities, and path of development of both fusion centers, but focused on the identification of best practices for responding to critical intelligence issues examined in the quantitative survey.

CURRENT STUDY

The current study seeks to explore relationships between relevant organizational constructs identified from an interdisciplinary review of literature and intelligence-led policing adoption. More specifically, types of diffusion, organizational structure and context, and performance evaluation are anticipated to facilitate the adoption of intelligence-led policing. To explore these relationships, the current study employs the methodology to follow. Given the methodology of the original evaluation project, the current study employs a cross-sectional design that features both strengths and weaknesses. Cross-sectional data cannot establish causal order in regard to organizational change, but observations of group differences are possible in this approach (de Vaus, 2001). Given the large array of law enforcement agencies in the sample, many agencies will be at different stages in the ILP adoption process and thus allow for the exploration of different variables across agencies at the same stage of adoption as well as those at different stages.

Survey Response Rate

The initial survey instrument was disseminated in June 2009 to 2,395 individuals. After each sampling wave, email addresses for persons who had already completed the survey or indicated they did not want to participate were removed from the next wave of emails. Only thirty agencies declined to participate in the study. An additional 313 of the email addresses that were provided to the Michigan State University research and training team were no longer valid. The final survey submission total was 456 responses. Furthermore, it should be noted that the sample for the present study is comprised of personnel drawn from only state, local, and tribal law enforcement agencies. Initial responses were received from a variety of federal law enforcement, such as the Federal Bureau of Investigation, Drug Enforcement Administration, Bureau of Alcohol, Tobacco, and Firearms, Transportation Security Administration, and Immigration and Customs Enforcement. These responses were removed from the sample. While these agencies certainly play a significant role in law enforcement intelligence (and especially national security intelligence) , the present study is focused on practices at the state, local, and tribal level - thus these agencies are not appropriate for comparison. Regional information sharing centers[23] were also removed from the sample as they are intelligence-mission specific as well as not related to state, local, or tribal law enforcement. Lastly, responses from private sector companies' security divisions were also removed as they do not represent state, local, or tribal law enforcement. Seventeen organizations were removed which were either information sharing centers of federal law enforcement agencies.

A challenge for the current study to examine intelligence-led policing adoption at the agency-level of analysis is that the data contain some survey responses that are multiples from a single agency. Specifically, there are 42 agencies that responded to the survey more than a single time. The dataset contains 351 cases - or survey responses. While an argument could be made that these different responses from within the same agency could stand alone due to the ambiguity of intelligence practices within state and local law enforcement, these multiple responses from within the same agency can

---

[23] Regional information system (RISS) centers that responded included: Middle Atlantic-Great Lakes Organized Crime Law Enforcement Network (MAGLOCLEN), Mid-States Organized Crime Information Center (MOCIC), and the Regional Organized Crime Information Center (ROCIC).

result in inaccurate standard errors for examining research questions (Lee *et al.*, 1986). As such, the most appropriate method to remedy the multiple response issue and establish the unit of analysis as police agencies is to account for a complex survey design which is by employing STATA statistical analysis software. Since standard errors affect levels of statistical significance, the conclusions drawn from an analysis that fails to employ a complex survey design may be misleading (Eltinge & Sribney, 1997; Lumley, 2004).

Table 2: Agency Descriptive Information (*n*=272)

	Median (Mean)
Agency Size	276 (1341)
	n (Valid Percent)
Agency Region	
Northeast	77 (22%)
Southeast	80 (23%)
Midwest	91 (27%)
Southwest	37 (11%)
West	60 (17%)
Respondent's Position	
Administrator	100 (30%)
Supervisor	79 (23%)
Investigator	107 (32%)
Analyst	51 (15%)
Respondent Years at Agency	
Less than 1 Year	1 (.3%)
1-3 Years	21 (6%)
4-9 Years	60 (18%)
10-15 Years	21 (21%)
More than 15 Years	185 (55%)

The complex survey design function in STATA adjusted the standard errors for all responses from the same agency. A unique identifier is assigned to each agency and STATA recognizes the unique number to adjust for the appropriate standard error. Once these multiple responses are accounted for, the dataset contained 272 unique responses at the agency level. Lastly, follow-up communications with agencies that did not complete the survey indicated that many agencies had multiple personnel receive the survey instrument, but rather than having each individual responding the agency tasked one person with completing the survey on behalf of the entire agency. Given the number of agencies that comprised the survey population was 967, this is the denominator for determining the response rate at the agency-level of analysis. As such, the adjusted response rate for the present study is 28% (N= 272 / 967) - an acceptable rate for an exploratory email survey on organizational implementation research (Kappelman & Prybutok, 1995; Sheehan, 2001).

Table 2 displays descriptive information for the agencies represented in the current study. The median agency size is 276 total sworn and non-sworn personnel while the majority of agencies are located in the Midwest region of the United States, followed closely by the Southeast and Northwest. Respondents are mostly investigators and administrators who have been employed by their agency for more than 15 years.

A Note on Missing Data

Perhaps more appropriate to discuss within the "Study Limitations" section of this study, a note on the handling of missing data is necessary at the outset. The current study utilizes variables that have a range of missing values[24]. The majority of the items on the survey instruments solicit for an affirmative response if the characteristic in question in present. Thus, the assumption is that where an agency does not have affirmation, then the characteristic is either not present or unknown within the agency and this likely reflects a less developed intelligence-led policing capability than would a response in the affirmative. Furthermore, some of the items included on the survey instrument simply do not apply to some of the responding agencies. For example, if an agency did not respond to items pertaining to analyst performance evaluation it is because they do not employ an intelligence analyst. This goes back to the idea of implementation fidelity in that some agencies have appropriate levels of intelligence-led policing, but the characteristics of their intelligence function are inherently different than others. As such, the values discussed above are not missing at random.

---

[24] The highest percentage of missing values is in the "performance evaluation" variable where 12% of agencies did not respond.

Data that are not missing at random create an issue as they make it impossible to obtain an unbiased estimate of parameters (Bryman, 2003). To most appropriately remedy such a shortcoming, a study would need to write an algorithm that accounts for the missing data that could then be incorporated into a more complex model for estimating missing values (Dunning & Freedman, 2008). Such an approach is beyond the scope of the current study. Given the intent of the current study to explore intelligence-led policing adoption among U.S. law enforcement agencies, these missing data can be coded into the lowest-response category - a method accepted in exploring organizational-level change (Hardy & Bryman, 2009; Maloney *et al.*, 2010).

As such, for each variable included in the current study missing values are coded into the lowest response category. If the variable is dichotomous, missing values are coded as zero. If the variable has a range, the missing value is coded as the minimum value of the range. Such an approach is most appropriate in the current study as it minimizes a reduction of statistical computing power. To employ listwise deletion of missing values would decrease the sample size. Moreover, to employ a method of imputation would be inappropriate given the nature of the current study. To develop an estimate on whether or not an agency has a privacy policy would conflict the intent of the study. Furthermore, in the context of the current exploratory study, agencies that do not respond to an item can be considered at the minimal level as they are likely to be missing this characteristic from a conceptual standpoint. For example, if an agency does not respond to having a privacy policy, it is consistent with the intent of the study and the operationalization of a measure to consider this agency as not having a privacy policy. Regardless if an agency responds for the reason of either not knowing if the agency has a privacy policy or not, or because of unwillingness to admit the agency is operating without a privacy policy, the value coded as not having a privacy policy would remain consistent with the operationalization of the measure.

RESEARCH QUESTIONS
The underlying objective of this study is to explore the adoption of intelligence-led policing by state and local law enforcement organizations in the United States. A review of the literature infers that certain organizational characteristics will likely affect the adoption of intelligence-led policing - much similar to the research discussed on

community policing. Specifically, the types of diffusion, organizational structure and context, and performance evaluation are anticipated to influence the adoption of intelligence-led policing. Predictive differences are also anticipated between adoption as measured in this study and adoption as self-reported by responding agencies. Research questions for this study are as follows:

RQ₁: Which types of diffusion are most likely to affect intelligence-led policing adoption?
It is anticipated that each of the four types of diffusion will positively affect intelligence-led policing adoption. These four types included threat awareness, risk mediation, peer emulation, and familiarity with the intelligence-led policing concept. It is anticipated that all four types of diffusion will have a positive influence on intelligence-led policing adoption.

RQ₂: Which organizational structure and context factors are most likely to affect intelligence-led policing adoption?
It is anticipated that variables measuring organizational structure and context will all have a positive effect on the adoption of intelligence-led policing. Structural characteristics include formalization, civilianization, and functional differentiation. Context characteristics include task scope, training, commitment, West region, and agency size. More specifically, agencies that have formal policies and an intelligence unit will more successfully facilitate adoption. Effects from civilization are expected to be positively related to adoption; however, the strength of this relationship is anticipated to be minimal as a result of the inability of the data to identify the non-sworn personnel as actually being intelligence-related personnel. Task scope, training, and commitment are anticipated to be the most salient context predictors of adoption. The influence of agency size on police change is mixed in the research literature (Zhao, 1996; Maguire *et al*, 1997; King, 2000, Wilson, 2006), but maybe even more so with intelligence-led policing as there has yet to be an established benchmark of practice for agencies of varying sizes and scopes of responsibility. With this in mind, it is anticipated that larger agencies will be more successful at adopting intelligence-led policing. Agency size serves as the control variable in most models as many relationships could potentially be explained as a function of agency size.

RQ₃: Are organizational diffusion, structure, and context effects on intelligence-led policing adoption consistent when integrated into a full model?

This research question combines research questions one and two. It is anticipated that when the relevant organizational diffusion, structure, and context variables are integrated to create a full model of intelligence-led policing adoption, the results indicated from the partial models will continue to have a positive relationship. Given expected correlations between the independent variables, it is anticipated that while the direction of the relationships will remain consistent, the strength of the relationships will be mitigated. As the variance is parceled out, the strength of the measures will decrease as the remaining variables are controlled for in the full model. Measures of model fit and explained variance is also anticipated to increase in the full model as compared to the partial models of diffusion and organizational structure and context.

RQ₄: Which methods of analyst performance evaluation are most likely to affect intelligence-led policing adoption?

Performance evaluation of intelligence analysts is measured on a quality continuum. These measures are no evaluation, evaluation based on the number of contacts an analyst has, the number of products an analyst produces, and the quality of the products an analyst produces. Based primarily on two reasons, performance evaluation is not appropriate for the full organizational model because: 1) a large proportion of local law enforcement agencies simply do not have analysts; and, 2) agencies that do have analysts are not yet well-informed as to what realistic expectations of analysts should be, and therefore have difficulty identifying appropriate evaluation methods (Cope, 2004). Despite these issues, evaluation is thought to have a significant impact on ILP adoption, and thus those agencies which have indicated making use of evaluation methods provide an opportunity to explore this anticipated relationship.

It is anticipated that qualitative methods of analyst evaluation will positively affect adoption. More specifically, agencies that utilize a qualitative approach rather than quantitative, to evaluate analysts are more likely to facilitate the adoption of intelligence-led policing. Evaluation of analysts' performance is not appropriate for the full model of intelligence-led policing adoption as the role and expectations of analysts are still uncertain within most law enforcement agencies (Cope, 2004; Root, 2006). Many agencies are unaware of what to expect from their analysts, let alone how to properly evaluate their performance.

Agencies that lack an evaluation method are likely to have a negative relationship with intelligence-led policing adoption. As agencies increase the comprehensiveness - or simply apply better techniques - of evaluation, the effect on intelligence-led policing adoption will be positive. As such, agencies that employ the number of contacts as the method of evaluation will have a slightly more positive relationship on adoption. Agencies that employ the number of products as the evaluation method will have a slightly more positive influence on adoption than those utilizing the number of contacts. Lastly, agencies that employ the quality of products as the evaluation method of will have the strongest positive effects on intelligence-led policing adoption.

It should be noted that methods of analyst evaluation can be interpreted to represent either a predictor or an indicator of intelligence-led policing. It appears logical to assume that if an agency is evaluating intelligence analysts, then analysts must be engaging in some activities and therefore intelligence-led policing is operating within the agency. This assumption has validity in that this certainly does occur. However, agencies that do have intelligence analysts are likely to lack an accurate understanding of analysts' roles in the intelligence-led policing process as a result of ambiguity and poor analyst standards. Moreover, if an agency does have analysts in place, this does not guarantee these analysts are actually engaged in creating intelligence products and therefore are not adopting intelligence-led policing. Agencies employing an increasingly quality-oriented method of evaluation are more likely than others to be agencies that are successfully adopting the new philosophy.

RQ$_5$: Do the relevant organizational variables identify differences between intelligence-led policing adoption as self-reported by each agency and adoption as operationalized by the present study?
It is anticipated that the variables identified as being predictors of intelligence-led policing adoption will predict adoption differently for agencies that self-report as having adopted intelligence-led policing versus the index measurement of adoption operationalized in this study. Anticipated differences are expected with respect to the predictor

variables that demonstrate active engagement in adopting intelligence-led policing. More specifically, some of the predictor variables are more likely to be representative of an agency that is "actively" - or having "more action than talk" - adopting intelligence-led policing. Such predictor variables include peer emulation, threat awareness, formalization, functional differentiation, and task scope as these are, to an extent, outcomes of an active adoption process. Simply put, you would expect an agency that was sincere about adopting intelligence-led policing to have an awareness of threats, intelligence-specific personnel, and be able to carry out a variety of tasks.

Other predictor variables demonstrate a passive - "more talk than action" - adoption process that is perhaps not as sincere as it should be within an agency that claims to be adopting innovations. Predictor variables consistent with planning for or passive adoption include familiarity with the intelligence-led policing concept, commitment, and training. Simply put, agencies that are not fully committed to adopting intelligence-led policing are likely to have in place characteristics that require little action, such as proclaiming a commitment and sending officers to training programs.

The difference between "active" versus "passive" adoption can certainly be examined as a continuum of adoption; however institutional theory lends itself to explaining the behavior of "passive" agencies which may be primarily seeking legitimacy rather than creating an operational intelligence capability. It is anticipated that the variables which are representative of active adoption will be significant when predicting the index measure of intelligence-led policing adoption. It is also anticipated that the variables which are representative of passive adoption will be significant when predicting both the index measure and the self-reported measure of intelligence-led policing adoption. As an exploratory study, this research question may also lend insight into the validity and reliability of the index measure of adoption.

RQ$_6$: Are the variables identified in the literature and quantitative analyses of the current study consistent with the contexts provided by the case study environments?
It is anticipated that the constructs identified through the review of literature will be reinforced by the information gathered during the case studies. More specifically, results from the quantitative analyses of the

current study should be present in the case studies. A caveat to this is that not all constructs are expected to be present in each of the case studies due to variability between organizations. Nonetheless, it is expected that between the two case studies featured in this study that the predictor constructs will be discussed in the context of a specific law enforcement intelligence environment, which increases the validity of the constructs (Tashakkori & Teddlie, 1998; Tashakkori & Creswell, 2008). While the results of this study cannot be generalized to the broad policing population, the case studies will assist in the application of the findings to agencies seeking to adopt intelligence-led policing. This research question will be addressed at the end of both case study chapters.

MEASUREMENT

This section will provide a discussion of relevant variables included in the study. This discussion will convey why each variable is relevant, as well as indicate how the variable is measured. While not specifically noted, agency size serves as a control variable in all regression models except for models incorporating organizational context as size is thought to be a predictor of adoption. A critical intent of this study is to establish a baseline of intelligence-led policing measures. This section will discuss these measures in detail.

Differential Indexes

In some instances, such as with community policing in the past and intelligence-led policing in the present study, observing some measures is not possible and thus they must be estimated through other measures from the survey. One approach researchers can take to remedy the lack of an observable measure - or latent variable - is by enhancing nominal-level dichotomous variables to create scales using reliabilities and correlations. This practice is rooted in strong psychometric research in psychology but is no stranger to criminal justice research. Using dichotomous variables to develop scales as a more precise measure has been done in a variety of policing (Maguire, 1997: King, 1998; Zhao, 1996; Wilson, 2006) and organizational (Damanpour, 1991; Kimberly & Evanisko, 1981) research studies. Wilson (2006:44) notes that the method of using additive item scales combines more information, has a greater range, and is more sensitive than either dichotomous or ordinal measures. Zhao (1996) draws reference to the work of Cole (1974) when justifying the use of scales with respect to organizational research. Specifically, Cole (1974:25) argued that this approach is most useful when applied to local government's adaptation to change since the use of additive scales provides a more comprehensive measure of the phenomena than is possible using any single measure.

Before scales can be developed, the measurement of the variables in question needs to be evaluated, most commonly done so by assessing the reliability and validity of the collected data. There are two types of reliability. The first pertain to the ability of the study to be replicated, while the second is concerned with the consistency of measurement determined by an item used to measure a phenomenon (Hagan, 2003:280). The consistency of measurement is the important evaluation with respect to developing scales. Cronbach's Alpha is perhaps the most widely used static and the most well accepted form of reliability measurement. The larger the alpha score, the more consistent the item is at measuring the desired phenomenon. While there is some debate over the question of how high this score must be to achieve acceptability in practice anywhere above .70 (Nunnally & Bernstein, 1994) to .80 (Carmines & Zeller, 1979) is typically considered acceptable in social science research. Factor analysis is used to confirm that the items load on a single factor. An acceptable measure related to this approach is an eigenvalue of more than 1.0 which indicate the presence of a single latent factor (Pett *et a.l*, 2003). If more than one eigenvalue of 1.0 or higher exists, it can be determined if the items are loading on different factors by assessing a scree plot as well as the variance between factors (Kim & Mueller, 1978).

Intelligence-Led Policing Adoption Dependent Variables
Intelligence-Led Policing Adoption Index
The intelligence-led policing adoption index represents a measure of an agency's adoption of intelligence-led policing as operationalized for the present study. Consistent with the approach taken by scholars examining community policing adoption (Zhao, 1996; Maguire *et al.*, 1997; Wilson, 2006), the present study creates an index to reflect an agency's adoption of an intelligence-led policing philosophy. An index measure is necessary in that you cannot observe whether or not an agency is engaged in ILP due to its varying degrees of implementation. Salient to this approach is the identification of programs and practices

that reflect an agency's engagement in ILP. At this point it is beneficial to reflect on the definition of intelligence-led policing:

> The collection and analysis of information related to crime and conditions that contribute to crime, resulting in an actionable intelligence product intended to aid law enforcement in developing tactical responses to threats and/or strategic planning related to emerging or changing threats (Carter & Carter, 2009:317).

This definition can be broken-down into its key components:

1) Collection of information
2) Analysis of information
3) Creation of actionable intelligence
4) Integrating intelligence for strategic planning
5) Sharing of information

These critical components of intelligence-led policing, combined with an operational plan to guide an intelligence-led philosophy, represent observable items to create an index of intelligence-led policing. Table 3 displays items from the original survey instrument, along with their means and standard deviations, which measure the critical components of ILP. These seven variables were used to create a scale to reflect intelligence-led policing adoption. Factor analysis produced one significant factor with an eigenvalue of 2.785, the remaining factors had eigenvalues at or below 1.097. While the factor analysis identified more than one factor with an eigenvalue above 1.0, analysis of a scree plot indicate the other factors with eigenvalues above 1.0 were not loading on the primary factor. Furthermore, the differences of the percentage of explained variance between the primary factor (41.766) and the subsequent factors (less than 15.978) reaffirm the identification of a single task scope construct.

Table 3: Intelligence-Led Policing Adoption Index Composition

Variable	*n*	Mean	S.D.	α if Item Deleted
Q28: Is intelligence formally integrated into your agency's decision-making process?	272	.92	.27	.730
Q50: Does the agency have defined goals and objectives for collecting, analyzing, producing and sharing information?	272	.42	.49	.718
Q64: Does your agency have processes in place for sharing relevant terrorism information with the public?	272	.44	.50	.710
Q66: Does your agency provide actionable intelligence?	272	.69	.46	.704
Q67: Does your agency receive information from outside agencies?	272	.95	.22	.722
Q88: Does your agency provide actionable intelligence in a timely manner to those constituents responsible for implementing prevention, protection, response and consequence management?	272	.67	.47	.696
Q86: Has your agency developed collection requirements?	272	.33	.47	.715

α = .745

Intelligence-Led Policing Self-Reported Adoption
The original survey instrument asked respondents indicate if their agency had adopted intelligence-led policing. In this instance, institutional theory and organizational learning are revisited. Even though respondents indicate the extent to which they have adopted ILP, this is potentially not the case. Institutional theory posits these agencies could be indicating they have adopted ILP in order to maintain

legitimacy among the public and their peers as they want to be an agency which appears to be maintaining the status quo by adopting intelligence-led policing.

Organizational learning posits this could be a possible indicator of agencies mistaking "talk" for "action". More specifically, agencies may be under a false impression that they are actively engaging in ILP due to having meetings, going to trainings, and developing an intelligence-led mission statement. However these agencies are not actually be doing anything intelligence-led such as collecting information, sharing information, and providing actionable intelligence products. It may be difficult to discern substituting "talk" for "action" from the beginning stages of adoption. It is anticipated that when the identified predictor variables of successful adoption are regressed on self-reported adoption the significance and strength of effects will be dramatically different from the ILP adoption index model.

Diffusion Independent Variables
The methods to "why" and "how" innovations are adopted within police agencies are perhaps most critical to the present study. Agencies that determine threats are present in their region and agencies that identify areas for potential civil liability are more likely to take the steps necessary to mitigate these problems – thus adoption of ILP as an innovation. It is assumed that how agencies innovate can be attributed to peer emulation and familiarity with the potential innovation. It is also assumed that agencies that seek assistance from other agencies on intelligence-related issues and agencies that increase familiarity with the concept of intelligence-led policing are more likely to facilitate adoption.

Threat Awareness
Threat awareness is defined as agencies that identify the need to adopt innovations as a result of determining threats in their geographic proximity. In the context of homeland security research, an agency's awareness of threats within its region has been found to increase the likelihood of adoption of innovation (Schafer *et al.*, 2009; Burress *et al.*, 2010). This same relationship is anticipated with respect to intelligence-led policing as a result of the conceptual foundation consistent with community policing and homeland security.

Risk Mediation
Risk mediation is defined as agencies that identify the need to adopt innovations in order to protect the organization from civil liability. Further explaining why agencies adopt innovations is the necessity to mitigate risk of civil liability.   Weiss' (1997) research supports this assertion.   In the context of intelligence-led policing, legal precedent has found law enforcement agencies liable under Section 1983 deprivation of civil rights lawsuits for collecting information on persons that could not be proved to be engaged in criminal activity. Information sharing across agencies has significantly increased since 9/11, however the practices and policies guiding such sharing are still on a steep learning curve.   In short, agencies now realize safeguards must be taken to protect against a potential Section 1983 lawsuit. Risk mediation is a latent construct that cannot be measured accurately through one item on a survey instrument. As such, a differential index was created to measure risk mediation within agencies.   These three variables were used to create an overall risk mediation scale. Factor analysis confirmed one significant factor with an eigenvalue of 1.979; the remaining factors had eigenvalues at or below .586.

Peer Emulation
Peer emulation is defined as agencies that learn about innovations by informally communicating with other agencies, typically of similar size and demographics. Agencies that reach out and communicate with other agencies and organizations for assistance on intelligence-related issues are more likely to facilitate adoption (Weiss, 1997). The process of peer emulation is primarily informal, and commonly consists primarily of telephone and email communications. Peer emulation is a latent construct that cannot be measured accurately through one item on a survey instrument. Once again a factor index was created to measure peer emulation within agencies. These nine variables were used to create an overall peer emulation scale. Factor analysis confirmed one significant factor with an eigenvalue of 5.412; the remaining factors had eigenvalues at or below .829.

Intelligence-Led Policing Familiarity
Intelligence-led policing familiarity is defined as agencies that determine the need to adopt innovations as a result of learning about the innovation and evaluating its benefits and fit within the

organization. Further enhancing an agency's ability to adopt innovation is familiarity with the potential innovation. While this may seem rather intuitive, an organization's familiarity with innovation conveys a sense of forward-thinking consistent with progressive and innovative organizations. An agency's innovativeness has been found to facilitate adoption (Weiss, 1997; King, 2000). It follows that an agency's increased familiarity with the intelligence-led policing concept should positively influence its adoption. Familiarity of ILP is a difficult construct to measure accurately through one item on a survey instrument, so another factor index was created to measure familiarity of the ILP concept within agencies. These three variables were used to create an overall ILP familiarity scale. Factor analysis produced one significant factor with an eigenvalue of 2.011; the remaining factors had eigenvalues at or below .665.

Organizational Structure and Context Independent Variables
Structural characteristics of police agencies have been found to have varying impacts throughout the literature on police change, innovation, and program adoption (Maguire *et al.*, 1997; Wilson, 2006). Salient structural constructs identified from across the innovation, policing, and organization literature included formalization, civilianization (also referred to as occupational differentiation), and functional differentiation. Agencies with formal policies, larger proportions of non-sworn to sworn personnel ratios, and an established intelligence unit are anticipated to be more successful in their efforts to adopt intelligence-led policing.

Organizational context for police agencies commonly encompasses task and institutional environments. These environments are comprised of elements that influence police activity to improve effectiveness and perceived legitimacy - either in the eyes of the public or peer organizations. Agency size, task scope, and training are elements that influence police activity. It is difficult to anticipate the effect agency size may have on intelligence-led policing adoption simply because the practice has yet to identify what intelligence-led exactly means across different types of police agencies. However, it is anticipated that agency size will facilitate ILP adoption. Increased task responsibilities, commitment and training are also expected to facilitate adoption. Regional influence is attributed to Western states traditionally being more progressive as compared to other regions in the U.S., while also perhaps explaining legitimacy as agencies will tend to emulate other agencies in their geographic proximity.   It is anticipated that commitment and Western region will facilitate adoption.

Formalization
Formalization is defined as the extent to which an agency has formal written policies to guide the innovation.   Formalization has received rather mixed results in the policing literature, and is subject to the criticism that formal policies stifle organic change to evolve with environmental demands (Zhao, 1996; Mastrofski, 1998; King, 1999). However, intelligence-led policing requires formal policies to guide more specific practices - such as collecting and maintaining legal information as well as sharing this information through the appropriate channels.   As such, formalization is anticipated to facilitate intelligence-led policing adoption.   Formalization is another latent construct that cannot be measured accurately through one item on a survey instrument.   Thus a factor index was created to measure formalization within agencies. These four variables were used to create an overall formalization scale. Factor analysis produced one significant factor with an eigenvalue of 2.211; the remaining factors had eigenvalues at or below .719.

Civilianization
Civilianization is defined as the ratio of sworn personnel to non-sworn personnel within the agency.   This construct is intriguing for intelligence-led policing research.   Generally, civilianization has been examined as a means to alleviate workload pressures from sworn officers (Skolnick & Bayley, 1986) and as a structural function of organizational size (King, 1998).   Currently, civilianization poses a potentially significant impact on intelligence-led policing adoption as the vast majority of intelligence analysts are non-sworn employees. While many agencies, especially as the local level, task an existing officer with the role of "analyst" these individuals are typically not truly analysts. Civilianization is a calculated, ratio-based variable where the researcher divided the number of non-sworn personnel by the number of sworn personnel - thus yielding the proportion of non-sworn to sworn employees.   Data on the number of non-sworn and sworn personnel were gathered from the Federal Bureau of Investigation's (2011) Uniform Crime Report Police Employee Data for 2009.   For

large state agencies, personnel data were gathered from the Bureau of Justice Statistics' (2011) Law Enforcement Administrative Statistics data for 2003.

Functional Differentiation

Functional differentiation is defined as whether or not an agency has a specific intelligence unit. In its most mature form, the practice of intelligence-led policing is an intersection of multiple units within a police agency. A study by Ratcliffe and Guidetti (2008) found improved information sharing between persons specifically tasked to carry out the intelligence function of the New Jersey State Police and the drug enforcement unit as a result of spatial proximity to one another. They noted the importance of direct communication as the two units commonly interacted on similar cases. While the spatial proximity in this circumstance is important, perhaps more important is the identification of an actual intelligence unit that is specifically tasked to carry out the intelligence function for a particular agency as opposed to simply assigning this task to an officer with multiple pre-existing responsibilities. It is important to reiterate that employing intelligence-specific personnel should not be mistaken for intelligence-led policing adoption. The presence of personnel to perform duties and tasks does not equate to these tasks actually being carried out. Outputs are necessary to determine if an intelligence-led approach has been adopted.

Functional differentiation is anticipated to be a function of agency size; larger agencies are more apt to have the resources and personnel to devote to an intelligence-specific unit than smaller agencies. Survey respondents were asked to indicate what form of personnel employment best describes their intelligence capability. This item does not directly measure whether an agency has an intelligence-unit or not, but it does indicate if the agency employs intelligence-specific personnel. As such, it can be assumed that if an agency employs either full- or part-time intelligence-specific personnel, then they have an intelligence unit. Taking into account the implementation fidelity of intelligence-led policing across police agencies, it is not an operational concern to consider part-time intelligence-specific personnel as an intelligence unit. The present study will not make a distinction between full- and part-time intelligence units. Functional differentiation as defined in this study is dichotomous; either an agency has an intelligence unit or it does not.

Task Scope

Task scope is defined as the extent to which intelligence personnel are responsible for conducting different tasks within the agency. Task scope, the variation of tasks an agency is able to carry out, is likely to facilitate adoption for two primary reasons. First, the more tasks intelligence personnel are able to perform, the more applicable their skills are to the intelligence-led philosophy. Second, the more tasks personnel are able to perform, the more products or activities will result and intelligence-led policing is driven by analysis and information products. Task scope is a culmination of multiple dimensions that cannot be measured through one item on a survey instrument. Instead, it is more appropriate to identify a latent construct of task variability. Thus a factor index was created to measure task scope within agencies.

Factor analysis produced one significant factor with an eigenvalue of 16.030; the remaining factors had eigenvalues at or below 1.476. While the factor analysis identified more than one factor with an eigenvalue above 1.0, analysis of a scree plot indicate the other factors with eigenvalues above 1.0 were not loading on the primary factor (Kim & Mueller, 1978). Furthermore, the differences of the percentage of explained variance between the primary factor (57.249) and the subsequent factors (less than 5.271) reaffirm the identification of a single task scope factor (Kim & Mueller, 1978).

Training

The training variable is defined as an agency that requires intelligence personnel to receive training on intelligence-led policing. Throughout the organizational literature training has consistently been a facilitator of adoption. This is somewhat intuitive as training serves as a means by which organizations can gain conceptual and practice knowledge of innovations or change. There are several ways to measure training for law enforcement intelligence practices - whether it is training attended by analysts or executives or training focused on technology for sharing information or more conceptual knowledge of intelligence. While the original survey instrument provided multiple items pertaining to training, the most appropriate measure was whether or not the agency required all persons responsible for the agency's intelligence function to receive specific intelligence-led policing training.

Commitment
Commitment is defined as the extent to which an agency is committed to the innovation through support and priorities. According to numerous scholars commitment to organizational innovation or change in general, is paramount to success (Brown, 1989; Yates & Pillai, 1996; Morabito, 2010). As noted earlier, commitment has been viewed as both a necessity to successful adoption as well as a potential tool for gaining legitimacy. The intent of this study is not to distinguish between the two, and takes the view that commitment is necessary for adoption. Once again it is difficult to measure an agency's commitment to a new policing philosophy. Common approaches to operationalizing commitment have included whether or not the chief has endorsed the change (Moore & Stephens, 1991). Organizational priorities are also an indicator of commitment, as priorities are consistent with organizational goals and desired outcomes (Ford *et al.*, 2003). The present study accounts for these aspects of commitment through the creation of a latent construct. These three variables were used to create an overall commitment scale. Factor analysis produced one significant factor with an eigenvalue of 1.996; the remaining factors had eigenvalues at or below .619. It is anticipated that commitment will facilitate intelligence-led policing adoption.

West Region
West region is defined as agencies located in the Western region of the United States[25]. Studies examining police innovation and change have consistently included measures of geographic region. Specifically, agencies in the Western region of the U.S. have traditionally been more progressive and more likely to be receptive to change (Wilson, 2006). Although regional effects may be significant in attributing to successful adoption - and for this reason they are included in this study - there is little that can be generalized from any finding. This is to say that even though Western region agencies may be more successful at adopting

---

[25] States in the Western region of the U.S. include: Oregon, Washington, California, Idaho, Nevada, Montana, Colorado, New Mexico, and Arizona.

intelligence-led policing; this is not a characteristic that other agencies across the country can alter to assist in their adoption process. Nonetheless, exploring this relationship supplements own knowledge of intelligence-led policing adoption and diffusion across the United States (cf. Wycoff, 1994; Zhao, 1996; Maguire *et al.*, 1997; Wilson, 2006). Indications of geographic region were not presented on the original survey instrument. Region was determined by utilizing multiple unique identifying datasets from the original evaluation project to determine precisely where each agency was located.

Agency Size
Agency size is defined as the sum of full-time sworn and full-time non-sworn personnel. Perhaps the most commonly included variable across all organizational research is size. As it has been noted, the anticipated impact of agency size on intelligence-led policing adoption is truly unclear. However, as larger agencies simply have more resources, more personnel, serve more complex jurisdictions and as a result have more complex responsibility, agency size is likely to facilitate the adoption of intelligence-led policing. Data on the number of non-sworn and sworn personnel were gathered from the Federal Bureau of Investigation's (2011) Uniform Crime Report Police Employee Data for 2009. For large state agencies, personnel data were gathered from the Bureau of Justice Statistics' (2011) Law Enforcement Administrative Statistics data for 2003. Given the presence of four extreme outliers, the median is a more appropriate descriptive of the variable. The median agency size was used for six agencies in which agency size was unable to be determined (cf. Schafer & Schenker, 2000).

Performance Evaluation Independent Variables
Intelligence-led policing is driven by analysis and the products analysts create. As found in the business literature (Griffin *et al.*, 1981), as well as industrial-organizational psychology (London & Smither, 1995), quality processes tend to lead to quality outcomes. Furthermore, if performance evaluation is based on an assessment of quality; the quality of products should increase. With respect to intelligence-led policing, analysts evaluated on their products' standard of quality should produce higher quality products to be integrated into the ILP function. If higher quality products are driving the intelligence-led

function, it can be assumed that the function itself should improve. As such, as the quality of analyst performance evaluation increases so should ILP adoption. The current study employs the following variables for performance evaluation:

> *No Evaluation Method*: Agencies indicate having no method of evaluation for intelligence analysts.
> *Number of Contacts*: Agencies indicates counting the number of contacts analysts have with other persons as the method of evaluation for intelligence analysts.
> *Number of Products*: Agencies indicates counting the number of products analysts create as the method of evaluation for intelligence analysts.
> *Quality of Products*: - Agencies indicates the use of a qualitative assessment of intelligence analysts' products as the method of evaluation for intelligence analysts.

Respondents were asked to identify which methods of analyst evaluation were critical. The variables are listed in order from the poorest quality evaluation method (no evaluation) to the highest quality evaluation method (quality of products produced). It should be noted that only 73% of the sample responded to analyst evaluation item; this is because the non-responding agencies do not have an intelligence analyst.

ANALYTIC STRATEGY
Measuring intelligence-led policing adoption is not a simple construct. Such difficulties are not new to social science and criminal justice research. In order for research on intelligence-led policing to progress, a baseline of measures needs to be created. As such, reliability alpha scores and factor analysis will be used to construct differential indexes for appropriate measures. Qualitative case studies will be integrated to provide context for the constructs examined. The present study will utilize descriptive and inferential statistics. Descriptive statistics will be provided to illustrate distributions while bivariate correlations will be provided to demonstrate the strength of relationships between the several variables. Ordinary least squares (OLS) stepwise regression is employed to test predictive relationships when the dependent variable is the index of intelligence-led policing adoption given the seven-value

continuum of adoption scores (Berk, 2004). Models employing OLS will report exponentiated coefficients - this is achieved by selecting exponentiated coefficients from the "Reporting" tab in STATA regression options. Ordinal stepwise regression is employed when the dependent variable is self-reported intelligence-led policing adoption since this variable has three categories of possible response (Allen, 1997). Models employing ordinal regression will report odds ratios. The index measure of intelligence-led policing adoption has a positively skewed distribution. Using the distribution diagnostic function in STATA, it was determined that the natural log of the index measure was the most appropriate transformation.

Models will include partial organizational models of diffusion, organizational structure, organizational context, and performance evaluation as well as a full model of all organizational predictor variables. The survey was sent to individuals who responded from the context of their agency as a whole. However, some agencies were represented multiple times. Employing regression without accounting for this unit of analysis error can skew the standard errors from the analyses (Eltinge & Sribney, 1997; Lumley, 2004). As discussed previously, to address this issue properly, a complex survey design was established using a specific function within the STATA statistical software[26]. Given that standard errors affect significance levels, the conclusions drawn from an analysis that does not take into account a complex survey design may be mis-specified. Qualitative case studies will also be provided to give context for the quantitative findings (Tashakkori & Teddlie, 1998; Tashakkori, & Creswell, 2008).

---

[26] For more information on the STATA complex survey design function, visit: http://www.stanford.edu/group/ssds/cgi-bin/drupal/files/Guides/software_docs_stata_complexsvy.pdf

CHAPTER 5

Empirical Findings on ILP Adoption

This present study primarily utilizes quantitative analysis of cross-sectional survey data. Results from these analyses will be reported and discussed within this section. The analyses in this section will include discussions of variable descriptive statistics, bivariate correlations of variables, as well as ordinary least squares and ordinal regression analysis to draw inferences from the data on the adoption of intelligence-led policing within state, local, and tribal law enforcement agencies in the United States.

DESCRIPTIVE AND BIVARIATE STATISTICS

Table 4 displays a summary of the distributions for variables included in the study. With respect to the intelligence-led policing adoption index, agencies responded on average to have more than half of the critical components of intelligence-led policing in place. More than half of the agencies (57%) self-reported that they have yet to adopt intelligence-led policing. Twenty-four percent of the agencies indicated they were currently in development, and 19% said they had adopted intelligence-led policing.

The distributions of the two dependent variables utilized in the present study require further discussion. The intelligence-led policing adoption index is not normally distributed; it is positively skewed. As a result, the natural log of this variable is used for the multivariate ordinary least squares models (Berk, 2004). Consistent with using a logged dependent variable, the outputs of these regressions to be conducted will present the exponentiated beta. On average, agencies self-reported being closer to not adopting intelligence-led policing given that the mean is closer to not adopting than adopting and of the continuum. Once again, given the limited response options for self-reported adoption, ordinal regression is employed for multivariate models.

Table 4: Descriptive Statistics for Dependent and Independent
Variables

Variable	N	Mean	S.D.
Intelligence-Led Policing			
Adoption			
Index	272	4.09	1.97
Self-Report	272	.61	.78
Diffusion Types			
Threat Awareness	272	3.77	.97
Risk Mediation	272	1.34	1.20
Peer Emulation	272	26.01	7.29
ILP Familiarity	272	7.54	2.20
Organizational Structure			
Formalization	272	1.88	1.46
Civilianization	272	.55	1.19
Functional	272	.74	.44
Differentiation			
Organizational Context			
Task Scope	272	13.41	10.35
Training	272	.20	.40
Commitment	272	7.73	2.09
West Region	272	.17	.38
Agency Size*	272	1341	3678
Performance Evaluation			
No Evaluation	272	.43	.50
Method			
Number of Contacts	272	.06	.23
Number of Products	272	.05	.23
Quality of Products	272	.04	.19

*Given four extreme outliers the median is a more appropriate descriptive
measure for agency size. The median for agency size is 276 total personnel.

With respect to the types of diffusion, on average the agencies in
the sample indicate being aware of threats, not having safeguards in
place to protect against civil liability, engage in peer emulation, and are
familiar with the intelligence-led policing concept. In terms of
organizational structure, sworn personnel outnumber non-sworn
personnel by approximately two-to-one (58%). Seventy-four percent of
agencies have either a full- or part-time intelligence unit, leaving 26%

that do not. On average the agencies in the sample are not formalized. While most variability is found between risk mediation and formalization, there is consistently high variability among the organizational context variables.

In terms of organizational context, the average agency size included in the sample is 1,478 total sworn and non-sworn personnel. However, this figure is somewhat misleading. There are four significant outliers within the sample - agencies with 13,195, 13,960, 16,580 and 50,688 personnel, respectively. To better understand the context of the agencies included, when these four largest agencies are removed, the mean agency size in the sample is 782 total personnel. More appropriately given the extreme outliers, the median agency size in the sample is 276 total personnel[27]. Only 60 (17%)[28] of the agencies in the sample are located within the Western region of the U.S., with the Midwest tallying the most at 90 (26%)[29]. On average, agencies participate in half of the available tasks measured by the construct which, given the number of tasks included in the measure, is still a significant number of intelligence-related tasks. Few agencies require training on intelligence-led policing, despite their stated commitment to the philosophy. In terms of analyst evaluation method, on average 43% indicated having no evaluation method, six percent on the number of contacts the analyst had, five percent used a quantitative approach by counting the number of products created, and four percent evaluated analysts using the quality of their analysts' products.

---

[27] The median agency size is similar to the mean agency size of agencies included in the 2003 Law Enforcement Administrative Statistics (LEMAS) study of 253 total full-time personnel.

[28] This percentage is slightly less than the average number of agencies located in Western states of the agencies included in the 2003 Law Enforcement Administrative Statistics (LEMAS) study which had 22% of the agencies in the West based on the same regional geographic breakdown.

[29] This percentage is equivalent to the average number of agencies located in Midwest states of the agencies included in the 2003 Law Enforcement Administrative Statistics (LEMAS) study which had 27% in the Midwest based on the same regional geographic breakdown.

In general, the bivariate correlations indicate the independent variables are consistently correlated.[30]   While not being able to draw conclusions regarding causality, many of the variables appear to be related to intelligence-led policing.   Agencies that do not have a method of analyst evaluation are less likely to engage in the other predictors of intelligence-led policing as demonstrated by the consistent negative correlations.   The strongest trend of relationships exists between risk mediation and formalization (r=.71); this is to be expected as the method by which agencies safeguard against civil liability is through formal policies and procedures.   A strong correlation also exists between analyst evaluation types.   This relationship is expected as well in as much as they are interrelated in that a component of a quality evaluation is likely to include the other types of evaluation. There is also a strong correlation between task scope and functional differentiation (r=.56).   This is also expected as an agency that has an intelligence unit it is likely to have versatile personnel to carry out multiple tasks.   These versatile individuals are most likely engaged in a variety of tasks to fulfill their mission objectives within an intelligence unit.

Not only are most of the variables highly correlated, but their interrelationships   are   statistically   significant   as   well.   Such intercorrelations are indicative of a multicollinearity issue in regression analysis (Fox, 1997).   The primary issue for testing hypotheses is that as the degree of multicollinearity increases, the regression model estimates of the coefficients associated with the independent variables become unstable and the standard errors for the coefficients can become inflated (Allen, 1997).   Regression diagnostics are required to determine   if   multicollinearity   exists.   Issues   of   collinearity (mulitcollinearity when two or more variables are considered an issue) imply that two variables are almost linear combinations of one another (Mansfield & Helms, 1982).

The two most commonly used diagnostic tests for multicollinearity are the variance inflation factor (VIF) and tolerance.   An established standard for acceptable VIF values is that values greater than 10 may require further diagnostics (O'brien, 2007) as there is likely conceptual

---

[30]Bivariate statistics not provided, but are available from the author upon request.

overlap. The established standard for tolerance is a value lower than one-tenth (0.1) - this is comparable to a VIF of 10 (often referred to as the "rules of 10" (O'brien, 2007)). In short, if a VIF value is greater than 10 or if a tolerance value is lower than one-tenth, collinearity is a likely problem and must be addressed directly. While VIF and tolerance are typically reported in a footnote to indicate the diagnostics had been run, they are provided here due to the many significant bivariate correlations and the conceptual ambiguity surrounding intelligence-led policing[31]. All of the diagnostic scores are well within the acceptable ranges - thus collinearity is not a concern despite the impression conveyed by the correlation matrix.

Furthermore, given the inter-relationships between the independent variables as demonstrated by the bivariate correlations, as well as the exploratory nature of the current study, further bivariate correlations are helpful in gaining an understanding of the data as the analysis moves forward. As such, Table 5 provides correlations between the independent and two dependent variables included in the current study. Diffusion types, organizational structure, and organizational context are all consistently correlated with the adoption index dependent variable, with the exception of civilianization, West region, and agency size. The highest correlation with the adoption index dependent variable is commitment; this indicates a potentially strong predictor of intelligence-led policing adoption consistent with previous policing research (Yates & Pillai, 1996; Morabito, 2010).

Generally, correlations between the independent variables and the self-reported adoption dependent variable are consistently lower as compared to the adoption index. The highest correlation with the self-reported adoption dependent variable is familiarity with the intelligence-led policing concept. This finding is consistent with the theorized position that some agencies will self-report being intelligence-led as a result of learning about and talking about adopting the new innovation, but they are not yet actually achieving ILP outcomes. With respect to the independent variables measuring analyst evaluation methods, the correlations are low. This finding reaffirms the

---

[31] Diagnostics were run using the "Collin" function in STATA statistical analysis software.

view that these variables are not yet appropriate to be included in the full organizational model of intelligence-led policing adoption.

Table 5: Bivariate Correlations of Independent and Dependent Variables

	ILP Adoption Index	Self-Reported ILP Adoption
Diffusion Types		
Threat Awareness	.435**	.276**
Risk Mediation	.545**	.420**
Peer Emulation	.492**	.131*
ILP Familiarity	.520**	.669**
Organizational Structure		
Formalization	.518**	.393**
Civilianization	-.050	.007
Functional Differentiation	.505**	.363**
Organizational Context		
Task Scope	.552**	.344**
Training	.381**	.439**
Commitment	.556**	.471**
West Region	-.001	-.085
Agency Size	.113*	.121*
Performance Evaluation		
No Evaluation Method	-.167**	-.104
Number of Contacts	.269**	.233**
Number of Products	.266**	.240**
Quality of Products	.355**	.324**

Note: All significance data are two-tailed
$*p < .05, **p < .01$

WHICH TYPES OF DIFFUSION ARE MOST LIKELY TO AFFECT INTELLIGENCE-LED POLICING ADOPTION?
Partial Model of Diffusion Types
Four measures of innovation diffusion were entered stepwise into the regression model as independent variables. Given the significance of prior organizational research (Zhao, 1996; Maguire *et al.*, 1997;

Wilson, 2006) - in both policing and innovation studies - it was necessary to control for agency size. This partial organizational diffusion model was significant with a rather strong predictive value explaining 50% of variance for the intelligence-led policing adoption index. All of the predictor variables were statistically significant, and in the expected direction. Given the logged dependent variable, table entries are exponentiated coefficients, standard errors, followed by corresponding t-scores. Table 6 presents effects of the independent variables on ILP adoption.

Table 6: Regression of Diffusion Types on Intelligence-Led Policing Adoption Index ($n=272$)

Variable	Exp(B)	S.E.	t
Threat Awareness	1.08*	.023	3.67
Risk Mediation	1.13*	.021	6.70
Peer Emulation	1.02*	.003	4.33
ILP Familiarity	1.05*	.012	7.02
Agency Size	1.00	.000	-1.07

F=83.18* / R^2 = .5045

*$p < .001$

Risk mediation has the strongest effects as agencies that increased their safeguard against civil liability indicate a 13% increase in intelligence-led policing adoption. Threat awareness was also a strong predictor; as agencies increase threat awareness in their region they indicate an eight percent increase in ILP adoption. Peer emulation and familiarity with the intelligence-led policing concept are more moderate predictors, with increases in each variable also increasing adoption of intelligence-led policing.

Results from the diffusion model of intelligence-led policing adoption are consistent with the results anticipated from the first research question. In short, while controlling for the size of agency, each of the four types of diffusion have a positive influence on the adoption of intelligence-led policing. The effect sizes are perhaps best explained by the logic behind diffusion. As discussed earlier, risk mediation and threat awareness are representative of "why" agencies decide an innovation is necessary. This is to say, agencies that become aware of threats in their region and/or identify practices that require safeguards to protect against civil liability are more likely to recognize the need to adopt an innovation to mitigate the identified threats and potential for civil liability.

This is perhaps a time to explain direction of causal order with respect to civil liability. As a result of the emphasis placed on sharing information among law enforcement, many agencies actively engaged in sharing information. However, there is a difference in simply sharing information and utilizing an intelligence-led approach. Heightened sensitivity on law enforcement intelligence brought upon by the American Civil Liberties Union (ACLU) created a sense of paranoia among law enforcement executives with respect to legal policies related to sharing information (Carter & Martinelli, 2007). This paranoia led agency executives to evaluate their legal policies guiding information collection, sharing, and records management. Rather than adopting intelligence-led policing, and as a result then drafting policies to guide legal information sharing, many agencies identified only the legal policies needed to guide information sharing to protect themselves against civil liability. Therefore, some agencies identified - or discovered - the philosophy of intelligence-led policing as a result of determining how to protect against civil liability. Many of these agencies then began to develop the rest of the intelligence-led policing philosophy. After agencies identify the need to adopt ILP they must then determine "how" to adopt by learning about the innovation. Peer emulation and familiarity with the intelligence-led policing concept are methods by which agencies learn about the ILP innovation, and variables representing their methods contribute moderate effects to ILP adoption.

While causal order cannot be determined with cross-sectional data, it can be logically deduced that the stronger predictors of intelligence-led policing are such due to the fact that agencies must first identify the need to adopt followed by learning how to adopt - as guided by a review of relevant literature. However, further logical consideration of the causal order of intelligence-led policing diffusion leads to the conclusion that each of the four diffusion types can serve as an initiator of innovation as well as a facilitator of innovation. Consistent with institutional theory, agencies may become aware of intelligence-led policing as a result of peer emulation and this is the method by which they identify "why" to adopt – this, of course, involves an agency recognizing this new approach as something of utility and worthy of adoption. Just as agencies learn about ILP as a result of informally communicating with peer agencies, they may learn about ILP as a result of reading reports and recommendations from the federal government or professional organizations. As an agency becomes more familiar with the ILP concept, its leadership recognizes the benefits of adopting the new philosophy. Furthermore, agencies can facilitate - or enhance - intelligence-led policing by identifying threats in their region and safeguarding against civil liability. Teasing out the order of these constructs is a major task for future research.

WHICH ORGANIZATIONAL STRUCTURE AND CONTEXT FACTORS ARE MOST LIKELY TO AFFECT INTELLIGENCE-LED POLICING ADOPTION?
Partial Model of Organizational Structure and Context
Given the significance of prior organizational research - in both policing and policy innovation studies - it was once again necessary to control for agency size (Zhao, 1996; Maguire *et al.*, 1997; Wilson, 2006). The analytical model was significant with a moderate predictive value, explaining 53% of variance of the intelligence-led policing adoption index. Given the logged dependent variable, table entries are exponentiated coefficients, standard errors, followed by corresponding t-scores. Table 7 presents effects of the independent variables on ILP adoption.

Table 7: Regression of Organizational Structure and Context on Intelligence-Led Policing Adoption Index (n=272)

Variable	Exp(B)	S.E.	t
Organizational Structure			
Formalization	1.09***	.018	5.18
Civilianization	.99	.017	-.72
Functional Differentiation	1.26***	.076	3.77
Organizational Context			
Task Scope	1.01***	.002	4.53
Training	1.12**	.042	3.05
Commitment	1.06***	.013	4.95
West Region	1.03	.045	.59
Agency Size	1.00	.000	.45

F=53.31*** / R^2 = .5282
*p < .05, **p < .01, ***p < .001

Two of the organizational structure predictor variables were significant controlling for organizational context variables. Functional differentiation had the strongest effects on ILP adoption; as expected, agencies with a full- or part-time intelligence unit were more likely to adopt intelligence-led policing than to agencies without an intelligence unit. Formalization also demonstrates a strong effect on intelligence-led policing adoption. As agencies increase formal policies to guide intelligence practices their intelligence-led policing adoption also increases. Controlling for organizational structure variables, three organizational context variables remain significant. An increase in task scope increased intelligence-led policing adoption. Training was the strongest indicator of intelligence-led policing adoption; those agencies that require training on intelligence-led policing increased their intelligence-led policing adoption as compared to agencies without such a training requirement. An agency's increase in commitment to an intelligence-led philosophy also increased intelligence-led policing adoption. While not statistically significant, agencies located in the Western region[32] of the U.S. appear to be more likely to adopt intelligence-led policing than agencies located across different regions of the United States. Contradictory to what was anticipated, agency size has no apparent effect on ILP adoption. It was thought that as size increased so would ILP adoption - given the resources and responsibilities commonly associated with agency size.

The partial model of organizational structure on intelligence-led policing adoption indicates two significant predictors at work while controlling for the size of agency. As it was anticipated, formalization and functional differentiation positively influenced intelligence-led policing adoption. Somewhat surprisingly, civilianization appears to have a slightly *negative* effect on adoption. This is counter-intuitive as the intelligence-led policing philosophy is driven by analysis, which is nearly universally provided by intelligence analysts who are nearly always non-sworn personnel. A potential mitigation of this influence on intelligence-led policing adoption is that many agencies, while they may employ civilians, are not yet actively engaged in intelligence-led

---

[32] The researcher conducted a separate regression of all five regions to examine effects on ILP adoption. The results presented no effects across all regions on ILP adoption.

policing. Therefore, that the agency's civilianization impact is not actually representative of an intelligence-specific civilian employee presence.

Functional differentiation - the presence of an intelligence unit - indicated dramatic increases in the adoption of intelligence-led policing. Once again a note on causal order is necessary to avoid undue confusion. The presence of an intelligence unit as a predictor of intelligence-led policing adoption may seem counter-intuitive to causal order as people may suggest the presence of an intelligence unit implies intelligence-led policing has already been adopted - thus explaining the dominant effect of functional differentiation. However, causal order could go in either direction. As it will be illustrated in chapter six and the Florida Fusion Center (FFC), agencies identify the steps needed to become "intelligence-led" in practice; they note that agencies with adequate resources will develop an intelligence unit tasked with the mission to operate the agency's intelligence function. Once this unit is in place, the intelligence-led philosophy and practices are developed by those persons within the designated unit. In the FFC example, intelligence units existed across the state of Florida before they were actually engaged in intelligence-led policing. The thought behind this approach was "let's get our people in place and then do the job" (FDLE, 2010).

It is broadly recognized and well understood that many local agencies will not have an independent intelligence unit simply given the severe resource restrictions the face. While these agencies may be adopting intelligence-led policing quite well, the intent of including this measure in the present study is based on the anticipation that if an agency is able to develop an intelligence unit they should do so to facilitate adoption. This is based on the assumption that the agencies with available resources to develop an intelligence unit may choose not to do so as they may be under the impression that simply assigning intelligence responsibilities to individual persons in the organization is adequate for intelligence-led policing. To reiterate, agencies that have the means to develop an individual intelligence unit should do so rather than task individuals with this added duty. Agencies that cannot devote resources to an intelligence unit are more appropriate for assigning intelligence responsibilities to individuals; this approach is in fact the norm - and it can certainly be successful. As indicated by the results noted here, facilitation of an intelligence-led policing capability is best achieved through the creation of an intelligence unit.

An increase in formalization also has a strong positive effect on intelligence-led policing adoption. While scholars have debated the impact formalization can have on adoption within police departments (Zhao, 1996; Mastrofski, 1998; King, 1999), each innovation must occur in context. For example, formalization was believed to stifle community policing as formal policies and procedures were viewed as a hindrance to the informal nature of community policing (Mastrofski, 1998). Intelligence-led policing requires a higher-level of formalization due to the legal and technical requirements of effective practice. Given the sensitivity to civil liability, agencies require detailed formal policies to guide the collection, retention, and dissemination of criminal intelligence. For some agencies to share criminal intelligence, connectivity to information sharing systems is necessary. These sharing systems require checks and balances for accountability - thus requiring formal procedures.

The partial organizational context model indicates three of the five variables were statistically significant- namely, task scope, training, and commitment. Training has the strongest effect on adoption, and commitment also indicates a strong positive relationship- as an agency's commitment increases the likelihood of successful adoption increases. Somewhat surprisingly, task scope is only marginally influential on intelligence-led policing adoption. Logically, it would seem that agencies which are able to carry out a variety of intelligence-related tasks would have greater success adopting ILP. Opposite of what was anticipated, agency size and Western region were not significant indicators of intelligence-led policing adoption. Surprisingly, agency size showed no effect on intelligence-led policing adoption - neither in strength nor in direction.

Full Model of Organizational Intelligence-Led Policing Adoption Index

All predictor variables of diffusion, organizational structure, and organizational context were entered stepwise into the full regression model as independent variables. Agency size is a predictor variable in the full organizational model, and therefore is also controlled for. The analytical model was significant with a strong predictive value, explaining 59% of variance of intelligence-led policing adoption index

- an increase of nine percent from the diffusion model and six percent increase from the structural and context model. Given the logged dependent variable, table entries are exponentiated coefficients, standard errors, followed by corresponding t-scores. Table 8 presents effects of all the organizational independent variables on intelligence-led policing adoption.

Table 8: Full Model Regression on Intelligence-Led Policing Adoption Index[33] (*n*=272)

Variable	Exp(B)	S.E.	t
Diffusion Types			
Threat Awareness	1.04	.021	1.81
Risk Mediation	1.07**	.023	3.02
Peer Emulation	1.02***	.003	5.04
ILP Familiarity	1.01	.012	.88
Organizational Structure			
Formalization	1.05*	.200	2.40
Civilianization	.98	.021	-.99
Functional Differentiation	1.20***	.066	3.23
Organizational Context			
Task Scope	1.01*	.002	2.42
Training	1.06	.039	1.71
Commitment	1.04**	.014	3.13
West Region	1.04	.040	.97
Agency Size	1.00	.000	-.51

F=46.40*** / R^2 = .5856
*$p < .05$, **$p < .01$, ***$p < .001$

The OLS model exploring intelligence-led policing adoption utilizing the index measure indicated significant fit statistics and yielded six statistically significant predictive variables. Peer emulation and risk mediation have the strongest effects among diffusion factors, suggesting agencies that reach out to other agencies for assistance and those safeguarding against civil liability are more likely to facilitate the

---

[33] Since a seven-value index does not have a large amount of variability, ordinal regression was employed as a diagnostic tool. The results were confirmed.

adoption of intelligence-led policing than their counterpart agencies. In terms of the organizational structure constructs, both formalization and functional differentiation have positive effects on intelligence-led policing adoption. These findings demonstrate the importance of written policies to guide the intelligence function and specific personnel to carry out the function rather than assigning intelligence responsibilities as additional tasks to other officers.

With respect to the organizational context indicators, task scope and commitment positively influence of intelligence-led policing adoption as well. Agencies demonstrating a commitment to the intelligence-led approach along with having the capability to produce a variety of analytic products are more likely to facilitate adoption. Although not statistically significant, it is worth noting relationships among the remaining predictor variables - with the exception of civilianization - demonstrate directional influence that was to be expected of agencies facilitating adoption. Agency size was not a significant indicator of adoption, a somewhat promising finding in that all agencies, regardless of size (Global Intelligence Working Group, 2003), are tasked with adopting an intelligence-led philosophy.

Familiarity with the intelligence-led policing concept is no longer significant when organizational structure and context variables are controlled. In terms of the organizational structure constructs, both formalization and functional differentiation continued to have positive effects on intelligence-led policing adoption. Lastly, task scope and commitment continue to be statistically significant predictor of intelligence-led policing adoption. Training is no longer significantly associated with intelligence-led policing adoption once diffusion types and organizational structure are controlled. Functional differentiation is the strongest predictor of intelligence-led policing adoption when controlling for all other factors.

As anticipated, the full organizational model of intelligence-led policing adoption remained rather consistent with the partial models. Interestingly, an agency's familiarity with the intelligence-led policing concept and an agency's training requirement are no longer significant predictors when controlling for the other predictor variables. Familiarity with intelligence-led policing is most likely a function of commitment and training, as possibly indicated by moderately high correlations. Agencies are likely to increase familiarity with an innovation prior to demonstrating a commitment to the innovation.

Training is a means by which agencies become more familiar with innovation. Familiarity with the intelligence-led policing concept in the partial diffusion model represents the only predictor related to knowledge of intelligence-led policing. However, in the full model, training s perhaps a more comprehensive construct to explain knowledge of intelligence-led policing, and therefore mitigates the effects of familiarity with the intelligence-led policing concept in the full model. Although not statistically significant, the results still indicate familiarity of intelligence-led policing has a slightly positive influence on intelligence-led policing adoption.

In terms of organizational structure, there was a sizeable decrease in the effect size of functional differentiation. In the partial model, the presence of an intelligence unit had a dramatically positive effect on intelligence-led policing adoption. In the full model, this effect has decreased somewhat, although it remains a strong predictor of intelligence-led policing adoption when parceled out. As indicated by moderately high correlations, a large proportion of effects from functional differentiation are mitigated by task scope. Agencies that are able to carry out multiple intelligence-related tasks are likely the same agencies that have personnel tasked specifically towards an intelligence function - thus having an intelligence unit.

Within the organizational context model, training indicates having a large impact on successful ILP adoption. However, when incorporated into the full model, the effects are statistically insignificant. Explaining this drop off in effect is, most likely, that other organizational constructs (especially in the context of intelligence-led policing) are a function of training. The development of skills to determine threat awareness, developing formal policies and procedures to guide an intelligence unit and legal safeguards, and even the informal network that allows for peer emulation can all be attributed to training programs. Moreover, the true effects of training are difficult to distinguish as a result of the key informant sampling method. As such, the entire population has participated in an intelligence-specific training program. The training construct is operationalized as agencies requiring intelligence personnel to receive training on intelligence-led policing. While this is a measure of the training construct, it is perhaps more accurately a measure of training as a priority rather than training seen as the amount of training taking place. This is best demonstrated by the simple frequency of the training variable; 20% of respondents indicated in the affirmative to having an ILP training requirement, while 78% indicated in the negative – this is despite the fact that all respondents had actually been trained on ILP.

Commitment remains significant in the full model, with continued strength and same direction. While very strong statistically, the effect size of task scope is rather minimal. While it is believed that functional differentiation is mitigated by task scope, it appears that task scope does not change when accounting for functional differentiation. Increased activity with respect to carrying out a variety of intelligence-related tasks would imply the presence of an intelligence unit. However, the presence of an intelligence unit would not necessarily imply active intelligence-activities. Lastly, agency size is not significant in the full model. This is a positive finding for law enforcement intelligence as all agencies, regardless of size, must adopt an intelligence-led policing philosophy (GIWG, 2003). The apparent lack of effect of agency size on the adoption of intelligence-led policing indicates police agencies of all sizes are adopting intelligence-led policing.

WHICH METHODS OF ANALYST PERFORMANCE EVALUATION ARE MOST LIKELY TO AFFECT INTELLIGENCE-LED POLICING ADOPTION?

Models of Analyst Performance Evaluation

Four variables of analyst performance evaluation were entered stepwise into the regression model as independent variables. While performance evaluation is anticipated to be less of a function of agency size as compared to the other independent variables, it is still controlled for in the model. The analytical model was statistically significant, however with a somewhat weak predictive value in explaining only 13% of variance of the intelligence-led policing adoption index. Given the logged dependent variable, all table entries are exponentiated coefficients, standard errors, followed by corresponding t-scores. Table 9 presents effects of analyst performance evaluation methods on ILP adoption.

The model of analyst performance evaluation on intelligence-led policing adoption is consistent with anticipated effects. Agencies without an evaluation method indicated no effect on intelligence-led policing adoption. Increases in intelligence-led policing adoption appear to result from agencies that indicated employing an evaluation method of counting the number of contacts by an analyst as well agencies that employed counting the number of products created as the evaluation method. The strongest effects on intelligence-led policing adoption come from agencies that employ quality evaluation methods of the products of analysts.

Table 9: Regression of Performance Evaluation on Intelligence-Led Policing Adoption Index (n=272)

Variable	Exp(B)	S.E.	t
No Evaluation Method	.99	.058	-.18
Number of Contacts	1.09	.061	1.57
Number of Products	1.11	.068	1.67
Quality of Products	1.36*	.070	5.92

F=18.35* / R^2= .1302
*$p < .001$

While the model presented in Table 9 is helpful - especially as it predicts relationships consistent with those anticipated - the effects can be teased out more precisely. The "no evaluation method" variable can serve as a baseline measure. Logically, if an agency does not have an evaluation method, then they will fall into one of the other three evaluation categories. By running separate regressions and removing "no evaluation method" from the model and creating it as a baseline measure, the effects of different evaluation methods can be more precisely predicted. Table 10 presents two separate ordinary least squares stepwise regressions. Alone, agencies without an evaluation method explain two percent of variance in the intelligence-led policing adoption index. The model with three possible analyst evaluation methods explains 13% of variance of intelligence-led policing adoption index.

When parceled out, the effects of agencies having no evaluation method are more profound as the decrease in intelligence-led policing adoption has continued in the same direction. Agencies that indicate employing some form of analyst evaluation method continue to have very similar effects on intelligence-led policing adoption. While the coefficients remain the same, the effect sizes are noticeably larger. Regardless of the model, a lack of performance evaluation indicates less intelligence-led policing adoption, whereas employing evaluation methods of increased quality will increase intelligence-led policing adoption[34].

Table 10: Different Regression Models of Performance Evaluation on Intelligence-Led Policing Adoption Index (n=272)

Variable	ExpB (S.E.) t	ExpB (S.E.) t
No Evaluation Method	.86* (.459) -2.90	
Number of Contacts		1.09 (.060) 1.63
Number of Products		1.11 (.068) 1.69
Quality of Products		1.36** (.065) 6.55
F	8.43*	24.14**
R^2	.0246	.1302

Note: Eponentiated coefficients are provided with standard errors in parentheses followed by t-scores.
*$p < .01$, **$p < .001$

Results from the analyst evaluation model of intelligence-led policing adoption are consistent with the anticipated relationships. While each variable is not statistically significant, the strength and direction of effects reaffirm theorized relationships. As the range of analyst evaluation method increases from no method to quality method, the effects on ILP adoption also range from strongly negative to strongly positive. Theory, and these findings, suggest that quality processes lead to quality outcomes (Griffin et al., 1981). The difficulty of generalizing these results is that most agencies will not have an intelligence analyst within their actual agency. Given a variety of resource limitations, misunderstanding of analysts' role, and simply a lack of necessity with respect to a large portion of the local law

---

[34] A supplemental analysis was conducted in which the three types of evaluation methods – number of contacts, number of products, and quality of products – were used to create an index of analyst evaluation methods. These three variables have an alpha of .787 as well as a factor analysis eigenvalue of 2.114. An OLS regression of "No Evaluation Method" and the constructed "Analyst Evaluation Index" regressed on the intelligence-led policing adoption index variable yielded consistent results with the models displayed in Table 9 and Table 10. No evaluation method remained significant with negative effects, while the index of evaluation types yielded a significantly positive relationship (Exp(B) = 1.19, S.E. = .027, t = 7.70).

enforcement community, many local agencies will not have an in-house intelligence analyst. Rather than invest in analyst personnel, agencies will utilize analytic resources provided by state and regional fusion centers and larger state and local agencies in their region. The findings on analyst performance evaluation are more applicable, and appropriate, for large municipal agencies, state entities, and for fusion centers.

ANTICIPATED DIFFERENCES BETWEEN A SELF-REPORT MEASURE AND AN INDEX MEASURE OF INTELLIGENCE-LED POLICING ADOPTION?

Self-Reported Intelligence-Led Policing Adoption

Consistent with the full model predicting the ILP adoption index, all predictor variables of diffusion, organizational structure, and organizational context were entered stepwise into the full regression model as independent variables. The dependent variable is a self-reported stage of intelligence-led policing adoption as discussed previously. This measure of adoption differs in that it is self-reported and a single item measure consisting of three levels. As such, ordered logistic regression will be employed for statistical analysis. The model fit statistics are significant. The differently shaped lines indicate relationships of interest between the predictor and dependent variables. Table 11 presents effects of all the organizational independent variables on self-reported intelligence-led policing adoption. Table entries are odds ratios and standard errors, followed by corresponding t-scores.

The full model of self-reported intelligence-led policing adoption indicates four statistically significant variables. Familiarity with the intelligence-led policing concept is the strongest indicator that agencies are more likely to self-report intelligence-led policing adoption. Peer emulation is also significant; however, the effects are minor in predicting self-reported intelligence-led policing adoption. Functional differentiation was the only significant structure variable, and predicts self-reported adoption. In terms of organizational context, task scope, West region, and agency size were not shown to be significant predictors of self-reported intelligence-led policing adoption.

Table 11: Full Model Regression on Self-Reported Intelligence-Led Policing Adoption[35] (*n*=272)

Variable	O.R.	S.E.	t
Diffusion Types			
Threat Awareness	1.04	.165	.27
Risk Mediation	1.00	.155	.01
Peer Emulation	.94*	.024	-.2.28
ILP Familiarity	2.49***	.302	7.53
Organizational Structure			
Formalization	1.17	.159	1.34
Civilianization	.97	.054	-.56
Functional Differentiation	3.53*	2.13	2.10
Organizational Context			
Task Scope	1.00	.018	-.21
Training	2.41**	.818	2.58
Commitment	1.23*	.106	2.43
West Region	.60	.239	-1.28
Agency Size	1.00	.000	-.25

F=12.11***
p < .05, **p* < .01, ***p* < .001

Training had a dramatic positive effect on self-reported intelligence-led policing adoption as agencies that require intelligence-led policing training are more likely to self-report intelligence-led policing adoption. Commitment also had a significantly positive effect as agencies who indicated being committed to intelligence-led policing were more likely to self-report intelligence-led policing adoption.

Results from the full organizational model of self-reported intelligence-led policing adoption are consistent with the results anticipated. Institutional and organizational learning theories best explain the differences found between the intelligence-led policing adoption index model and the self-reported model. In short, institutional theory posits that agencies will indicate they are adopting new innovation to seek to establish legitimacy in the eyes of their peers

---

[35] Since the mean and variance of self-reported ILP adoption were almost equal, poisson regression was employed as a diagnostic tool. The results were confirmed.

and constituents (Wilson, 2006). These types of agencies may have no true buy-in or interest in the innovation other than not wanting to be identified as the agency that is not seeking improvement or maintaining consistency with its environment.

The present study does not imply, nor does it assume, that these agencies are trying to deceive others into believing they are intelligence-led. This is simply an approach to organizational behavior explained by theory. A more appropriate approach is put forth by the organizational learning framework. Approaches within this framework determine some organizations have the misconception that planning for, talking about, and committing to change one day in the future is actually change occurring (Pfeffer & Sutton, 2000); sadly, this is not the case. Change, or adoption/implementation, occurs when purposeful actions actually result from the talk, planning, and commitment. These agencies are not engaged in the "window dressing" approach as institutional theorists posit - they are simply either stuck in place or are in the beginning stages of adoption and have yet to yield any form of actionable productivity.

Familiarity with the intelligence-led policing concept and training were the two strongest indicators of self-reported intelligence-led policing adoption - consistent with anticipated effects. So too are commitment and peer emulation, both of which indicated weak, yet nonetheless statistically significant findings. Commitment and familiarity with intelligence-led policing demonstrate the beginning stages of adoption where agencies establish an understanding of the innovation and determine if the innovation is consistent with the operational mission and objectives of the agency. It is logical to assume the next step in the adoption process would be putting into place a training requirement.

Training effects can possibly be explained in that these are agencies that have identified intelligence-led policing as a desired innovation, and therefore they are seeking a more comprehensive understanding above and beyond familiarity. This hopefulness is perhaps not without cause as, it was mentioned, every agency within the sample attended at least one training session on intelligence-led policing - a fact which would indicate actually attending training programs. This is a particularly key distinction with respect to the operationalization of training inasmuch as it does not measure a quantity of training but rather taps into an agency's requirement to attend intelligence-led policing training. It is also possible that respondents representing their agency's perspective when filling out the original survey instrument interpreted their agency as having adopted ILP given their agency had invested in the time to send a person to the Intelligence Toolbox training program. Peer emulation indicated a slight decrease in self-reported intelligence-led policing adoption. As this finding is contrary to institutional theory, it perhaps gives reason to assume agencies are not consciously "going through the motions," but rather are sincere about their intelligence-led policing adoption efforts and are simply in the beginning stages of the adoption process.

The variables that were not significant, specifically threat awareness, risk mediation, functional differentiation, and task scope, are all indicative of actionable intelligence capabilities. Threat awareness and risk mediation require an assessment of risks to determine if innovation is necessary - thus implying the agency is sincere in its adoption intentions. Functional differentiation implies the existence of an intelligence unit - which is unlikely to be found in agencies that are not sincerely interested in intelligence-led policing or remain "stuck" on the planning stages. Lastly, task scope is operationalized as the variety of intelligence-related tasks an agency is capable of carrying out; once again, this trait is not likely to be found in agencies that are unable to translate "talk" into "action".

CHAPTER 6

Case Study: Florida Fusion Center

INTRODUCTION

Currently, the majority of state, local, and tribal law enforcement agencies in the U.S. are either unaware of, or struggling with, the adoption of intelligence-led policing. These ambiguities are compounded by the implementation fidelity of ILP - best practices in one agency may not translate to another. Such a problem creates an obstacle for conducting case studies on law enforcement intelligence practices. One solution is to identify an environment where intelligence practices are most likely to be applied in a manner consistent with federal guidelines and recommendations and be most generalizable to the broad law enforcement community. Fusion centers provide such an environment as they are law enforcement organizations specifically structured to engage in law enforcement intelligence practices. While the average fusion center has significantly different organizational characteristics as compared to the average local law enforcement agency, the principles of engaging in information sharing are the same.

This chapter provides a case study from the Florida Fusion Center as a means to provide context for the conceptualizations and empirical findings of the present study. The Florida Fusion Center is somewhat unusual unique given its rich tradition of law enforcement intelligence within the state of Florida, as well as the state's geographic location and diverse demographic composition. Once again it should be acknowledged that this case study is not provided as a source for data extraction or further empirical analysis; rather, this case study is provided as a means to provide context for understanding law enforcement intelligence practices generally and intelligence-led policing in particular. Moreover, little is known about the operations and administration of fusion centers, and while this study is not intended to examine these aspects the narrative to follow provides a useful overview of the fusion center environment. Intersections between the case study and relevant constructs and empirical findings will be discussed.

The Florida Fusion Center

The Florida Fusion Center (FFC) is physically located within the Florida Department of Law Enforcement's (FDLE) Office of Statewide Intelligence, located at FDLE headquarters in Tallahassee, Florida. Officially created in January 2007, the FFC operates under the authority of FDLE as recognized in the Florida State Statute 943[36]. The mission of the FFC is to protect the citizens, visitors, resources, and critical infrastructure of Florida by enhancing information sharing, intelligence capabilities and preparedness operations for all local, state and federal agencies in Florida in accordance with Florida's domestic security strategy. The FFC serves as the state node in that it provides connectivity and intelligence sharing among the regional fusion centers as well as the regional domestic security task forces.

For forty years the FDLE has operated a centralized intelligence unit that supported criminal investigative efforts of local, state and federal law enforcement agencies. This rich history of law enforcement intelligence practices within the state of Florida presents a unique environment in which FDLE was able to respond quickly to emerging initiatives and flourish in a dynamic intelligence environment where in other agencies have encountered challenges and endured difficult struggles. This context provides a unique opportunity for this study to examine law enforcement intelligence practices within an intelligence environment that has evolved over a good amount of time. As a result of this evolving intelligence environment, the structure of intelligence and information sharing among law enforcement agencies and other organizations within the state of Florida has also evolved, and as a consequence requires a step-by-step explanation of how the different entities of the information sharing structure have been established and communicate.

Structure of Law Enforcement Intelligence in Florida

The Office of Statewide Intelligence and the Florida Fusion Center

While the State of Florida has been actively sharing information for decades, the heart of Florida's intelligence operations was established

---

[36] 943.0321 The Florida Domestic Security and Counter-Terrorism Intelligence Center and the Florida Domestic Security and Counter-Terrorism Database. This statute can be accessed at: http://www.leg.state.fl.us/Statutes/

in 1996 with the creation of the Office of Statewide Intelligence (OSI). This new office within FDLE was designed to refine the analytical and investigative efforts of FDLE to be centered on an intelligence-led approach. The OSI is comprised of multiple intelligence divisions created to support the over-arching function of intelligence-led policing. To further enhance this intelligence-led approach adopted by FDLE, the Florida state fusion center was created in 2007 to expand information sharing to include a broad "all-threats, all-hazards" approach to threat prevention. While the OSI and FFC are staffed by similar personnel, and both serve as a threat-prevention function of FDLE, they are separate entities operating together, separated by a key distinction that will be discussed below.[37]

The primary mission of the OSI is to provide FDLE leadership with sufficient information so that they may make informed decisions on the deployment of resources to best carry out FDLE's mission. The OSI plays a primary role in the planning and direction, analysis, reporting, and evaluation of FDLE intelligence products and serves as the core resource of the Florida Fusion Center. The OSI is responsible for the coordination of FDLE's intelligence efforts, analysis of intelligence and crime data information, and dissemination. Although other functions take place in OSI, its primary focus is to ensure timely information is available so that critical decisions can be made based on the best available intelligence.

The OSI has had an all-crimes approach since its inception, an approach that was reflective of FDLE's investigative strategy and focus areas. This approach was enhanced with the addition of a domestic security mission after the attacks of September 11th, 2001. Under the coordination of FDLE, seven regional domestic security task forces (RDSTFs) were created along with an analytical unit within OSI to enhance domestic security and counter terrorism investigative efforts. Each task force is co-chaired by an FDLE Special Agent in Charge and a sheriff from the region. Beyond the RDSTFs, the OSI also contains strategic and operational focus teams that interact with and support regional intelligence centers as well as state, local, and federal

---

[37] For a complete FDLE organizational chart visit: http://www.fdle.state.fl.us/ Content/getdoc/f3f99431-903b-4209-8d00-b3e0e4bc4be4/Org-Chart.aspx

agencies; together they monitor public safety issues that could affect the state of Florida.

Seven Regional Fusion Centers
In 2007, FDLE conducted a gap analysis of the state of Florida's information sharing processes. The findings and recommendations from this gap analysis identified insufficient cooperation and information sharing with local law enforcement agencies within the state of Florida. While this gap analysis will be discussed in more depth to come, its importance to the information sharing structure of the state of Florida pertains to the creation of seven regional intelligence centers[38]. An infrastructure and resources foundation for these regional intelligence centers had already been established in the seven critical regions of Florida with the RDSTFs and RIAs. Logistically, financially, and functionally it made sense to place the regional fusion centers in these same seven regions. The regional intelligence centers do not replace the existing RDSTFs or RIAs; rather, they are separate entities which work alongside one another to enhance law enforcement effectiveness across the board.

In March 2008, Florida Governor Charlie Crist designated the FFC to serve as Florida's primary fusion center. While the regional fusion centers are in the process of becoming operational, the FFC provides resource and instructional assistance. Regional fusion centers may provide operational support and situational awareness to local and state law enforcement agencies in their jurisdiction, but only the FFC handles this function for the entire state. The FFC also has a 24/7 investigative support center for situational awareness and some after-hours tactical support. It should be noted that while the primary state fusion center is in Tallahassee (the FFC), a regional fusion center is

---

[38] The terminology throughout this case study uses the termsregional fusion center and regional intelligence center interchangeably. There is a notable difference between fusion centers and intelligence units within agencies, however. Fusion centers represent an amalgamation of personnel and resources to collect, analyze and share information with a primary focus on terrorism and "all hazards". This is distinguished from an intelligence unit in a state or local agency that supports only that agency on all crimes that pose a threat to the jurisdiction served by the agency in question.

also located in Tallahassee. The RIAs serve as the primary communication mechanism between the FFC and regional centers. At the time of the site visit, the regional fusion centers in Miami Dade County and Orlando / Orange County were fully functioning with the other five centers becoming operational in the near future. The FFC has begun to conduct quarterly meetings that include representatives (ILO's) from each of the regional fusion centers.

Information collection requirements and priorities are established through two-way communication between the FFC and regional centers. For purposes of protecting the state of Florida, the FFC establishes information collection requirements for the regional centers and requires information relative to the established requirements be pushed back to the FFC for further analysis and dissemination. For example, the FFC may have information relevant to a certain type of insurance fraud occurring throughout the state of Florida and pushes out requirements pertaining to these activities to the regional centers. Once the regional centers are aware of this emerging trend and identify information that may be relevant to the insurance fraud scheme, they push their intelligence products back to the FFC for further analysis. Once all seven regions are functional they will begin pushing information back to FFC where it can be analyzed, the FFC can begin to create an entire state-wide picture of how insurance fraud is occurring in Florida and push this information back out to the seven regions for the officers and analysts respond to more accurately. Moreover, if information comes in from Miami on specific individuals involved with insurance fraud, and this information matches closely or is specifically related to other information provided from another regional center, this information can be fused together and pushed back to each region to provide a more comprehensive understanding of the individuals and actions involved.

Beyond collecting information consistent with requirements established by the FFC, regional fusion centers are also tasked with the responsibility of collecting and analyzing region-specific information on all-crimes and all-hazards. Region-specific reports are then pushed on to the FFC in order for that body to maintain a conscious awareness of crimes, individuals, and activities across the state of Florida as well as allocating necessary resources to specific regions when in need. Each regional center is responsible for establishing partnerships with the community and private sector within their respective regions. For example, the FFC will not have an established formal partnership with the Disney Corporation directly - this would be the responsibility of the Orlando/Orange County regional fusion center. Information provided by or requested from Disney would be managed by the regional center, and then pushed to the FFC in Tallahassee in the form of an intelligence product.

The Difference between the Florida Fusion Center and the Office of Statewide Intelligence
Once again, the OSI is responsible for providing intelligence products to FDLE executives to guide the planning and direction, analysis, reporting, and evaluation of FDLE operations. Even though all of the OSI assets support the FFC, the two entities have distinct missions. The OSI provides intelligence products to support FDLE cases and investigations, cases which are standard criminal investigations, such as those related to criminal enterprises. The FFC on rare occasions may lend support to FDLE cases; however, the FFC's mission is to provide strategic intelligence products related to terrorism, critical infrastructure, and all-threats and all-hazards[39]. This structure can be explained by FDLE's adherence to the Baseline Capabilities for State and Major Urban Area Fusion Centers (DHS, 2008). The guiding purpose of these baseline capabilities is fusion centers to establish operating procedures consistent with the Program Manager's Information Sharing Environment's (ISE) model.

According to the ISE model, fusion centers are responsible for terrorism, crimes that have a terrorism nexus, and threats to critical infrastructure and key resources (GIWG, 2005). This ISE context is the approach adopted by Florida to operate their fusion centers. From a functional perspective it is expected that there will be some investigation overlap between the OSI and FFC. This overlap is due to the fact that some crimes may or may not have a terrorism nexus, and until the investigation can reach a point at which a terrorism nexus can be identified, both the OSI and FFC will continue to work the

---

[39] An "all-threats, all–hazards" approach is commonly applied to critical infrastructure and key resources threat prevention. This approach also applies to natural disasters and homeland security intelligence. For more information visit http://www.dhs.gov/xabout/structure/gc_1220886590914.shtm

investigation simultaneously and in conjunction with one another. If the investigation indicates a terrorism nexus, the OSI will turn the investigation over completely to the FFC. Likewise, if the investigation indicates a lack of a terrorism nexus, the FFC will turn the investigation over completely to the OSI.

INFORMATION SHARING FACILITATED BY THE FLORIDA FUSION CENTER
Gap Analysis

As Mentioned, in 2007 FDLE conducted a statewide assessment of their information sharing capabilities to identify gaps for potential improvement. The critical gap identified through this evaluation was the need for improvement in the relationship between the FFC and local law enforcement agencies; more specifically, a gap was pinpointed in information collection provided via local agencies and local analyst products. Many of the local agencies tended to interpret intelligence-led policing as being focused within their own agency (FFC, 2010a) as opposed to a broader philosophy of being part of the information sharing culture where locals think beyond jurisdictional boundaries. This is critical given the FFC's strong emphasis that for successful intelligence-led policing to occur, agencies must understand trans-jurisdictional responsibilities (FFC, 2010a). Less than optimal relationships with local law enforcement were not uniform present as FDLE experienced a variation across the regions with respect to these relationships. For example, the FFC has a strong relationship with local law enforcement agencies in Pensacola, one developed though their collaborative experience managing both natural disasters (hurricanes) and drug-related criminal investigations.

Relationships with local law enforcement appeared to hinge on two factors; 1) local agencies recognizing what information needed to be pushed to the FFC, and, 2) a lack of awareness of what the FFC actually provides. This is not to say that local agencies in Florida are opposed to developing consistent standards for information sharing, but rather that a gap exists with respect to understanding the intelligence-led policing philosophy and the resources available to assist them in achieving an operational intelligence capability. This lack of knowledge is coupled with insufficient commitment from local law enforcement executives. As noted by FFC personnel, the lack of support and buy-in at all levels of the organization is a key obstacle to effective information sharing. The sub-par commitment is not in the form of unwillingness to share information, but rather in the provision of insufficient resources needed to meet the standards for information sharing outlined by the FFC to ensure quality, legality and effectiveness. Despite the identified gaps in communication with local agencies, many of them are involved in some form or fashion, be it having a formal ILO or simply maintaining an informal relationship to pass along information. In fact, information overload from local agencies is a challenge both in terms of the FFC managing this information but also communicating the importance to local law enforcement of the need to analyze and evaluate the information as it relates to their region. Similarly, the information overload issue arises as a result of needing a clearly defined dissemination strategy, one which has identified recipients and mechanisms are in place to provide for appropriate two-way information flow.

In response to these concerns, the FFC recognizes the need to market their products and resources with local law enforcement to increase awareness of what that entity can provide for local law enforcement, and *vice versa*. Currently, this is being achieved through FFC personnel who meet continually with local law enforcement to provide region-specific information as well as keep them up-to-date on resources available to them through the FFC. The creation of the seven regional fusion centers is also at the heart of the solution to this issue. These regional centers are tasked with the responsibility of marketing their resources to local law enforcement within their region while developing and maintaining active information sharing channels.

The collective mission of the seven regional centers is to build the grass-roots partnerships for two-way communication flow, and the FFC relies upon these regional centers to provide information from the community-level. This information flow allows the regional centers to identify region-specific crime/hazard/terrorism trends and provide this information to the FFC in the form of an intelligence product that can be used to allocate resources to that region to respond to the identified local needs. Moreover, the FFC can use this locally-gathered information to track crime/hazard/terrorism trends throughout the state of Florida and disseminate this information across the state and to national-level agencies as appropriate.

Intelligence Liaison Officers (ILOs)

A critical component to the success of fusion centers across the country is the establishment of intelligence liaison officers (ILO). An ILO is intended to be a communication channel of raw information from his or her agency/organization who can integrate that agency/organization-specific information into the collective body of information for analysis. When the fusion center has intelligence requirements, the ILO is the communication channel back to the agency/organization to share, monitor, and process the new information needs (Carter, 2009). The ILO's may be physically assigned to fusion centers, but a more common arrangement is for the ILO to perform his or her fusion center responsibilities simultaneously to those of their home agency/organization from that location.

The previously discussed information sharing gap analysis conducted by FDLE in early 2007 identified the need to establish ILOs in the state of Florida. By December 2007, 12 state agencies formally committed to the FFC by signing memoranda of understanding (MOU) with FDLE to contribute members to serve on the Executive Advisory Board and to serve as ILOs to support FFC operations. All formal ILOs meet with FFC personnel each Wednesday of the week to maintain consistency of intelligence requirements and identify emerging issues. These ILOs represent multi-discipline partners from education, fire rescue, communications, law enforcement and emergency management. Below is a list of the agencies and entities which participate as ILOs in the FFC:

- Department of Agriculture
- Department of Business and Professional Regulation
- Department of Corrections
- Department of Education
- Division of Emergency Management
- Department of Environmental Protection
- Fish and Wildlife Conservation Commission
- Department of Financial Services
- Department of Health
- Department of Highway Safety
- Department of Transportation
- Office of the Attorney General

- National Guard
- Department of Homeland Security
- US Attorney's Office
- Federal Bureau of Investigation
- Drug Enforcement Administration
- Florida Chiefs of Police Association
- Florida Sheriffs Association
- Florida Fire Chiefs Association
- Agency for Enterprise Information Technology

To formally become an ILO with the FFC, agencies/organizations must enter into an MOU with FDLE. The MOU requires the ILO to recognize rules, regulations, and laws pertaining to the disclosure of information, as well as comply with the operating policies and procedures and meet the performance expectations of FDLE/FFC. This MOU also requires a minimum time dedication of one ILO day per week. Additionally, ILOs must complete a background investigation, successfully obtain a secret-level security clearance (including civilian personnel), and complete a formal ILO training program set forth by the FDLE and the Fusion Executive Advisory Board.

All FFC members (and FDLE members assigned to the FFC) must also complete these trainings requirements. These training requirements are supplemented by monthly training schedules that address emerging issues in information sharing - such as 28 CFR Part 23 reviews, information sharing systems and privacy concerns. Moreover, each ILO is responsible for an established benchmark for standard tasking that includes, but is not limited to: monthly encounters report (e.g., repeat offenders, traffic stops and tickets), review of their agency/organization databases[40], actively push information back to the FFC, and complete strategic assessments for monthly encounters.

Formal ILOs assigned to the FFC are expected to participate in a capacity deemed appropriate by the ILO's agency/organization and will

---

[40] Florida Fusion Center personnel may ask for Intelligence Liaison Officers to run all the checks of their databases for persons which they are legally authorized to conduct. For example, a database search may identify a name from a terrorism watch list that also appears in the Department of Education or Public Health information systems.

have the ability to be virtually connected to the FFC via electronic information sharing systems. The intelligence system utilized by the FFC as well as other local, state and federal criminal justice agencies throughout Florida is known as the Statewide Intelligence Site - InSite. This system operates on the secure information portal administered by FDLE, the Criminal Justice Network (CJNet). InSite provides law enforcement agencies (federal, state and local) a secured computerized database of active criminal intelligence and active criminal investigative information to the legally authorized users across the state of Florida. The FDLE is responsible for system administration to include audits for the use of both CJNet and InSite. Access to the portal and the system requires MOUs, Agency Agreements and Individual User Agreements.

All users of InSite are required to undergo additional background investigations and training before being granted access to the system. All agency executives and individual users of InSite must acknowledge in writing an adherence to the FFC Privacy Policy as well as all applicable federal or state laws. Individuals assigned to the FFC from agencies outside FDLE are also bound by the Non-Disclosure Agreement. Civilians may be provided access to the system on a case-by-case basis for those who have a need to know and a right to know the information contained within the system.

The ILOs not only provide additional terrorism information, but they also enhance the all-hazards perspective adhered to by the FFC given their proximity to threats that can emerge outside of the traditional law enforcement purview. A unique example from the FFC of this all-threats approach was working with emergency management personnel for hurricane evacuation plans. Beyond the obvious threats posed by hurricanes, FDLE and emergency management planners have taken another step in collaboration and are examining registered sex offenders living within the projected hurricane damage areas to determine an appropriate evacuation and contingent living options. Together, the FFC and emergency management personnel identified the increase of a potential threat involving registered sex offenders being evacuated during a hurricane and directed to shelters where there may be large numbers of children with minimal adult oversight - such as many schools that serve as evacuation shelters during hurricanes. As such, the FFC and emergency management personnel are working together to create appropriate hurricane

evacuation plans for registered sex offenders living within high-impact
hurricane areas in the state of Florida.

Threat Assessments, Intelligence Products, and Dissemination
Utilizing information and intelligence products received from other law
enforcement agencies, fusion centers, and ILO's the FFC has developed
a comprehensive process for intelligence and information sharing in
support of the completion of strategic assessments, criminal
investigations and, as emphasized the most at the FFC, situational
awareness. These processes are at the heart of the FFC function to
facilitate communication across organizations (FFC, 2010a). Within
their first six months of operations, the FFC completed 12 strategic
threat assessments and responded to 53 requests for information.
During 2009, approximately 250 intelligence assessments on subjects
and topics of interest were produced.

As with any emerging initiative there has been improvement, but
some issues and concern still remain. For example, when the Super
Bowl was held at Raymond James stadium in Tampa, FL in 2009, the
FBI requested the FFC to conduct a threat assessment of possible
threats, actors, targets, and methods that could impact the Super Bowl.
Within this threat assessment, the FFC included a brief section on
serious domestic threat groups in the Tampa area. Once the assessment
was disseminated to the FBI it was decided this information should not
be included in the final threat assessment for the Super Bowl given the
FBI's threat prevention concerns were focused on international threat
groups. Despite a significantly higher likelihood of potential attacks
coming from domestic groups/crime, this information was not included
in the threat assessment and thus resulted in a less comprehensive
intelligence product for dissemination.

The FFC utilizes a "user-friendly, short and concise" (FFC, 2010a)
format for their intelligence products, and it disseminates these
products in multiple ways electronically. Intelligence products are
posted to the Homeland Security Information Network Intelligence[41]
(HSIN-Intel) website and Homeland Security State and Local
Intelligence Community of Interest[42] (HS SLIC) website. Beyond

---

[41] For more information visit https://government.hsin.gov/
[42] For more information visit https://hsin-intel.dhs.gov/

these major Regional Information Sharing System websites, the FFC maintains an updated email distribution list for awareness products as well as an internal secure portal to share information with other law enforcement agencies on request.   Moreover, the ILOs receive information on how to disseminate products during their ILO training program.   However, maintaining a consistent and timely standard for disseminating intelligence products has its challenges.   One primary obstacle faced by FFC personnel is that every 35-40 days the FFC's access to federal databases gets automatically deleted to particular system nodes.   For example, HSIN has a variety of nodes that remove access on a regular basis for security purposes.   After a couple of days the FFC's access is restored, but this becomes a routine inhibitor to information flow.   Information sharing inhibitors are not only technical, but can be bureaucratic in nature as well.   The process of receiving timely products from federal agencies is a rather complicated process due to the fact that there are so many layers of review and sign-off on intelligence products before they are permitted to go out.   This prolonged review process often results in stale information that is no longer applicable to current situations.

Relationships with the Private Sector
The importance of establishing public-private partnerships with fusion centers is reiterated in a variety of reports and recommendations.   The extent of participation and format of these partnerships can vary considerably across fusion centers nationally.   The approach taken by the FFC reflects the structure of the information sharing system in the state of Florida.   To begin with, active information sharing with the private sector occurs both at the state and regional fusion center levels. At the state level, the FFC administers a website specifically designed to facilitate information exchange with private sector entities. "Business Safe" is a program that includes an outreach program and a website open to the private sector.   BusinesSafe is designed to involve local businesses in protecting the safety and well-being of Florida's residents and visitors from threats - both man-made and natural. Florida's seven RDSTFs have launched BusinesSafe to provide businesses with the necessary tools and resources to facilitate two-way communication with the regional fusion centers.   BusinesSafe provides

sector-specific fact sheets for businesses to reference[43]. These sheets are categorized by the type of business and are patterned after a program that was created by the New York City Police Department after the attacks of September 11th - the NYPD Shield initiative[44]. More specifically, the information provided via BusinessSafe is designed to help local businesses identify suspicious activities which may result in a threat to those businesses. Private sector members can also sign up to receive electronic alert notifications via e-mail, cellular phones, and PDAs. These notices provide information about breaking news, possible threats, suspicious activity and specific preparedness techniques pertinent to the local businesses. Currently there are approximately 4,000 local businesses in the state of Florida connected to BusinessSafe (FFC, 2010a).

Additionally, businesses can register with a US Department of Homeland Security website[45] which provides vital information on how to better protect their business from threats. To register for this secure website, private sector members must apply via the website and identify their regional protective security advisor (PSA). The regional PSAs are representatives from the RDSTFs[46]. Beyond the US Department of Homeland Security secure website, local businesses may also register to become a member of multiple other websites designed for sharing threat information[47] - all of these websites can be reached via the BusinessSafe website. For example, the website "Business Owners Against Terrorism" (BOAT) provides local business owners connectivity with the North Florida Regional Domestic Security Task Force. The BOAT website allows business owners, managers or

---

[43] For a list of specific sectors and fact sheets visit: http://www.fdle.state.fl.us/ Content/getdoc/77cd6c85-8eed-4888-855c-715de12dcaef/Sectors-Key-Resource-Areas-(1).aspx
[44] For more information visit http://www.nypdshield.org/public/
[45]For more information visit http://cvpipm.iac.anl.gov/
[46] For more information visit: http://www.fdle.state.fl.us/Content/getdoc/ 5a336d9b-cf38-4979-bd03-d9bfe0f52738/DHS_Protective_Security_Advisor.aspx
[47] To view a list of additional private sector sharing websites visit: http://www.fdle.state.fl.us/Content/getdoc/b46536cc-bd2d-4008-8023-4d27f427da63/Related-Links.aspx

employees to anonymously report suspicious behavior or activities to local law enforcement authorities.

Consistent with the approach that local business must identify their protective security advisor - the representative from the RDSTF - to gain access to secure websites, regional fusion centers are responsible for establishing and sustaining active two-way information flow with the private sector within their region. The state fusion center (FFC) does not maintain partnerships with private sector companies - only the BusinessSafe website; the FFC relies upon the regional intelligence centers for these partnerships. The regional fusion center personnel push intelligence products from the private companies in their region to the FFC for further review and integration into other intelligence products. If additional information is needed from a private organization, the FFC will communicate with the regional center in which the business is located and the regional fusion center will then reach out to the business where information is sought.

INTELLIGENCE ANALYST PERFORMANCE AND STANDARDS
Analysts at the Florida Department of Law Enforcement
Law enforcement intelligence is reliant upon the analysis of raw information and thus, intelligence analysts. The FDLE and the FFC are sensitive to the importance of quality intelligence products. The FDLE defines a law enforcement analyst as "any person who is employed or contracted by a municipality, state or political subdivision thereof whose primary responsibility is to collect, analyze and disseminate data in the form of operational, strategic, investigative, intelligence and crime analysis to support, enhance and direct law enforcement missions (FFC, 2010a). When asked what character traits FDLE looks for in an intelligence analyst, the FFC personnel indicated the importance of credibility, excellent written and oral communication skills, and the ability to think critically. Moreover, FDLE believes analysts are not just people who sit behind a desk and operate computer software, but rather have a genuine ability to reach out to others and be proactive about the case they are working on and how it may relate to other cases they are aware of but might not be assigned (FFC, 2010a). Despite hiring analysts with these characteristics, FDLE is cognizant of the need for professional standards to train and evaluate analysts in order to achieve quality intelligence products.

A critical issue facing FDLE and the FFC is that the regional fusion center structure presents challenges with respect to how to coordinate and ensure the quality of intelligence products throughout state. This challenge of coordination and quality control is the result of the fact that some of the regional fusion centers were developed by local agencies that are currently being incorporated into a state-wide regional structure. Moreover, regional fusion centers operate, for the most part, separate from the FFC, and even though the FFC provides an FDLE analyst in all regional fusion centers the FDLE will not dictate to the regional centers.

Analyst Training
One way of addressing the analyst quality and standards challenge is through the development of a required analyst training academy. In 2003, the Florida Department of Law Enforcement developed the Florida Law Enforcement Analyst Academy (FLEAA). This academy was the first of its kind in the nation. Analysts learn criminal and intelligence analysis skills that are used by law enforcement and other emergency responders to prevent crime and conduct complex investigations. The FDLE's long-term goal in creating the FLEAA was to establish and provide a uniform training curriculum in the area of criminal intelligence and law enforcement analysis. During this six-week academy, analysts are challenged with hands-on training, work assignments, and weekly quizzes. They develop the skills necessary to complete individual and group research projects. Following the completion of all course work, analysts take a comprehensive examination. Successful academy graduates receive a state certification as a law enforcement analyst. The FLEAA is traditionally offered twice a year. To better prepare analysts for the academy, FDLE also developed two pre-requisite courses. The first course is a 40-hour Florida Basic Analyst Training (FBAT) class. This course is designed to train newly and recently hired analysts in the field of law enforcement analysis. The course offers instruction blocks that lay the groundwork for their career in criminal or intelligence analysis. There is a very high demand for this course, and it is usually offered two to four times a year.

During 2005, FDLE developed a new course titled "Computer Applications and Analytical Techniques" which is also a 40-hour course designed to train analysts in using computer applications to conduct investigative analysis. Once again there is a very high demand for this course as well, and it is normally offered two to four times a year as well. The basic and computer courses serve as training "stepping stones" and are required to be completed prior to attendance in the FLEAA. Currently, other acceptable prerequisites are being considered. The FDLE has been planning the launch of an advanced course since fall 2005. This course will fill an existing void between the basic course and the FLEAA. The intent is for this training to concentrate on the applications and techniques taught in the basic course and allow for more hands-on, advanced investigative analysis. The advanced course is delivered to analyst academy graduates and will focus on emerging topics of concern in criminal intelligence analysis - such as fusion centers, suspicious activity reporting, and intelligence-led policing.

Currently, the FDLE training program is funded through Law Enforcement Terrorism Prevention Program funds issued from the Department of Homeland Security. Students attending these courses must be assigned to an analyst position with a local or state law enforcement agency in the state of Florida. This funding allows FDLE to offer the FLEAA training courses free of charge to all state, county and municipal law enforcement and investigative agencies.

Analyst Performance Evaluation and Analyst Promotion
To reinforce and maintain consistent quality among intelligence analysts, FDLE has employed the use of both qualitative and quantitative methods for analyst performance evaluations. To begin with, the entry-level analyst at FDLE is a "Crime Intelligence Analyst I" (CIA I). The position of CIA I can be attained following the successful completion of all the applicable application/selection processes, which include approved exercises and interviews as well as meeting the minimum qualifications for the position. Prior to the expiration of the CIA I probationary period, the analyst must successfully complete the 40-hour FBAT and the 40-hour "Computer Applications and Analytical Techniques" course. The next analyst level at FDLE is a "Crime Intelligence Analyst II" (CIA II). A CIA I may be upgraded to a CIA II upon attaining one year of analytical experience and successfully completing the aforementioned training requirements. Any promotion from the position of CIA I to CIA II is be contingent upon the satisfactory completion of all probationary

requirements, a minimum rating overall of "Achieves"[48] on the analyst's work plan and the recommendation of the analyst's supervisor and approval via the analyst's chain of command to the Special Agent in Charge or equivalent.

The next progression for analysts at FDLE is to become a "Certified Crime Intelligence Analyst" (GA I). A CIA II may be promoted to a GA I upon attaining two years of analytical experience as a CIA II with the FDLE and successfully completing the FLEAA. The final progression for analysts at FDLE is to become a "Senior Crime Intelligence Analyst" (GA II). A GA I may be promoted to a GA II upon attaining five years of analytical experience as a GA I as well as becoming a certified analyst instructor; successfully completing an additional 40 hours of advanced analyst training; maintaining membership and active participation in a professional organization, which is pertinent to the analyst's job assignment and approved by the member's supervisor, and lastly maintaining a minimum rating of "Achieves" on the analyst assignments. Upon becoming a GA II, the analyst will have additional responsibilities that include, but are not limited to: assisting in the development and approval of curriculum for all course work in the FLEAA; assisting in the development and monitoring testing processes within the FLEAA; and administering proficiency exams for CIA candidates and FLEAA candidates.

In addition to the minimum requirements of evaluation for career progression, FDLE goes beyond evaluating their analysts at pre-determined intervals. Analyst products are not only reviewed when they are tested for the progression of their skills, but also on a day-to-day basis as senior personnel examine daily intelligence products and investigative support work. If an analyst's quality of work is thought to be less than sufficient, the inadequate product is returned to the analyst with comments and a follow-up discussion from senior personnel on the areas for improvement. The FDLE emphasizes the importance of quality over quantity (FFC, 2010a).

---

[48] Analysts receive one of three evaluations of their intelligence products as related to FDLE's benchmark for quality analysis; "Excels", "Achieves", and "Below"

PROTECTING CITIZENS' CIVIL RIGHTS

As many fusion centers across the country have come under public scrutiny for information sharing practices, whether legitimate or not, the FFC emphasizes transparency with respect to their operations. The FFC has a vigorous privacy policy which is open for public review and posted to the FDLE public website[49]. As explained in the FFC privacy policy document, the intent of the FFC is to:

> The Florida Fusion Center (FFC) is committed to the responsible and legal compilation and utilization of criminal investigative and criminal intelligence information and other information important to protecting the safety and security of the people, facilities, and resources of the State of Florida and the United States. All compilation, utilization, and dissemination of information by FFC participants and source agencies will conform to requirements of applicable state and federal laws, regulations and rules, and to the greatest extent practicable be consistent with Fair Information Practices. The intent of this policy is to abide by all privacy, civil rights and civil liberties guidance issued as part of the Intelligence Reform and Terrorism Prevention Act of 2004, National Fusion Center Guidelines, State and Major Urban Area Fusion Center Baseline Capabilities and the National SAR Initiative. All local, state, tribal and federal agencies providing suspicious activity reports (SAR) with a nexus to Florida or participating with the Florida Fusion Center (FFC) by virtue of submitting, receiving or disseminating SAR information, criminal intelligence or criminal investigative information via the FFC are required to adhere to the requirements of the Florida Fusion Center Privacy Policy (FFC, 2010b:3).

All members of the FFC are required to review, acknowledge and adhere to the FFC Privacy Policy. All participants and source agencies, which include all individual users of the InSite system, are required to review and adhere to the FFC privacy policy. The FFC provides a

---

[49] http://www.fdle.state.fl.us/Content/Florida-Fusion-Center/Menu/Privacy-Policy.aspx

printed copy of their policy upon request to all entities participating in the FFC and InSite and requires a written acknowledgement to comply with this policy and the provisions it contains. All FFC personnel, participating agency members, personnel providing information technology services to the agency, private contractors, InSite users and any other information sharing partner are required to comply with applicable laws protecting privacy, civil rights, and civil liberties. The FFC has adopted internal operating policies and procedures that are in compliance with applicable laws and regulations protecting privacy, civil rights, and civil liberties, including but not limited to, the U.S. Constitution and state, local, and federal privacy, civil rights, civil liberties, and legal requirements applicable to the FFC. Florida State Statutes 119[50] - Public Records - is one applicable law pertaining to the criminal intelligence and criminal investigative efforts of the FFC and participating agencies. In order to maintain consistency and adherence of the privacy policy by all actors involved, the FFC has created an internal Standing Privacy Review Board that actively reviews information sharing policies.

A noteworthy aspect of the FFC in response to a heightened suspicion of fusion center activities with respect to civil rights issues is that the Director of the FFC receives guidance from a Constitutional Protections and Privacy Advisory Board (CPPAB) that collaborates with community privacy advocacy groups to ensure that privacy and civil rights are appropriately protected by the FFC's information acquisition, dissemination and retention practices as defined by the FFC's written policy. The CPPAB is comprised of three members not actively associated with or employed by an FFC participating agency. The members of CPPAB are individuals with well-established credentials in the fields of criminal justice and/or the law. Currently the CPPAB members are comprised of an ACLU Director from the state of Florida, a retired Special Agent in Charge with the Federal Bureau of Investigation, and the Director of the Center for Advancement of Human Rights at Florida State University. The members are appointed by the FFC Executive Advisory Board to serve

---

[50] For more information visit
http://www.leg.state.fl.us/Statutes/index.cfm?App_mode=Display_Statute&
URL=Ch0119/ch0119.htm

for at least two years. The CPPAB will periodically review and recommend to the FFC Executive Advisory Board updates or changes to the FFC's policy and procedures for protecting civil rights and civil liberties in response to changes in applicable laws, or as otherwise necessary. The CPPAB may be consulted to participate in any independent inquiry into complaints alleging violation of the privacy rights policy and it will advise the FFC Executive Advisory Board of their findings and any recommended corrective action.

CONTEXT FOR ILP ADOPTION FINDINGS

This overview of the administration and operation of the Florida Fusion Center has provided the necessary context for validating relevant conceptual constructs discussed in this study. To clarify once again, the intention of this case study is to bring to the forefront an environment where law enforcement intelligence practices are most likely being applied in a manner consistent with established guidelines and recommendations. While fusion centers differ from most local agencies, their role in the intelligence/information sharing process sheds light on the likely facilitators and inhibitors of information sharing at the local level.

Perhaps the best illustration of information sharing and intelligence-led policing that can be extracted from this case study is the process and communication channels established throughout the structure of Florida's intelligence system. In the context of an individual agency at the local level, establishing communication channels for information sharing would essentially involve that agency to develop a process to manage collection requirements, develop partnerships with the private sector, and from partnerships with elements of the community. These steps represent the information collection infrastructure of police agencies that allow an agency to maintain the "pulse" of their community while also allowing for two-way communication of raw information. While this form of infrastructure aids the single agency is applying ILP to their specific needs, this also allows the single agency to engage in information sharing across jurisdictions and report on the types of trends and threats they feel are relevant. Such a process also allows for information to be pushed on to state fusion centers. This model is consistent with that of Florida's state fusion center and its seven regional fusion centers. Simply put, each regional fusion center acts independently and is responsible for their regional issues - just as independent local agencies would be responsible for their jurisdiction and report to the state fusion center or to other agencies seeking information they might feel is useful.

With respect to how intelligence-led policing is conceptualized, both in practice and in philosophy, elements of the Carter and Carter (2009a) model are integrated throughout Florida's intelligence structure. To begin with, the FFC adheres to an "all threats, all hazards" philosophy intended to prevent threats from reaching fruition. "Threats" is an all-encompassing term which refers to street crime, complex criminality, terrorism, and natural disasters. In short, the goal of this philosophy is to not only remain cognizant of traditional threats, but threats that have been outside the traditional law enforcement purview. Such a philosophy requires a variety of information sources and communication channels. These sources of information are consistent with those described within the "threat and crime environment" of the C&C model. The FFC has established sources consistent with this information collection environment that include public-private partnerships with the Disney corporation and "BusinessSafe". Moreover, the "BusinessSafe" portal allows for the submission of suspicious activity reports (SARs) - a threat-based source of behavioral information endorsed by practitioners and the C&C model of intelligence-led policing. Lastly, the importance of trans-jurisdictional information gathering and sharing was reinforced as a necessary function of intelligence-led policing. Once again, the philosophy of information being collected and for purposes of focusing on threats across jurisdictions - not just the jurisdiction in which an agency is located.

In terms of intelligence-led policing specifically, the "gap analysis" conducted by the FFC to identify shortcomings of information sharing among local agencies as well as with the fusion center itself reaffirms constructs identified in this study as predictors of intelligence-led policing. Diffusion of best practices, consistent with peer emulation, is present in the form of intelligence liaison officers. While ILOs are typically established once the ILP is present in an agency, the regular meetings among ILOs in Florida represent a continued effort to maintain contemporary practices as policies and recommendations guiding law enforcement intelligence are constantly evolving. Furthermore, the lack of understanding among local agencies is synonymous with limited familiarity of the ILP concept. It appears the lack of familiarity with the ILP concept inhibited the agencies from engaging in information sharingwith the FFC.

From an organizational structure perspective, all intelligence (and crime) analysts were civilian (non-sworn) personnel. An obvious caveat to the civilianization of the FFC as compared to local agencies is that it can be assumed logically that civilian employees within an intelligence-specific agency will be responsible for intelligence-specific tasks whereas civilian employees within a general local agencies may be tasked with responsibilities other than intelligence - thus clouding the effect of civilianization on ILP within local agencies. The FFC relies on many formal policies and procedures to guide their intelligence practices - thus being high in formalization. Perhaps the best example of formalization is the memorandum of understanding (MOU) that is required by agencies/organizations that formally partner with the FFC. This detailed MOU guides requirements for information sharing, collection, retention, and dedication of personnel and resources.

The influence of organizational context presented itself when the gap analysis indicated a significant lack of administrative commitment to the ILP philosophy as well as a requirement for comprehensive training on intelligence-related issues. It was noted by FFC personnel that the lack of support and buy-in at all levels of the organization is a key obstacle to effective information sharing. It is also worth noting that insufficient commitment is not in the form of unwillingness to share information, but rather insufficient resources needed to meet the standards for information sharing outlined by the FFC - most likely a result of too little executive buy-in. Training is greatly valued and required within the Florida intelligence system. While all intelligence-related personnel are required to receive training on intelligence issues, analysts receive the most timely and comprehensive training. This aspect of the FFC is also related to the importance of quality performance evaluation. Executives of the FFC acknowledge the importance of quality intelligence products to guide decision making. In order for quality products to be made available, analysts that create the products must be trained consistent with professional standards and expectations. Moreover, beyond the exhaustive training requirements, analysts are evaluated on the quality of their products as opposed to the number of products. The quality of products is determined by senior intelligence analysts in the form of a blind-review.   If an apparent decrease in quality is observed, the analyst can be required to attend further training programs.

In terms of the operationalization of the ILP adoption index as the dependent variable, the items used to compose the index were observed. Specifically, the need to share and receive information with the community and private sector constituents, identify and communicate collection requirements, and develop a mission and goal for the ILP capability were identified in the gap analysis. Moreover, the FFC personnel communicated the goal of being able to educate local agencies within Florida as to how to integrate intelligence into their decision making and how to share actionable products effectively. At the time of the case study these aspects were viewed as a goal because local agencies within Florida did not have an appropriate understanding of ILP, let alone the infrastructure and operational knowledge to carry out these aspects.

The Florida Fusion Center identified a significant lack of understanding as to the concept of intelligence-led policing among local law enforcement agencies across the state of Florida. As noted throughout this study, ambiguity of ILP is one of the largest hurdles of adoption and research. This lack of understanding further demonstrates the need for exploratory research on law enforcement intelligence practices.

CHAPTER 7

Case Study: Southern Nevada Counter-Terrorism Center

INTRODUCTION
This chapter provides a case study from the Southern Nevada Counter-Terrorism Center (SNCTC) as a means to build on the concepts observed in the Florida Fusion Center to provide context for the conceptualizations and empirical findings of the present study. While commonalities exist across the SNCTC and FFC, the SNCTC has a different structure for carrying out its mission. Furthermore, the SNCTC is designed to facilitate information sharing across a much different geographic and demographic area as compared to the FFC. The SNCTC is largely focused on activities within Clark County - specifically the city of Las Vegas, NV and the tourism/hospitality industry whereas the FFC is designed to manage multiple large cities, a large, spread-out geographic area, as well as a large tourism base. This different structure will provide another useful insight into an intelligence-specific organization. Just as with the previous case study, it should be noted that this case study is not provided as a source for data extraction or further empirical analysis. This case study is provided as a means to provide context for law enforcement intelligence practices and intelligence-led policing. Intersections between the case study and relevant constructs and empirical findings will be discussed.

The Southern Nevada Counter-Terrorism Center
Housed in a 24,000 square-foot, non-descript airport office park, the SNCTC became operational on October 1, 2007. On March 18, 2009, Las Vegas Metro Police Sheriff Doug Gillespie testified before the U.S. House of Representatives Subcommittee on Intelligence, Information Sharing, and Terrorism Risk Assessment during a session titled "Homeland Security Intelligence: Its Relevance and Limitations" (HCHS, 2009). During his testimony, Sheriff Gillespie stated that the Las Vegas Metro Police Department and the SNCTC were committed to the key components of an effective fusion center - intelligence-led

policing and an "all-threats, all-hazards" mission.   Sheriff Gillespie explained that the Las Vegas Metropolitan Police Department employs the intelligence-led policing philosophy and that analysis of crime data, coupled with the execution of innovative policing tactics, is the cornerstone of their efforts to prevent risks to society.

All-Threats, All-Crimes Approach to Fusion Centers
Despite the name of the SNCTC as a "counter-terrorism center" Sheriff Gillespie explained that the SNCTC could be more effective by taking a more broad "all-crimes, all-hazards" focus since law enforcement does not want to miss out on the criminal element that eventually turns out to be a terrorist. The SNCTC's core mission is to provide tactical and strategic analytic support to regional stakeholders. The tactical analysis section provides timely and actionable information to command staff and field personnel. The strategic analysis section complements tactical operations by developing long-term analytical products. Specific units exist to target gangs, counter terrorism, and narcotics as well a criminal analysts section to produce a variety of issue-specific products on issues facing the Clark County region. The SNCTC has established strong relationships with local industry, the public health community, and emergency management agencies to further enhance this approach.

     Awareness training is provided to private sector businesses on how to identify and report suspicious behavior. Co-located with the analysts, the SNCTC houses a 24/7 watch station capability, investigators that handle tips, leads and suspicious activity reports, critical infrastructure protection group, and the All Hazards Regional Multi-Agency Operations and Response (ARMOR) unit. This ARMOR team consists of local, county, state and federal experts in chemical, biological, radiological, nuclear, and explosive (CBRNE) response, detection, and identification. The SNCTC has developed a privacy policy that is founded on 28 CFR Part 23.

MISSION
The mission of the SNCTC is to improve communication and coordination among international, federal, state, local, tribal, and private agencies. This mission is achieved through the combining of relevant information from disparate databases concerning terrorism, critical infrastructure, and raw information pushed from the

community. The SNCTC is the regional hub for receiving information, providing analysis and dissemination of actionable intelligence to the participating agencies, Joint Terrorism Task Force (JTTF), All Regional Multi-Agency Operations and Response (ARMOR), and other appropriate law enforcement, public safety and intelligence entities. The SNCTC produces written reports concerning criminal trends and threat assessments in the Southern Nevada region and provides analytical case support and tailored analytical products.

MANAGEMENT AND STRUCTURE
The SNCTC defines a "member agency" as an entity that contributes at least one full-time employee or one full-time contractor that is co-located at the SNCTC site dedicated to fulfilling the SNCTC's mission. A "contributing agency" is defined as an agency that contributes personnel on a part-time or surge (as needed) basis. Any local, state, or federal agency with statutory law enforcement, public safety, or public health jurisdiction may join the SNCTC upon approval by the board of governors. In general, all agencies that have invested in the SNCTC are referred to as "participating agencies". Each of these participating agencies must agree upon and enter into a memorandum of understanding (MOU) with the SNCTC that outlines responsibilities and commitments to the center. On the average work day, the SNCTC houses 60 employees from various agencies and organizations.

Board of Governors
The SNCTC is overseen by a board of governors comprised of agency executives, who all have equal voting rights, from each of the participating agencies. The chairperson of the board of governors is the executive of the agency that is designated as the fiscal agent for the SNCTC, currently the Las Vegas Metro Police Department. The board of governors, which convenes as a whole twice a year, provides mission guidance and policy direction. Additionally, they resolve conflicts or disputes that might arise related to policies or the mission. The board of governors appoints the executive director for the SNCTC who has day-to-day command authority over members assigned to the center. As staffing patterns change and full-time employees are added, contributing agencies may change their status to become member agencies. Each agency executive who sits on the board must possess,

or be eligible and apply for a minimum security clearance at the level of "secret."

Collections Section

The deputy director of collection leads the collections section, which is responsible for the collection of hazard, threat, and suspicious activity information from a wide variety of sources and the distribution of the finished analytic products to the appropriate customers. There are two groups that comprise the collections section- namely, the collection management group and the operations group, each of which is supervised by a first-line supervisor. The primary function of the collection management group (CMG) is to ensure that the SNCTC has a constant, robust situational awareness of all threats, hazards and crimes occurring in Clark County and the state of Nevada. The CMG also coordinates all matters associated with the terrorism liaison officer program (TLO), and is responsible for the content and implementation of the SNCTC website and SAR programs. The operations group (OG) is responsible for the development of information sources, and the lawful collection of this source information. The OG is also responsible for the investigation and follow-up activities on suspicious activity reports, and on other tips and leads. On occasion the OG is called upon to provide dignitary protection liaison for U.S Secret Service protection details, and other high-level dignitaries.

Analysis Section

The deputy director of analysis leads the analysis section and is responsible for the collation, synthesis, analysis, and production to meet the intelligence needs identified by the requirements committee (to be discussed subsequently), or any ad hoc intelligence need established by the SNCTC. The analysis section consists of two distinct, but inter-related groups- the crime analysis group and the counter-terrorism analysis group. Personnel assigned to the crime analysis group are responsible for strategic, operational, and tactical crime analysis, hence fulfilling the crime analysis requirements established by the requirements committee. The counter-terrorism analysis group is responsible for the analysis of terrorism threat information, and the production of situational awareness, threat assessment, strategic, and tactical analytical products, and in so doing meeting the requirements established by the requirements committee.

Intelligence Requirements Committee
As noted by a SNCTC executive, intelligence-led policing is fueled by intelligence requirements (SNCTC, 2010). The most significant approach taken to identifying intelligence requirements for the SNCTC is the creation of a requirements committee. The purpose of this committee is to establish the information, intelligence and production requirements of the SNCTC and to establish the priority in which these requirements are addressed by personnel assigned to the SNCTC. Moreover this committee is responsible for ensuring that agencies receive the intelligence products that meet their needs - whether these products are related to organized crime, motorcycle gangs, or terrorism. Requirements for information collection fall into three categories;

1) Ad hoc requirements (highest priority, information related to a wide-range of possible emerging threats).
2) Priority requirements (information related to an identified, time-sensitive threat).
3) Standing requirements (information related to an identified, on-going threat).

This intelligence requirements committee is comprised of command-level managers who are responsible for designing, approving and/or implementing initiatives, and who possess decision-making authority for their employing agency. Personnel who are assigned to the SNCTC are not permitted to be members of the committee in order to reduce potential conflicts of interest. In general, the positive outcomes of this committee are wide-ranging. Though more specifically, the result of the inclusion of the requirements committee into the business process of the SNCTC is better coordination of the human and technological resources available to the participating agencies of the SNCTC. Arguably the most important outcome of this committee is the assurance that the intelligence needs of each of the participating agencies are met. Also, with improved communication on the daily activities of the SNCTC, the partner agencies will realize a greater return on their personnel investment.

The requirements committee is responsible for providing four necessary outputs. The first, standing intelligence needs, are semi-permanent and enduring information and intelligence needs that will change very little over time. Examples of this need are the weekly

LVMPD action reports and analysis of every terrorist attack on a hotel or tourist destination. Second are the priority information needs that are requests for information or intelligence that are assessed and determined by the requirements committee to have a high priority. Third are the top priority information needs which occur during times of crisis or emergency and require immediate attention and the suspension of work focused on standing and/or priority information needs. Lastly, a matrix of priorities, comprised by the committee, reflecting the priorities assigned to each standing or priority information need. SNCTC executives use this matrix as a guide in prioritizing and allocating work to SNCTC personnel.

From a procedural perspective, the requirements committee meets on the second and fourth Wednesdays of every month at the SNCTC. The executive director of the SNCTC is responsible for facilitating the meeting, and provides the committee with updates relative to the progress made towards completing each of the existing requirements. Each member of the committee is responsible for briefly summarizing any initiative or action that resulted from a completed requirement. This type of feedback ensures that the intelligence and information needs of the participating agencies are being met by the SNCTC, as well as ensuring that the requests for intelligence align with intended actions.

Quality Assurance Section
The deputy director of quality assurance leads the quality assurance section that is comprised of three groups. The first is the security group that is responsible for the operational and physical security of the SNCTC and all classified environments, the maintenance of all access and alarm systems, and the proofs of compliance for all security matters. This group is also the single point of contact for all applications for security clearances, and maintains a roster of security clearances- including dates for renewal investigations. The second group is the privacy protection group that is responsible for ensuring that the SNCTC adheres to all pertinent laws, rules, and regulations relating to the protection of personal privacy and civil liberties. This group is also responsible for implementing the program and systems necessary, through the training of personnel, to provide regular and periodic audits to ensure compliance and provide proofs of compliance for all SNCTC investigations and intelligence products. Finally, the

third group is the performance measurement group which is tasked to develop and collect the data necessary to measure the ability of the SNCTC to perform its established mission. This group seeks to determine if the work accomplished by the SNCTC aligns with the intelligence requirements set forth by the requirements committee.

Direction of SNCTC and Resource Control

Oversight and specific control over an agency's SNCTC resources and the continued dedication of resources to the SNCTC are retained by the participating agencies which are kept fully informed of all analytical developments by their respective subordinates, as appropriate security clearances permit. The salaries of the SNCTC personnel are paid by their respective agencies, and the LVMPD, in the role of the fiscal agent provides office space, equipment, and supplies to carry out the administrative operation of the SNCTC. Once the original seed money from federal and/or state grant funding is no longer available, sustaining the SNCTC will be the responsibility of all participating agencies. This provision for long term operation includes any additional equipment required by a participating agency, which will be the responsibility of that agency to supply. Any and all expenditures by each participating agency are subject to the home agency's budgetary processes and to the availability of funds and resources pursuant to applicable laws, regulations, and policies. When entering into a memorandum of understanding with the SNCTC, agencies expressly acknowledge that the language in the agreement in no way implies that Congress or the Federal government will appropriate funds for such expenditures.

Supervision of SNCTC

Day-to-day supervision of matters assigned to the SNCTC is the responsibility of the LVMPD. Analysts are assigned based upon subject matter expertise and serve the entire southern Nevada region. As additional analytical resources become available, supervisory personnel from other member agencies are added. Each participating agency is subject to the personnel rules, regulations, laws and policies applicable to their respective agencies and abides by appropriate security agreements concerning the handling of classified and sensitive material. If a complaint is made against any SNCTC member while acting within the scope of their SNCTC assignment, it is reported to the SNCTC director. The executive director reports the complaint to the board of governors and the respective agency's direct supervisor of the SNCTC member under complaint. The executive (from the board of governors) of the complaint member's agency is responsible to conduct an investigation with assistance of the SNCTC executive director.

The SNCTC initially consisted of a combined body of the LVMPD supervisory and management staff, analysts, and support personnel, together with agents, analysts and support personnel assigned from the participating agencies. The MOU utilized by the SNCTC establishes and outlines the intent of the participating agencies to centralize and co-locate. This fusion is intended to provide resources, expertise, and information to maximize their ability to detect, prevent, investigate, and respond to all crimes and all hazards in the greater Clark County, southern Nevada region. The benefits of collaboration and communication between the contributing agencies are readily apparent and widely recognized as absolutely essential. Further, the MOU established a framework for the organization of the SNCTC and to address issues that are common to the participating agencies. The MOU is to set out a common understanding of the policies and procedures that the SNCTC follows in providing intelligence and coordination of service to the citizens encompassed by the populated areas of southern Nevada.

Analyst Environment
Analyst personnel at the SNCTC are comprised of a senior analyst to oversee all analytic functions, a private sector-specific analyst (to be discussed forthcoming), and four full-time analysts, both crime and intelligence analysts. Crime analysts are responsible for providing tactical and/or operational assessments to decision makers whereas intelligence analysts are responsible for providing case and/or strategic products. The analyst room is physically structured in the form of a "news room" with cubicle walls that stand only a few feet tall. This physical layout is to enhance awareness of each analyst's work in that each analyst will be in an environment where they will over-hear other analysts talking about cases or queries that they may also have information on and a connection can be made. This approach is consistent with the idea of eliminating barriers (such as bureaucracy) for more direct communication and thus, more effective information sharing.

Law Enforcement and Public-Sector Partnerships
The SNCTC has participating agencies from the public sector that go beyond the traditional law enforcement arena. Maintaining the "all-threats, all hazards" approach to intelligence, the SNCTC has engaged in extensive partnerships with emergency response/preparedness agencies, local public schools, and federal law enforcement agencies. At the time of the case study, the SNCTC had entered into formal partnerships with the following public sector agencies and organizations:

- Las Vegas Metropolitan Police Department (LVMPD)
- Federal Bureau of Investigation (FBI)
- Henderson Police Department (HPD)
- North Las Vegas Police Department (NLVPD)
- Clark County School District Police Department (CCSDPD)
- Clark County Fire Department (CCFD)
- Las Vegas Fire & Rescue Department (LVFR)
- Nevada Department of Public Safety (NDPS)
- United States Federal Air Marshals Service (FAMS)
- United States Transportation Security Administration (TSA)
- Las Vegas Convention and Visitors Authority (LVCVA)
- City of Las Vegas Department of Law Enforcement and Detention (LVDLED)
- Southern Nevada Health District (SNHD)
- North Las Vegas Fire Department (NLVFD)
- Nevada High Intensity Drug Trafficking Area (NV HIDTA)
- Clark County District Attorney (CCDA)

Partnerships with the Private Sector - Suspicious Activity Reporting
One of the SNCTC's greatest strength is the ability to collect SARs from the community and private sector. Even though there is a constant need to improve SAR education and awareness for identification and reporting - being achieved by the SNCTC through the "See something, Say something" campaign - the SNCTC has one of the most sophisticated, user-friendly, and effective methods of both identifying and collecting SARs. The means by which SARs reach the SNCTC are the product of a formal partnership with the Las Vegas

Convention and Visitor Authority (LVCVA), a successful partnership with the hospitality industry in Las Vegas as a whole, and a user-friendly website interface that will be discussed in the following section.

The LVMPD entered into a formal agreement[51] with the LVCVA to enhance the private-sector SAR initiative. This agreement outlines the responsibility for both agencies to provide certain services to the public in accordance with their respective statutory authority. More specifically, the LVMPD is responsible for the day-to-day supervision of matters assigned to the SNCTC, which was established to improve communication and coordination among public safety agencies to maximize their ability to detect, prevent, investigate and respond to all crimes and all hazards in the greater Clark County and southern Nevada region. The LVCVA determined that being a formal and active participant of the SNCTC was in the best interest of and a direct benefit to the hospitality industry in Clark County. As such, the LVCVA is now a member of the board of governors of the SNCTC and is required to contribute personnel or provide the financial support to hire personnel in order to fulfill the mission of SNCTC.

In order for this formal partnership to work effectively, the participatory role of the LVCVA in the SNCTC was adapted to allow participation without violating any statutes or laws regarding confidentiality and privileged information that only law enforcement agencies have access and right to access to in terms of certain classified and/or criminal information. To best serve this purpose, the LVMPD hired a private-sector specific intelligence analyst, dedicated to the interests of the hospitality industry, whose position is financially supported by the LVCVA. This intelligence analyst is an employee of LVMPD and is assigned to the SNCTC for the purpose of responding to the needs and security of the hospitality industry. Moreover, this intelligence analyst is not considered an employee of LVCVA for any purpose and only serves as a liaison between the LVCVA and SNCTC to represent the interests of the hospitality industry. The LVCVA does not have any right to control the work of the intelligence analyst, their assignments, work schedules, conditions of employment or any other aspect of the relationship with LVMPD.

---

[51] Inter-local Agreement pursuant to the provisions of 277.180

Even though the private sector is primarily concerned with criminality related to gaming in Nevada, they are committed to an all-threats approach with the SNCTC. A highly successful example of this partnership is the SAR awareness program the SNCTC has with the hospitality industry in Las Vegas. In partnership with The University of Nevada Las Vegas Institute for Security Studies, state and local public safety, and homeland security agencies, the SNCTC developed a terrorism SAR awareness video titled "Nevada's Seven Signs of Terrorism[52]". The video, which is available in both English and Spanish, provides an informative walk through key behaviors and activities that are the hallmark of terrorist planning and preparations. While the video uses local examples in order for viewers to personally relate to the information, the key to the success of the terrorism SAR video is the fact that hotels in Las Vegas now require all employees to view the video; there is a very promising indication of commitment to the partnership between the SNCTC and the private sector hospitality industry.

INFORMATION SHARING AND RECORDS MANAGEMENT
Collection
The SNCTC recognizes intelligence information as defined by the Fusion Center Guidelines (GIWG, 2005) and National Criminal Intelligence Sharing Plan (GIWG, 2003) as the product of systematic gathering and evaluation of raw information on persons or activities suspected of being criminal in nature. Criminal intelligence information submitted and stored within the SNCTC system/network is required to minimally meet the following three criteria:

1) Reasonable suspicion
2) Be obtained legally
3) Have relevance to a subject's suspected terrorist or criminal activity

Reasonable suspicion - or criminal predicate - means there is enough information to establish sufficient facts or basis to believe a subject or group is involved in definable illegal activity. This includes,

---

[52] This video is available at: http://www.snctc.org/View-DVD.asp

but is not limited to, an enterprise that represents a significant/recognized threat to the population; is undertaken for the purpose of seeking illegal power or profits or poses a threat to the life and property of citizens; involves a significant permanent criminal organization or is not limited to one jurisdiction. Legally obtained refers to the information gathered and maintained through lawful means with authorized access that is relevant to the identification of a subject and the individuals' or groups' known or suspected involvement in terrorist or criminal activities. The SNCTC does not retain information related to political, religious, social views, associations (businesses, partnerships, etc.) or activities that are not related to criminal conduct or activity.

The SNCTC also utilizes different sources of information to enhance the intelligence fusion process. Many of the resources commonly accessed for information do not meet the criteria established for criminal intelligence and are not subject to 28 CFR Part 23[53]. Non-intelligence information may include data from law enforcement resources, public information outlets, and open sources such as the internet, newspapers, and other publications. Sources of information typically accessed by the SNCTC include:

- Criminal history records
- Warrants
- Case or investigative information from other systems
- Tips and leads
- Field Contacts
- De-confliction systems
- Driver's license, telephone subscriber, etc.
- Identification systems (AFIS, finger prints, mug shots, etc.)

In an effort to reduce the duplication of records and diminish the probability of maintaining dated, inaccurate information, to the extent

---

[53] Codified as 28 CFR Part 23 "Criminal Intelligence Systems Operating Policies", this regulation governs inter-jurisdictional and multi-jurisdictional criminal intelligence systems that are operated by or on behalf of state and local law enforcement agencies and that are funded by or receive federal funds.

possible the SNCTC uses links and pointing tools to connect identifying data to a subject and the individuals' or groups' known or suspected involvement in terrorist or criminal activities. The SNCTC utilizes the collection and storage of non-criminal identifying information as applicable by 28 CFR Part 23, which allows for the collection and storage of non-criminal identifying information in criminal intelligence systems under the following specific conditions.[54]

- Information must be clearly labeled as non-criminal.
- The field in which it is entered must be searchable.
- Information must be relevant to subject's identification or criminal activity.
- Data cannot be used as the independent basis for meeting reasonable suspicion threshold.
- Political, religious, social views, associations (businesses, partnerships, etc.) or activities that are not related to suspicious conduct or activity are not permitted to be maintained.

Storage
The submission of information to the SNCTC system/network is critical to the overall success of its mission. As previously mentioned, criminal intelligence and non-intelligence data must be maintained separately in accordance with federal regulations. The SNCTC determined all data shall be kept in electronic format to ensure the security of information, minimize vulnerability, control audit activities, and expedite search and analysis activities. The originating agency is responsible for identifying information, attaching the correct labels, and saving or storing information in the designated criminal intelligence and non-intelligence areas of the SNCTC system/network. Paper documents are only available when electronic format is not an option, and they are stored under appropriate measures.

All criminal intelligence files contain a minimum of core information fields. In addition, the originating agency may include

---

[54] Complete 28 CFR Part 23 information is available at: http://www.iir.com/ 28cfr/Laymensguide.pdf

relevant and pertinent information as consistent with 28 CFR Part 23. The SNCTC intelligence files include:

- Name of subject (e.g. individual, organization, business, or group)
- Subject identifiers
- Suspected criminal activity
- Officer(s) involved
- Agencies/Bureaus involved
- Source
- Date of original submission
- Date of revision(s)
- Description of Activity
- Analysis
- Recommended Action

Information contained in working files can only be non-intelligence data. It is important for the SNCTC to minimize duplication of information. Information received by the SNCTC that is relevant to a file already on record is recorded by documenting the link to its location. In the event that data or information received is in paper form, it is scanned to an electronic format, labeled, and stored appropriately. The original paper hard copy is destroyed or returned to the originating agency depending on their policies or agreement with SNCTC. The SNCTC employs multiple classifications types for analytic products as well as certain pieces of raw information.

In addition to the core file fields, the SNCTC requires the submitting agency to label appropriately all information intended for storage in the SNCTC systems/network. Both criminal intelligence and non-intelligence information is required to be labeled to denote the *level of sensitivity* or classification (restricted, limited, controlled, for official use, open source), *level of confidence* (reliable, usually reliable, unreliable, unknown), and *validity* (confirmed, probable, doubtful, unknown). Moreover, every named subject included in any submission must be reasonably suspected of direct involvement in criminal activity and must be properly labeled to identify the association, such as subject, associate, relative, or employee. For organizations or groups to be identified, a significant portion of the subject's activity must be criminal.

Dissemination

Information on the SNCTC system/network is disseminated using an established automated notification system to key personnel and participating agencies. This process maintains an electronic audit trail of notifications for security and auditing purposes. Participating agencies that receive electronic notifications are responsible for maintaining the appropriate security of all information as outlined by their agreements with the SNCTC. The SNCTC staff documents the release of all information, excluding the automated notifications mentioned above, using the appropriate form. Release of information requires verification of the inquirer's identity, right-to-know[55], need-to-know[56], and may be required to necessitate approval from the original source and/or an SNCTC executive. Recipients of intelligence/information/data from the SNCTC must agree to comply with 28 CFR Part 23 regulations. Each release form is maintained electronically and linked to the associated intelligence file being requested. In the event of an emergency or critical incident, the SNCTC director may approve the dissemination of information classified as restricted, limited, or controlled to law enforcement agencies, public safety, and emergency personnel who are coordinating information with responders on the scene. The release of information to private individuals for non-law enforcement purposes is restricted by Nevada Revised Statute (NRS) 239C[57] and requires the SNCTC director's approval.

---

[55] The "right to know" dissemination standard is determined valid in a circumstance where the individual requesting the sensitive information is determined to have the official capacity and/or statutory authority to receive the information being sought.

[56] The "need to know" dissemination standard is determined valid in a circumstance where if the information to be disseminated is pertinent and necessary to the recipient in order to prevent or mitigate a threat or assist and support a criminal investigation.

[57] Full reference for NRS 239C is available at: http://www.leg.state.nv.us/nrs/NRS-239C.html#NRS239CSec010

Under NRS Chapter 239C Homeland Security (subsection 210), the Governor of Nevada declared certain documents prepared and maintained for the purpose of preventing or responding to an act of terrorism to be confidential. Further, documents (including records or other items of information) are not available for inspection by the public if such a disclosure creates a substantial likelihood of compromising, jeopardizing or otherwise threatening the public health, safety or welfare. Protected information under this statute includes, but is not limited to, the following:

- Critical infrastructure (maps, drawings, plans, etc)
- Emergency response plans
- Emergency radio transmission information
- Training, handbooks, manuals related to emergency response plans
- Other documents as determined by Executive Order

Original Documentation - Third Party Prohibition
The SNCTC does not allow original documentation obtained from an outside agency to be released to a third party by SNCTC staff without prior approval from the originating agency. However, there are some MOUs between the SNCTC and member/participating agencies which feature this on-going approval. This includes both criminal intelligence information and data considered to be non-intelligence. The SNCTC staff has the discretion to choose to refer the requestor to the originating agency for further assistance. If the SNCTC believes original documentation received from an outside agency should be released, a SNCTC executive coordinates with the originating agency to request permission to disseminate, or request that a modified or redacted version that can be reclassified for release purposes. Only the originating agency can redact, modify information, and/or authorize release of their information. If the SNCTC is the original source of the information marked restricted, limited, controlled, or for official use only, and a request is received or determination is made to provide the information to agencies outside of law enforcement, SNCTC executive may approve modification and redaction for the purposes of reclassifying the information for distribution to other non-law enforcement entities as appropriate.

Approved Methods for Information Dissemination

The SNCTC disseminates information using the most secure methods available based on the sensitivity level of the information, available mechanisms for sharing information with the inquirer, and timeliness. Based on the criteria discussed previously, the SNCTC has approved the following mechanisms for the dissemination of information:

- Verbal communication; via telephone or in person.
- Hand delivered; appropriate labeling.
- Interoffice mail; appropriate labeling required.
- Approved secure electronic mail, using appropriate encryption applications.

Access to the SNCTC system/network maybe directly available to participating agencies not located within the SNCTC. Appropriate security controls to prevent unauthorized access or damage to information stored in the system have been adopted by the SNCTC.

Public Request for Information

All public requests for information made to the SNCTC must be directed to the records compliance administrator. Only a SNCTC executive, under the guidance of the SNCTC board of governors, SNCTC policies, and in accordance with all established agreements, has the authority to approve the release of information to the public. Only the subject of the information on record, or a legal representative, may obtain access to the requested information. A legal representative's authorization must be written and notarized and the person authorized must have picture identification to receive the information. The SNCTC follows a strict dissemination policy. The requestor will be advised if he or she is not entitled to the information. Juvenile information and certain victim and witness information are protected from disclosure by law and are not be provided upon request. The SNCTC reserves the right to redact and delete information it deems prudent to protect from public disclosure in accordance with all laws, regulations, and policies.

An individual making a public request for information must fill out a form at the SNCTC and provide the following:

- Name
- Copy of driver's license or other government issued photographic identification (e.g. military id, passport, alien card)
- Name of employer
- Citizenship
- A statement of the purpose for the request to inspect the information. (Note: Nothing in the supporting statutes prohibits an SNCTC employee or public officer from contacting law enforcement to report suspicious or unusual requests to inspect information).

The SNCTC observes persons during inspection of information they have requested in a location and in a manner that ensures the information is not copied, duplicated, or reproduced in any way. Restricted documents may be copied, duplicated or reproduced only under the following circumstances and in compliance with all other laws, rules, and policies governing information requested:

- Lawful order of a court of competent jurisdiction.
- As reasonably necessary in the case of an act of terrorism or other related emergency.
- To protect the rights and obligations of a governmental entity or the public.
- Upon request of a reporter or editorial employee, affiliated with a news association, or commercially operated and federally licensed radio or television station for use in the course of this employment or affiliation.
- Upon request of a registered architect, licensed contractor (or designated employee of) for use in their professional capacity.

Information Review and Purge
In an effort to preserve citizens' civil rights related to the retention of information, the SNCTC has in place an ongoing review of criminal intelligence and non-criminal intelligence (SARs) files for relevancy, importance, and sensitivity required to delete inaccurate or outdated information and remain in compliance with federal regulations. Automated system audit trails, purges, and reports are periodically

reviewed. Additionally, manual review and destruction processes are followed to ensure both electronic files and hard files remain in compliance with the SNCTC's privacy/records policies.

As mandated by 28 CFR Part 23, there is a five-year maximum retention of criminal intelligence information. The SNCTC determines the start date by the initial date information (subject record or file) is stored in the SNCTC system/network. Any significant change or update to the information resets the purge date to be five years from the point of change; the changing of an address, phone number, or noncriminal associations are not considered significant changes. As such, if a criminal intelligence file remains without significant changes during the five-year period it is removed from the SNCTC system/network. This system automatically generates a report at six months prior to purging for files meeting this criterion. The originating agency reviews the file scheduled for destruction for currency and accuracy, and then an approval decision for removal of the document, along with an explanation as to why the information shall remain, is made.

Non-intelligence information is consistent with the same review period and purge criteria as are intelligence data. Information scheduled for purge is returned to the originating agency or disposed of in accordance with the originating sources' requirements. These purging requirements from the originating agency must be in writing with the SNCTC. Information/intelligence/data that is approved for purging is documented as such and removed from the system by the originator of the information. Any paper documents containing criminal intelligence information approved for destruction are disposed of using approved destruction methods. Electronic files are purged (deleted) from the SNCTC system/network by the originating agency, supervisory authority, or information technology authority at their request. Paper documents are destroyed by shredding to prevent the reconstruction of any of the documents. Approved shredders are located in the SNCTC facility, and all files and record destruction take place on site at the SNCTC.

Information Security Inside the SNCTC
The electronic storage of information on the SNCTC system/network is the most secure and therefore the recommended method for retaining all information. As stated previously, paper copies are kept to a

minimum at the SNCTC and any paper documents classified at the restricted, limited, and controlled level are kept in a locked cabinet in a designated secure area of the SNCTC. Less highly classified documents - such as For Official Use Only - are kept secure within a locked area (e.g., file drawer) or office. The SNCTC has gone to great lengths to secure the facility and its equipment from unauthorized access. However, additional responsibility for protecting information lies with those individuals working within the SNCTC. The following safeguards are required to be adhered to by SNCTC staff:

- Do not leave documents in clear sight when in work areas.
- Always remove and store documents in a manner appropriate to their classification when leaving the work area.
- When using photocopiers, facsimiles, etc. do not leave originals behind.
- Be aware of others in the immediate area when documents are open for viewing on computer screens. Use the minimize function to limit exposure.
- Follow computer protection policies when setting passwords. Change passwords immediately if suspicion of compromise arises.
- Do not provide your password to anyone.
- Always turn your computer off when leaving the area for an extended period of time; and at the end your work day.
- Immediately notify the appropriate authority if you suspect information is missing, has been altered, or has been accessed without authorization.

Information Access
Each participating agency retains sole ownership, exclusive control over, and sole responsibility for the proprietary information it contributes to the SNCTC. All work that is the product of and originates from an employee of a participating agency clearly identifies the contributing agency and also clearly states that the information is and remains the sole property of the contributing agency under that agency's exclusive control. All joint reports or products of collaboration between participating agencies and the SNCTC are considered property of the SNCTC. However, the dissemination of

joint products is dependent upon approval from any of the contributing participating agencies. Each participating agency has the sole responsibility to ensure the accuracy of information it has contributed to the SNCTC. If the participating agency becomes aware of any inaccuracy in information it has contributed, it has the responsibility to correct that information and communicate this correction to the SNCTC. Each participating agency is responsible for ensuring that all shared information is collected for legitimate law enforcement purposes to investigate, prevent or mitigate suspected criminal activity and/or threats.

All participating agencies' information and records system designs must ensure that audit trails, system security, and information dissemination correspond to the mission of the SNCTC. The following are key aspects that must be incorporated into each participating agency's information and records system design:

- Collection Limitation
- Data Quality
- Use Limitation
- Security Safeguards
- Openness
- Individual Participation
- Accountability

Any report prepared by a participating agency must be classified at the level of the highest classification of any material it contains and cannot be disseminated to any party who does not possess that clearance level as well as the right-to-know and/or need-to-know.

The SNCTC handles both "classified" and "sensitive but unclassified" law enforcement/public safety information. Participating Agencies are only granted access to classified or sensitive information if they have the appropriate security clearances. Any SNCTC members seeking access to classified information who do not possess secret/top secret clearances, depending on the level of access to classified information sought, are subject to a full background investigation with access to the sensitive information contingent upon receipt of an appropriate security clearance. In these circumstances where a background investigation is required, the participating agency is responsible for all costs associated with obtaining the necessary security clearance for their member.

All participating agencies, their employees, and their contractors must agree not to disclose classified or sensitive information to anyone not authorized to receive information at the specified classification level, and who does not also have a need- and right-to-know, without the express written permission of the originating agency. Moreover, all intelligence products and intelligence sharing must comply with 28 CFR Part 23 standards.

Intelligence Reports and Products
The SNCTC has an established system of report production and dissemination for other public safety agencies and non-government consumers. To begin with, the SNCTC utilizes a web portal called "All-Data Virtual Information Sharing Environment" (ADVISE) to disseminate products and other communications. The ADVISE system allows the SNCTC to disseminate and/or post a wide-range of general information products. Information typically available through program reports are; tips and leads, case files, intelligence files, SNCTC products, and a reference / research library. For agencies or organizations soliciting information from the SNCTC, their initial point of contact is the watch station. This point of contact is a phone line staffed by trained personnel to provide constant situational awareness and identify emergent patterns in crime, hazards and risks.

The type of products provided by the SNCTC follow an intelligence/information production plan. A standardized format is required for all products. This format includes a single banner that is agency-neutral across the top of the documents. Agencies that provide joint cooperation for compiling products are identified in the product narrative. Furthermore, the production plan identifies three categories of products:

- Situational Awareness Reports
- Periodic Reports
- Ad hoc Reports

Situational awareness reports are the most general and straightforward product from the SNCTC. These reports include a synthesis of open-source information and typically include the latest and most pertinent information related to breaking news, significant crime events, and bulletins from the National Operations Center (NOC).[58] In short, these reports are intended to provide the SNCTC community with a rich situational awareness of their areas of responsibility. Periodic reports are centered on counter-terrorism analysis. These reports are broken down into five sub-categories of types of terrorism. Even more specifically, these five sub-categories have their own methodology for crime analysis that incorporates 42 categories of analysis. Periodic reports are disseminated to SNCTC consumers on daily, weekly and monthly intervals. The final type of reports is ad hoc. Somewhat similar to the situational awareness reports, ad hoc reports provide more detailed crime advisories, tactical intelligence support, Homeland Security alerts (urgent), Homeland Security advisories (important), threat assessments (less important), and requests for analysis from other agencies.

Information Sharing Functional Exercise
From November 2-12, 2009, the SNCTC spearheaded a functional information sharing exercise with three Nevada Fusion Centers, the U.S. Department of Homeland Security / FEMA, and the State of Nevada / Clark County / City of Las Vegas Emergency Management; this exercise was referred to as "Operation Silver Rogue". The objectives of the exercise were to: 1) detect, recognize and act upon indicators and warnings of potential criminal/threat activity; and, 2) properly share and conduct investigations and operations related to potential terrorism. The exercise indicated strengths and weaknesses.

---

[58] The National Operations Center provides real-time situational awareness and monitoring of the homeland, coordinates incidents and response activities, and, in conjunction with the DHS Office of Intelligence and Analysis, issues advisories and bulletins concerning threats to homeland security, as well as specific protective measures. The NOC – which operates 24 hours a day, seven days a week, 365 days a year – coordinates information sharing to help deter, detect, and prevent terrorist acts and to manage domestic incidents. Information on domestic incident management is shared with Emergency Operations Centers at all levels through the Homeland Security Information Network (HSIN).

The most significant strength exhibited during the exercise was that intelligence sharing and coordination between the three Nevada fusion centers was effective. The Terrorism Liaison Officer program with the private sector provided effective information sharing. Participants in the exercise found the analyst and executive briefings to be effective. Lastly, the SNCTC staff made effective use of predictive and geo-spatial analysis and discussed various modes and locations of attack. Weaknesses identified during the exercise included a critique of the ADVISE system given its limited search capacity. Moreover, there was a lack of a formalized reporting, vetting and storage process for SARs. The SNCTC lacked a formal Request for Information (RFI) tracking system. Lastly, there was disconnect in the information flow between the analytical staff and the investigative staff.

Access to the SNCTC via Internet
To enhance communication for information sharing between the SNCTC and its public/private partners, they have created a comprehensive and extremely user-friendly website by utilizing federal funds. The SNCTC's website - www.SNCTC.org - is multi-tiered. Tier access is as follows:

- Tier 1: Public Access
- Tier 2: Private Access
- Tier 3: Public Safety Access

The first tier, designed for the public to access, is the information displayed without having to login to the website. This is where the public can learn more about what the SNCTC is and its mission. Anyone who visits the website also has the ability to submit a SAR form to report anything they may have witnessed. The second tier, designed for the private sector to access, requires login information to move beyond the public realm. Access and login credentials are granted by the SNCTC upon review when requested by persons who are not already affiliated with the SNCTC.

Second tier information that can be viewed after signing into the website is typically information that is pertinent to the private sector/hospitality industry. While specific information cannot be disclosed here, this information is typically "need-to-know" or "be on the lookout" to increase the level of preparedness/prevention among private sector organizations. Tier three is the most restricted access tier and is accessible only by public safety and law enforcement personnel. Once again login access must be granted by the SNCTC after a more comprehensive vetting process. This information typically includes access to SAR reports, intelligence products/reports, and additional sensitive information posted by the SNCTC for other law enforcement. This portion of the website is also referred to as the *SNCTC Trusted Information Exchange (STIX)*.

Homeland Security Hotline - SNCTC Watch Station
The SNCTC manages a toll-free Homeland Security Hotline that is staffed twenty-four hours a day, seven days a week by watch station personnel. The purpose of the hotline is to facilitate the collection of suspicious activity reporting (SAR). It is the policy of the SNCTC that every suspicious activity report is investigated by the collection branch or the operations group. The Federal Bureau of Investigation (FBI) retains the statutory authority to investigate terrorism cases, and all SARs are immediately transmitted to the FBI personnel assigned to the SNCTC.

The watch station is staffed by personnel from the analysis section, regardless of job classification and/or employing agency. The primary responsibility of the watch station is to maintain constant situational awareness of the southern Nevada metropolitan area as well as the State of Nevada. This situational awareness is made possible by integrating the computer-aided dispatch displays of each of the participating agencies. It is the responsibility of the watch station personnel to report to the appropriate jurisdiction any emergent public safety or public health issues as soon as they become evident.

The watch station position is one of the most critical operational positions within the SNCTC. It is responsible for recognizing significant public safety events locally, nationally, and globally. It is one of the centerpieces to help achieve the SNCTC's mission to prevent, reduce, and disrupt crime and terrorism through the early warning of all-crimes, all-hazards, and all-threats. The watch station also assists in the support of critical incidents, emergency responses, and investigations. The watch station is where real time analysis begins, and it is therefore critical that personnel assigned are actively engaged monitoring events. The person manning the position has the responsibility and authority to direct the completion of time-sensitive requests to and from other members of the analysis section, all SNCTC partners, and to coordinate the dissemination of such information to decision makers.

PRIVACY AND CIVIL LIBERTIES PROTECTION

The SNCTC has developed a privacy policy that utilizes 28 CFR Part 23 as a foundation, and with the guidance provided by the U.S. Department of Justice Privacy Policy Development Guide, Law Enforcement Intelligence Unit Intelligence File Guidelines, and the Global Justice Information Sharing Initiative. The SNCTC is transparent with their privacy policies, and welcomes review and input from local civil liberties communities. The SNCTC expects participating agencies to share their informational databases with other participating agencies to the extent allowable and authorized by the individual agencies guidelines, Nevada law, and Federal law. Personnel from participating agencies utilize their own forms, recordkeeping, and reporting methods. Reports prepared by the SNCTC are shared with all SNCTC analysts and sworn personnel, with the proper security clearance and the need to know. Moreover, the SNCTC's privacy policy draws upon the eight privacy design principles developed by the *Organization of Economic Cooperation and Development's Fair Information Practices*[59]. These principles are:

- Purpose Specification - Define agency purposes for information to help ensure agency uses of information are appropriate.
- Collection Limitation - Limit the collection of personal information to that required for the purposes intended.
- Data Quality - Ensure data accuracy.
- Use Limitation - Ensure appropriate limits on agency use of personal information.
- Security Safeguards - Maintain effective security over personal information.
- Openness - Promote a general policy of openness about agency practices and policies regarding personal information.

---

[59] For more information visit: http://www.oecd.org

- Individual Participation - Allow individual's reasonable access and opportunity to correct errors in their personal information held by the agency.
- Accountability - Identify, train, and hold agency personnel accountable for adhering to agency information quality and privacy policies.

The SNCTC has established mechanisms (interagency connectivity, public records subscription services, etc.) to create access to existing data sources from participating and member agencies to share data with the goal of identifying, developing, and analyzing information and intelligence related to terrorist activity and other crimes for investigative leads. This capability facilitates the integration and exchange of information between the participating and member agencies.

Collection Limitations

Given the mission of the SNCTC is to develop information and intelligence products by cooperating with other agencies and organizations. The decision of these agencies to participate with the SNCTC, and the information they provide, is voluntary and is governed by the laws and rules governing the individual agencies as well as by applicable federal laws. Because the laws, rules, or policies governing information and intelligence that can be collected and released on private individuals will vary from agency to agency, limitations on the collection of identifying information is the responsibility of the collecting agency and the original source information. Each agency that contributes information is to abide by the collection limitations applicable to it by law, rule, or policy. Information contributed to the SNCTC must be done in conformance with those limitations. The SNCTC does not store information that has been collected in violation of these laws, rules or regulations.

Data Quality

The agencies participating or coordinating with the SNCTC are responsible for collecting the information, remain the owners of the information contributed, and are responsible for its quality and accuracy. Since inaccurate and/or identifying information can have a damaging impact on the individual concerned and on the integrity and functionality of the SNCTC, any information obtained through the SNCTC must be independently verified with the original source from which the information was extrapolated before any official action (e.g., warrants or arrests) is taken.

Limitation of Information Use
Information obtained from or through the SNCTC is only used for legitimate law enforcement investigative purposes. A legitimate law enforcement investigative purpose means the request for information can be directly linked to a law enforcement agency's criminal investigation or is a response to a confirmed lead that requires follow-up to prevent a criminal or terrorist threat. The board of governors takes the necessary measures to make certain that access to the SNCTC's information and intelligence resources is secure and have the authority to prevent any unauthorized access or use. The board reserves the right to restrict the qualifications and number of personnel who can access the SNCTC and suspend or withhold service to any individual violating the SNCTC's privacy policy. The board also reserves the right to conduct inspections concerning the proper use and security of the information received from the SNCTC to further ensure the integrity of their information sharing practices.

All personnel who receive, handle, or have access to information from the SNCTC receive training on information/intelligence requirements. Every authorized personnel with access to the SNCTC understand that this access can be denied or rescinded for failure to comply with the applicable restrictions and use limitations. All such personnel must agree to the following rules:

- Data will be used only to perform official law enforcement investigative-related duties in a manner authorized by the SNCTC.
- Individual passwords will not be disclosed to any other person except as authorized by SNCTC management.
- Individual passwords will be changed if authorized personnel of the SNCTC or members of the Center suspect the password has been improperly disclosed or otherwise compromised.

- Background checks will be completed on personnel who will have direct access to the Center by the participating agency for which the individual is employed.
- Use of data in an unauthorized or illegal manner will subject the user to penalties established by the board of governors, discipline by the user's employing agency, and/or criminal prosecution.

Transparency

The SNCTC is intent on promoting transparent information sharing practices. As such, the SNCTC, and its participating agencies, are open with the public concerning data collection practices when such openness does not jeopardize ongoing criminal investigations. The SNCTC and participating agencies refer citizens to the original collector of the data as the appropriate entity to address any concern about data accuracy and quality; once again, this occurs only when this can be done without compromising an active inquiry or investigation.

Accountability

When a request for information is made to any of the SNCTC information applications, the original request is automatically logged by the system identifying the user initiating the request. When information is disseminated outside of the agency from which the original request is made, a secondary dissemination log is maintained in order to track information for audit purposes and provide notification in the event errors are identified or corrections are necessary. Secondary dissemination of information is only allowed by a law enforcement agency for a law enforcement investigative purpose or to other agencies as provided by law and in accordance with SNCTC policies. The originating agency from which the information is requested maintains a record of any secondary dissemination of information. This record reflects (at a minimum):

- Date of release.
- Name of releasing individual.
- Name, verification of inquirer (need-to-know and right-to-know will also be documented).
- Information released.

Recipients of SNCTC information are advised on, and agree to protect, its confidentiality and restrict its access based on right and need to know. SNCTC information cannot be disseminated outside the recipient's organization without the written permission of a SNCTC executive. Given the nature of law enforcement intelligence, the need for such protective use is necessary as any unauthorized disclosure of SNCTC information could damage or compromise ongoing or future investigations and operations. Furthermore, SNCTC information that is disseminated remains the property of the SNCTC and recipients must agree to comply with requests to immediately seal or destroy information obtained upon notification by a SNCTC executive. The SNCTC may request a recipient to sign a non-disclosure agreement prior to the release of any information. Refusal to sign such an agreement can limit or prohibit disclosure of requested information to that particular recipient. The SNCTC director, deputy director of quality assurance, and/or privacy protection officer is responsible for conducting or coordinating audits and investigating misuse of the SNCTC's information under the oversight of the board of governors.

INTELLIGENCE-LED POLICING: REQUIREMENTS-DRIVEN
In order for the SNCTC and their respective partners to have an effective intelligence-led policing (ILP) philosophy, a formal requirements process is necessary to guide information collection; this particular process is controlled by the requirements committee. Intelligence requirements are designed to fill intelligence gaps, typically with respect to case-specific information (case requirements) or on-going threats (standing requirements). It has become increasingly evident that many agencies working with the SNCTC are uncertain as to what requirements actually are and how they can benefit their investigative efforts. In order to address this uncertainty, the SNCTC has urged other agencies to formulate their intelligence requirements as questions. This is a straightforward approach to identifying what information is necessary to analyze and thus input into the intelligence-led policing cycle. An example of an intelligence requirement question may be "Is there radicalization in Nevada prisons?" Agencies working with the SNCTC are urged to compose their requirement questions and forward them to the SNCTC with the intent of identifying emerging threats and issues.

STRENGTHS AND WEAKNESSES

While an estimate on quantity or sources was not provided, one of the SNCTC's greatest strengths is its ability to gather raw information from the community in the form of suspicious activity reports. This improvement of increasing intelligence and information "receptors" is the result of the growth of awareness within the community and other public safety agencies above and beyond the SAR initiatives. For example, it is important for the SNCTC – and for fusion centers in general - to market their resources and products to all law enforcement and the public. Given that fusion centers are a fairly new concept in the law enforcement arena, a great deal of misunderstanding and/or misconception exists as to the utility of fusion centers. Most local agencies are unaware of the resources and products provided by fusion centers and the applicability these products have for their everyday public safety missions - not just terrorism.

An additional strength of the SNCTC is that it contains multiple capabilities under a single roof. As it has been discussed, a variety of agencies and organizations are represented within the SNCTC, ranging from law enforcement and the public/private sectors. Arguably the three most unique capabilities are the All Regional Multi-Agency Operations and Response (ARMOR) that focus on CBRN threats, the private-sector specific analyst funded by the LVCVA, and a representative from the Clark County Public Schools. The ARMOR unit consists of a multitude of advance technological and strategic equipment for not only responding to CBRN threats, but also equipment that aids everyday law enforcement in a variety of situations and special events. The school representative is funded by the Clark County school dispatch to increase the level of school preparedness as well as aiding law enforcement's awareness of issues and threats arising from and taking place in Clark County schools. Another strength indicated by the SNCTC is their ability to leverage funding from federal sources and through the commitments of the LVMPD and other agencies/organizations.

Lessons learned have also resulting in making some SNCTC weaknesses into strengths. The previously discussed watch station was created to serve as a primary point of contact for those reaching out to the SNCTC. Rather than speaking to "anyone who picks up the phone" this watch station personnel has a working knowledge of the different on-going initiatives and current issues within the SNCTC and can direct the inquiry to the correct person in a timely manner. Moreover, the watch station personnel maintain the most heightened sense of awareness as to emerging threats in the southern Nevada region. Additionally, an experienced senior analyst was hired by the SNCTC to supervise all analysts, and their function is to improve the efficiency and the effectiveness of the intelligence products associated with SNCTC.

CONTEXT FOR ILP ADOPTION FINDINGS

As compared to the Florida Fusion Center, the Southern Nevada Counter-Terrorism Center is quite different in character, but has similar baseline commonalities. With respect to the current study, the SNCTC is perhaps a further disconnect from how most local agencies would engage in law enforcement intelligence practices; however, relevant constructs are once again observed within this environment.

To begin with, the philosophical approach of intelligence-led policing adopted by the SNCTC is consistent with the Carter and Carter (2009a) model. More specifically, the SNCTC subscribes to an "all threats, all crimes, all hazards" perspective. Moreover, this approach emphasizes the importance of collection requirements that incorporate suspicious activity reports (SARs). Such an approach requires the development of partnerships with the community and private sector in order to educate them on SARs as well as establish channels for two-way communication of this information. Similar to the FFC, this perspective is exemplified through formal partnerships with non-public safety participating agencies such as the Southern Nevada Health District, Clark County School District, and Las Vegas Convention and Visitors Authority.

The importance of SARs was further demonstrated after the functional field exercise "Operation Silver Rogue" when one of the concluding recommendations was to further educate the community and private sector on SARs. Furthermore, sharing information across jurisdictional boundaries was deemed imperative. An "all-threats/hazards" philosophy, combined with SARs, community policing, and trans-jurisdictional communication are characteristics entirely consistent with the C&C model of intelligence-led policing.

In terms of the predictor variables of ILP adoption - namely, risk mediation, threat awareness, formalization, functional differentiation, task scope, commitment, and performance evaluation - all appeared to be relevant observations. Diffusion of intelligence-led policing was not easily observable in the SNCTC case study. Despite this, the importance of risk mediation and threat awareness were communicated by SNCTC executives to be critical to intelligence-led policing. More specifically, the SNCTC has detailed policies and procedures guiding the legal sharing of information as to mitigate the possibility of being held civilly liable. Furthermore, the SNCTC conducts threat assessments for Clark County as well as specific agencies and organizations within Clark County and throughout Nevada. The SNCTC executives communicated the importance of agencies and organizations being cognizant of the threats in order to develop appropriate information collection requirements to aid in the prevention of a threat as well as develop a plan for emergency response in case a threat reaches fruition.

Structurally, the SNCTC is reliant upon a high degree of formalization. A variety of formal personnel positions, committees, advisory boards, and policies/procedures guide the center. As previously noted, this is anticipated to be the nature of many comprehensive intelligence capacities across the country, whether they are fusion centers, state agencies, or large local agencies. Simply put, the more bureaucratic an agency is, the more likely they are to be formal. Interestingly, it was noted by a SNCTC executive that formalization might play a role as an inhibitor of successful intelligence-led policing. An identified weakness , the SNCTC faces are the institutional inhibitors of getting policies put in place in a timely and effective manner. As with all large law enforcement bureaucracies, a certain amount of red tape can be expected. However, the landscape of intelligence and information sharing relies upon expedient decision making and the operational hierarchy of large agencies, at times, can inhibit the sharing of information in a manner consistent with the "need to know". This view is shared by organization theorists who argue that formalization more often than not stifles innovation (Mastrofski, 1998).

Formalization is perhaps explained to an extent by functional differentiation. The SNCTC relies upon a variety of specialized units to vary out specific tasks. These units include the Collections Section (comprised of the Collection Management Group and Operations Group), Analysis Section, Intelligence Requirements Committee, and the Quality Assurance Section. Furthermore, the development of the multi-tier web portal that allows for two-way communications further enhances this capability. Interviews with the SNCTC personnel indicated these units greatly enhanced the ability of the SNCTC to carry out their intelligence-led mission as a result of having specialized persons responsible for specialized tasks, thus increasing effectiveness and efficiency. Just as it was anticipated and found to be statistically significant, functional differentiation has a positive effect on the adoption of intelligence-led policing.

In terms of the organizational context of the SNCTC, task scope and commitment appear to be relevant observations. Perhaps a function of the multiple specific units, the SNCTC requires analysts to maintain responsibility for a variety of analytic products as well as services. Products include those that have been discussed previously, such as risk assessments, trend patterns, and executive reports; however, the services aspect is somewhat unique and is primarily concentrated on what the SNCTC calls the "watch station". A lesson learned from "poor practice" was rather than having an operator be responsible for incoming calls directly to the SNCTC, these calls are now answered by analysts or intelligence-specific persons with knowledge of the operations and different units. The phone calls received by the watch station are typically SARs, requests for information, or a tip from another law enforcement agency. When an operator was answering these calls they were not knowledgeable about the actual operations of the SNCTC and this created a barrier in the communication channels, as well as increasing issues due to quality of interpretation on behalf of the operator. With analysts or intelligence-specific personnel answering the calls, the information coming in was immediately entered into system and could also be acted on immediately if a tactical response was required. Commitment is rather straightforward and was demonstrated by the lead law enforcement executive, Clark County Sheriff Doug Gillespie.

The importance of commitment to note in this observation is in reference to two aspects: 1) the commitment towards intelligence practices as the forefront of law enforcement; and, 2) the devotion of resources from Las Vegas Metro Police Department to be the primary fiscal agency of the SNCTC dedicating finances, personnel, and equipment. Lastly, the importance of quality intelligence products is demonstrated by the Data Assurance Section and importance of data quality. This section of the SNCTC (which is made up of three groups) is tasked with the responsibility of securing the physical security of the

SNCTC as well as making sure the SNCTC is compliant with legal information collection, dissemination and retention. Of more relevance is the performance measurement group that is tasked to develop and collect the data to measure the ability of the SNCTC to perform its established mission and determine if the SNCTC outcomes align with the intelligence requirements set forth by the requirements committee. These performance measures are at the organizational-level and not the analyst level as operationalized in the current study. However, it can be logically assumed that as analysts are responsible for the creation of intelligence-products on which the SNCTC bases its decisions for strategic and operational planning that the SNCTC recognizes the importance of quality analyst performance evaluation, even though this was not directly observed or documented.

Once again, the SNCTC has provided a useful example of an intelligence-environment that is different from most local agencies. Despite this difference, relevant theoretical constructs remain consistent as the underlying philosophy of law enforcement intelligence practices should remain consistent regardless of size of responsibility. Just as it is expected that different local agencies will have locally-tailored intelligence-led policing philosophies, fusion centers will as well. These differences will play a critical role in future research as the most influential factors leading to successful adoption and practice are identified across different environments.

CHAPTER 8

Recommendations for ILP Adoption

The current study has explored intelligence-led policing as an innovative philosophy in law enforcement agencies across the United States; its findings provide insights for scholars and practitioners alike. No one theoretical model exists to provide guidance for such a study. An overriding framework for the study is the concept of *program fidelity*, a construct which requires proof of successful replication while allowing necessary variance across different organizations for an appropriate organizational/environmental fit. While observing this aspect of adoption, salient factors attribute to a greater likelihood of successful adoption and can be identified and applied across organizations. The intent of this study has been to explore both the organizational and policing literatures to develop a theoretical framework that could identify such pivotal factors as they relate to the adoption of intelligence-led policing. Moreover, the current study employed case studies to provide strategic context for the findings. This final chapter applies the most significant of the exploratory findings to: 1) the employed theoretical framework; 2) the process of adopting intelligence-led policing; and, 3) future research needed for improvement in the ILP dissemination process. Limitations of the current study will follow to give it appropriate boundaries of certainty and uncertainty of conclusions drawn.

SIGNIFICANT FINDINGS

The current study developed one full organizational model to predict intelligence-led policing adoption. However, this one model was used to predict two types of adoption - one as an operationalized index measure and the other a self-reported measure. A preponderance of this current discussion will focus on the index measure of adoption inasmuch as it is a more theoretical and substantive representation of intelligence-led policing adoption. Unless otherwise specified, findings discussed here are in reference to the index measurement of adoption. At the outset it is important to note that each predictor variable, except for civilianization and agency size, had a positive influence on the adoption of intelligence-led policing. The theoretical framework employed for the current study shows promise. While each of these variables was not statistically significant, their "significance" is still worth mentioning as the intent of this exploratory research is to identify factors that facilitate adoption of intelligence-led policing; it appears from the evidence presented here that these factors do just that. More refined measures in future studies may be able to paint a more accurate picture of these relationships; however, these exploratory study findings establish a reasonable starting point for such research.

Three of the four diffusion types were statistically significant, with threat awareness and risk mediation having the greatest effects on adoption followed by peer emulation demonstrating a more moderate effect. Threat awareness and risk mediation are representative of more formal processes of identifying the need, and means, to adopt intelligence-led policing. These findings suggest that law enforcement agencies may be making a good faith effort at adopting intelligence-led policing given that the process of conducting a threat assessment and reviewing legal policies requires the dedication of substantial organizational resources. Moreover, conducting assessments of threats and legal liability are indicative of forward thinking on the part of law enforcement executives. These progressive thought processes provide an environment to cultivate successful innovations.

Not surprisingly, peer emulation was the strongest statistical finding. Perhaps the most default human nature response to learning about something is to ask someone you believe to know the answer or be struggling with the same problem. This thought holds true for police agencies seeking to work their way through problems of adopting new practices. Beyond being a successful method of problem solving, in the context of intelligence-led policing - and thus information sharing - agencies that reach out to other agencies in search of information, and who receive the information they are looking for, represent the epitome of successful law enforcement intelligence practices.

From a structural perspective, formalization and functional differentiation were strong facilitators of intelligence-led policing adoption. Aside from being statistically strong indicators, these constructs were observed at both the Florida Fusion Center and the Southern Nevada Counter-Terrorism Center where both organizations were guided by a litany of formal policies and comprised of multiple task-specific units. It bears repeating, law enforcement intelligence has many conceptual similarities to community policing and problem-oriented policing; however, the analytic component and legal ramifications that are associated with intelligence-led policing require formal policies and procedures to avoid predictable pitfalls. These formalities also allow for a strategic division of labor for specialized persons to perform specialized tasks, thus improving effectiveness and efficiency (the positive attributes of the scientific management approach). This is not to say analysts are equivalent to persons working on an assembly line, but that they are responsible for specific tasks that require professional training and knowledge.

These specialized persons are typically found within an agency's intelligence unit. Consistent with logic is the notion that an agency which has an intelligence unit will be more likely to adopt intelligence-led policing successfully. This finding is not as relevant from the perspective of actually having a specific intelligence unit, but that law enforcement managers should acknowledge the importance of positioning persons responsible for intelligence practices within a structured intelligence unit rather than having them operate independently of one another. This may sound simple, but in practice many agencies are assigning personnel to be "one of the intelligence people" while going about thier business as usual. Rather than having two persons "wearing the intelligence hat" for an agency and being physically located on different floors from one another, it would be beneficial to physically position these persons next to one another in an effort to facilitate communication - simply for purposes of "being on the same page" and sharing knowledge acquired in their respective jobs. This same approach was found to have a significant impact in the New Jersey State Police by Ratcliffe and Guidetti (2008).

In terms of organizational context, task scope and commitment were statistically significant factors. Despite not being statistically significant, both a training requirement and Western region had predicted directional effects. Leadership commitment to the intelligence-led policing philosophy was the strongest context indicator of adoption. This construct was observed to be at play in the case studies as well. The Florida Fusion Center conducted an assessment of information sharing gaps between law enforcement agencies within the state of Florida. One of the findings from this gap analysis was that local law enforcement was not engaging in information sharing as a result of poor, or nonexistent, commitment to the intelligence-led approach. At the Southern Nevada Counter-Terrorism Center, a strong administrative commitment to an intelligence-led approach was established when Sheriff Doug Gillespie announced (multiple times) that the Las Vegas Metro Police Department (the primary agency of the SNCTC) was going to fully embrace this new philosophy. Both the LVMPD and SNCTC are successfully engaged in intelligence-led policing.

Task scope was statistically the strongest facilitator of intelligence-led policing adoption. Intelligence-led policing does not rely upon the production of one or two standard intelligence products, but rather entails a variety of products ranging from simple to complex. A detailed threat assessment is a more comprehensive product than an executive report/briefing; however, both products are important to the intelligence-led policing philosophy. Agency composition and responsibility also affects the types of tasks intelligence personnel are responsible for completing. State and large municipal agencies will require more complex tasks than smaller departments. The influence of training on intelligence-led policing adoption was positive, but difficult to examine in this study for a variety of issues which will be discussed in the limitations section of this final chapter. Police agencies in the Western region of the U.S. indicated positive adoption[60]; however, this finding yields little applicable value to police practitioners. The value added element is for future research, specifically with respect to why innovations diffuse more successfully in the states of the West. Lastly, agency size was not a significant predictor of agencies adopting intelligence-led policing. This finding is positive for law enforcement as the intent of intelligence-led policing is that it should be developed by all agencies regardless of size (GIWG, 2003).

Performance evaluation was an interesting construct to explore in the arena of law enforcement intelligence. Consistent with the notion of intelligence-led policing as the "business model" of policing is an

---

[60] Full organizational regression models were run substituting each of the five regions. The results indicated the following effects of agencies in the: Northeast was negative three percent, Southeast was positive six percent, Midwest was negative four percent, and Southwest had no effects.

emphasis on quality products. The ability of an agency to utilize intelligence products requires them to (for the most part) be actionable. In order to be actionable, analysts must have well developed critical thinking skills along with technical knowledge of certain information sources and software. As illustrated by the analyst training requirements of the Florida Fusion Center, quality evaluation methods are critical to ensuring the most valid products are available to be integrated into the intelligence-led policing process. The old adage describing organizational processes as "crap in, crap out" is perhaps the most simplistic way of describing the effects of poor quality control of analyst products. Once again, intelligence-led policing is reliant upon the integration of analyzed information into the decision making process. If analysts are producing poor products of no significance, the intelligence-led policing function is hindered from the beginning.

The findings reported in this study supported this assertion quite soundly. As agencies move along the continuum of evaluation methods from having no evaluation method to employing an assessment of quality, the success of intelligence-led policing adoption increases with each step along the continuum. The two statistically significant findings were at each end of this continuum – namely, agencies that indicated having no evaluation method decreased intelligence-led policing adoption by 22% while agencies that indicated using a quality assessment of analyst products increased intelligence-led policing adoption by seven percent.

The second full organizational model explored self-reported adoption of intelligence-led policing. Statistically significant variables in the positive direction included familiarity with the intelligence-led policing concept, training, and commitment. Peer emulation was significant with a slightly negative effect - perhaps due to perceived difficulties communicated by agencies which had struggled with adoption. Beyond the differences of a comprehensive measure versus a self-reported single item, theory anticipates differences between agencies that adopt innovations and agencies that in actually "adopt" innovations. Table 12 displays the difference between the intelligence-led policing adoption index measure and the self-reported adoption of intelligence-led policing.

Table 12: Differences between Adoption Index and Self-Reported Adoption

	Index	Self-Report
Diffusion Types		
Threat Awareness		
Risk Mediation	+	
Peer Emulation	+	-
ILP Familiarity		+
Organizational Structure		
Formalization	+	
Civilianization		
Functional Differentiation	+	+
Organizational Context		
Task Scope	+	
Training		+
Commitment	+	+
Agency Size		
West Region		

Note: Directional relationships are indicated in the columns.

Institutional theorists are inclined to argue that agencies are attempting to gain legitimacy from the community and peer organizations by labeling themselves as an intelligence-led policing agency while organizational learning theorists posit that these agencies are mistaking the process of talking about innovating with the actual actions needed to innovate. A crude example would be agencies that incorporate an intelligence-led component in their mission statement and have meetings discussing the intelligence-led approach, but do not actually engage in the analysis of information or other actions consistent with practicing intelligence-led policing. Familiarity with the intelligence-led policing concept, requiring training on intelligence-led policing[61], and committing to an intelligence-led policing

---

[61] Requiring training on intelligence-led policing could go in either direction with respect to active or passive adoption. Agencies sincerely attempting to adopt intelligence-led policing would develop this training requirement, and most likely require newly acquired skills and knowledge to be applied to intelligence-related outcomes. Conversely, agencies that are aligning

philosophy are factors that can be associated with "window dressing" and public relations work. The negative relationship between peer emulation and self-reported intelligence-led policing adoption is interesting. Agencies may be in the process of gathering information on the intelligence-led policing concept from peer agencies and during this process they learn how difficult the adoption may be and as a consequence they do not pursue it (cf. Armenakis & Bedeian, 1995; Barnett & Carroll, 1995). This thought is also supported by the high correlation between familiarity with the intelligence-led policing concept and peer emulation.

It is difficult to disentangle the difference between an agency that self-reports being intelligence-led in an effort to seek legitimacy and mimic peer organizations from an agency in the beginning stages of sincere adoption efforts. Further clouding these waters is the fact that many agencies simply don't know what intelligence-led policing is, what they should be doing in terms of advancing toward intelligence-led policing, and they may feel they are sincerely engaged in the philosophy without outward signs of that good faith effort. To take this a step further at the risk of completely confusing this study findings, program fidelity is also at play in this model. The multitude of small municipal agencies in the U.S. will not necessarily engage in many of the facets of intelligence-led policing; they do need to be cognizant of the intelligence-led policing concept however, and should have an operational plan to collect information and pass it along to the appropriate parties. Such a capacity could be mistaken for inadequate, not yet adopted, or even "window dressing" in lieu of innovation adoption, but this capacity in a small agency is indeed appropriate for the agency's needs and the role they can play in the larger intelligence picture. Such a dilemma presents challenges, and opportunities, for future research as it is beyond the scope of the current study. Disproving the notion of agencies simply seeking legitimacy versus beginning their adoption efforts would require a panel methodology where progress, or lack thereof, towards a more actionable intelligence-led philosophy could be observed.

---

themselves as "intelligence-led" in an attempt to be perceived as intelligence-led will likely lack the translation of training to implementation and action.

Lastly, from a conceptual perspective the philosophy of intelligence-led policing as subscribed to in the current study appears to be applied faithfully in practice. The Carter and Carter (2009a) model of intelligence-led policing has basic tenets observed during the case study site visits at both the Florida Fusion Center and the Southern Nevada Counter-Terrorism Center. These tenets include an "all threats, all hazards" approach to prevention, a broad threat/crime/hazard environment, inter-jurisdictional focus, utilization of a variety of information sources, partnerships with the community and private sector, and community policing as a foundation for intelligence-led policing. Both the FFC and SNCTC designate their approach to prevention as "all threats, all hazards," featuring a focus on street crime, complex criminality, terrorism, and natural disasters (such as the FFC example of sex offender evacuation plans during hurricanes).

An inter-jurisdictional focus is somewhat a given due to the mission of fusion centers as being designed to synthesize information from multiple sources/organizations. However, as it was noted specifically in the gap analysis conducted by the FFC in the state of Florida, the lack of communication across boundaries was identified as a common shortcoming of local law enforcement. Both the FFC and SNCTC expressed the critical importance of suspicious activity reporting (SARs), a process which is made possible through a commitment to establishing and maintaining community and private sector partnerships. Furthermore, both case studies acknowledged the movement to build upon community policing with additional intelligence-led components such as systematic analysis and open source information gathering.

IMPLICATION FOR PRACTICE

Criminal justice scholars engage in applied research to assist practitioners in accomplishing their profession goals more effectively and efficiently. There would be a significant disconnect between academia and professionals if the research could not be translated into applications for improvement in practice. With this thought in mind, this section will discuss how law enforcement can benefit from the findings derived from this exploratory study.

To begin with, there are significant differences between an agency's self-reported perception of having adopted intelligence-led policing and a multi-item index measure of intelligence-led policing adoption[62]. A multitude of theoretical explanations are plausible for these differences, but the principal implication for practice is the need for further education on ILP on the part of both academics and practitioners. Academics learn about intelligence-led policing primarily as it emerges from those persons in the field and attempt to refine the concepts and put them into perspectives for the most effective outcomes. Practitioners in the field learn about intelligence-led policing primarily from their peers who then communicate it to academics in the hopes of receiving a more comprehensible plan or strategy in return. Simply put, both academics and practitioners are continuing to educate themselves on intelligence-led policing as best they can through established networks, but there is a lack of common ground with respect to understanding its true application. Whether the differences between agencies' self-reported adoption and index measurement of adoption is attributed to achieving legitimacy or gaining funding, or a reflection of the beginning stages of adoption, a purer assessment requires further education and training. It is believed that a few (not all) of the common misunderstandings of intelligence-led policing are (from a local law enforcement perspective):

1) What is intelligence-led policing?
2) How does intelligence-led policing fit into my agency?
3) Can we do intelligence-led policing without an intelligence analyst?
4) Does intelligence-led policing replace community policing?
5) What are intelligence products?
6) How will intelligence-led policing benefit my agency?

Further research similar to the current study would not only provide a baseline of fundamental knowledge of intelligence practices, but it would also establish a foundation for future research by which

---

[62] Bivariate correlation between the intelligence-led policing adoption index and an agency's self-reported adopting of intelligence-led policing was .377 and was significant at .01 (two-tailed). Such a correlation indicates a lack of inter-relationship and perhaps lends insight that agencies may be doing less actual adoption of intelligence-led policing despite their self-reported intentions.

academics and practitioners alike can continue to tease out methods for success for adoption of ILP practices. With this in mind, the organizational factors identified in this study are a place for persons in both fields to begin advancing knowledge of the intelligence-led policing.

Identifying threats proved to be a strong facilitator of intelligence-led policing adoption. Beyond an agency becoming cognizant of potential threats, identifying criminal/terrorist threats in the region helps to facilitate other aspects of intelligence-led policing. For example, if an agency is able to identify specific threats as a result of their assessment, they can then develop intelligence requirements for these threats. As identified in the case studies and conceptual framework, an intelligence requirement - or an information collection plan - is the driving force behind intelligence-led policing. Collection requirements allow for agencies to identify specific domains for gathering information from multiple environments to feed into the intelligence cycle.

For example, if a department identifies an emerging threat of outlaw motorcycle gangs in their region they are able to develop more specific means of gathering information to guide decisions on how to prevent threats arising from the group. More specifically, an agency is able to reach out to the motorcycle community and begin to not only extract information that may benefit the analysis process, but establish a communication channel to aid in prevention. An intelligence requirement for an outlaw motorcycle gang may involve an agency going to local motorcycle businesses, bars, or communities to begin to collect raw information that can be input into the analysis process to identify potential members, criminality engaged in by the group, and determine the severity of the threat posed by the group. Collection requirements narrow the focus of desired information to avoid information overload. Furthermore, this information allows law enforcement to develop strategic, operational, and tactical intelligence products that enable law enforcement to "maintain the pulse" of identified threats while initiating steps to prevent threats from reaching fruition. In short, identifying threats is a starting point for law enforcement to pinpoint specific collection requirements, build community and private sector partnerships/relationships, and produce analytic products of high quality.

Many agencies will not have the staff resources such as an analyst to conduct a threat assessment. However, state fusion centers can provide a threat assessment of a local agency's region. As identified in both the FFC and SNCTC case studies, the majority of local law enforcement are unaware of what the fusion center is responsible for and the resources they can provide to local departments. This was documented in both fusion center case studies, where the individuals in key roles stated that if they could hire any type of "luxury personnel" that would benefit intelligence-led policing the most it would be a person to go around the state and market the fusion center's capabilities to local agencies. Local agencies need to take advantage of the resources fusion centers provide in order to identify threats and create the stepping-stones for facilitating an intelligence-led policing capability.

Risk mediation was also a strong facilitator of intelligence-led policing adoption. Safeguarding against civil liability implies a focus on protecting the agency financially as well as emphasizing the importance of the human rights aspect of intelligence-led policing – that is, the notion that law enforcement will not violate an individual's civil rights in carrying out its duties. It is important to note that all law enforcement agencies, regardless of size or responsibility, should have comprehensive legal safeguards. Regardless of how advanced an agency's intelligence-led policing capability is, the baseline activity is collecting, retaining, and sharing information; there are activities which can be a liability under a section 1983 lawsuit. An underlying influence that may be attributed to risk mediation and facilitating intelligence-led policing adoption is the agency knowing they have taken the legal steps necessary to engage actively in the practice of intelligence-led policing. Simply put, an agency with appropriate legal safeguards is more likely to engage in the activity that is safeguarded by those policies than one that is lacking such safeguards.

Applying risk mediation in practice involves multiple checks and balances. An agency must make sure they are compliant with 28 Code of Federal Regulation Part 23 - the guiding regulation of law enforcement intelligence practices. The key element of this regulation is that in order for personal identifying information to be included in the criminal intelligence records system information on the individual must meet a criminal predicate threshold. Criminal predicate is a threshold of engaging in criminal behavior. There is ambiguity as to what exactly meets this threshold and the Supreme Court has yet to provide precedent for clarification. In practice, and from a legal perspective, criminal predicate is essentially reasonable suspicion. In order for law enforcement agencies to legally identify an individual in a criminal intelligence records system they must be able to go in front of a judge and establish a level of reasonable suspicion that designates an individual as engaged in criminal behavior. Other steps law enforcement should take in ensuring risk meditation are review and purge intelligence records systems on a scheduled basis, maintain consistency with court decisions relating to intelligence practices, and have a legal professional review legal policies and procedures.

The presence of formal policies guiding intelligence practices indicated increased intelligence-led policing adoption. This finding is logical; it is expected that policies guiding an innovation would allow for the innovation to be more successful. However, when put into practice, intelligence-specific policies are required. A mission statement indicating the agency is intelligence-led is not a formal policy. Practices requiring specific policies should include how the agency engages in intelligence-led policing. Rather than stating this vaguely, agencies must outline a step-by-step process from information collection and analysis to dissemination and integrated decision making. Policies under these larger auspices also include the handling of classified information, collecting and retaining suspicious activity reports (SARs), and engaging in memoranda of understanding (MOUs) with other agencies. These MOUs should be applied in more formal partnerships where the agency and, for example, private sector entity share personnel or other resources. The extent of formal policies is obviously contingent upon the comprehensiveness of the agency's intelligence function. Once again, going back to implementation fidelity it is clear that different agencies will have different needs and thus will create somewhat different intelligence-led policing functions.

Implementation fidelity issues create a challenge for the present study. To identify how different agencies across the U.S. would apply these findings would be a formidable task as there is simply too much variance across the matrix of local agency sizes and responsibilities. In an attempt to provide a general guide for how different levels of intelligence-led policing can be adopted or transitioned into, the following discussion will identify key aspects and steps from not having an intelligence-led policing capability (or minimal) that is likely encountered by most rural agencies to a comprehensive capability experienced by some of the largest municipal and state agencies.

The following broad generalizations of classifications for intelligence-led policing levels are developed under the context of accepted practices at the time of the present study. These levels are classified as *minimal, basic, advanced,* or *mature* intelligence-led policing. It is assumed that the majority of rural local agencies will have a minimal (or absent) capability. It can be reasoned that these agencies have not developed intelligence requirements, lack intelligence policy or procedures, and have no defined intelligence goals or objectives. In order to begin adopting intelligence-led policing, agencies relating to this minimal capacity must become familiar with the intelligence-led policing concept, attend training programs, develop goals and objectives for sharing information as well as putting into place legal policies guiding these objectives, and finally establish informal partnerships with the community and businesses. Many mid-size, and even some larger, agencies could be considered to have a basic intelligence-led policing capability. Building from the minimal intelligence capacity, it is assumed that these agencies will have had limited intelligence training in which they likely assigned a person from investigations to attend and be the "intelligence person".

Furthermore, these agencies will likely have a generic intelligence policy, but no system for managing information. To adopt a more comprehensive intelligence-led policing capability, these agencies must refine policies related to intelligence operational plans, provide some form of awareness training to all members of the agency, and establish formal community and private sector partnerships. It is this transition from a minimal capacity to a basic capacity where future evaluations will be able to tease out the slippery slope of institutional theory's view on legitimacy and mimicry versus agencies sincerely in the initial stages of adoption or having arrived at an appropriate level of adoption.

Agencies falling under the general advanced capacity are assumed to have in place the factors previously discussed. These agencies are likely to be large municipal and even many state agencies. Consistent with this level is the assumption that agencies also have intelligence-specific personnel such as analysts. As such, further training is required to enhance analysts' critical thinking, connectivity to information systems, and task variability. It is also assumed these agencies will have liaisons in place for the state fusion center, intelligence and terrorism liaison officers, and detailed privacy policies guiding each mechanism within the capacity. Lastly, few agencies are likely to be considered to have a mature intelligence-led policing capacity, especially as practices still struggle with ambiguity and government resources remain sparse. State and large municipal agencies are likely to be the only agencies to achieve the most comprehensive level of intelligence-led policing as they have the resources and mission responsibility for such a capability. Fusion centers will also be at this most comprehensive level. The Florida Fusion Center and Southern Nevada Counter-Terrorism Center serve as examples of agencies that are towards the most mature end of the adoption continuum.

For purposes of adoption or enhancement, it is assumed these agencies will have in place the aforementioned factors from the previous levels. Beyond these factors, mature intelligence-led policing agencies are assumed to have multiple intelligence analysts, multiple connections to information sharing systems, and a comprehensive records management system. Moreover, these agencies are likely engaged in a resource-based partnership with private sector organizations and fusion centers, thus requiring more formal policies and procedures. These examples have been somewhat crude, but demonstrate the chronology of not only adopting intelligence-led policing but of further enhancing this philosophy as the needs and responsibilities of agencies increase. It should be noted that small or rural agencies are not excluded from being able to have an advanced or mature intelligence-led policing capacity; such a status is simply unlikely due to resource constraints and a lack of necessity.

DIRECTIONS FOR FUTURE RESEARCH
Up until the present time, intelligence-led policing had only been conceptualized in the literature. Natural progression of research on a new phenomenon requires a period of conceptual clarification within the literature. It is once this conceptual clarification begins to present itself that systematic when empirical explorations can begin. Following exploration, more robust empirical evaluations can be achieved and a specific literature solidified. Intelligence-led policing is currently in the transition from conceptual to empirical exploration, with this study serving as one of the initial empirical examinations of intelligence-led policing in the context of state, local, and tribal law

enforcement. The study has provided a useful foundation on which future research can be based. Further exploration is certainly required as the breadth of understanding is far from being at a stage to allow for a comprehensive evaluation of the efficiency of ILP. Some directions for this future exploration are discussed here.

Future research on adopting intelligence-led policing would benefit from including a measure of the status of community policing practices as a predictor variable. As it is conceptualized in the present study, and by scholars identified in the review of relevant literature, community policing is a critical foundational component of an intelligence-led policing capability. Furthermore, the innovation diffusion research identifies an organization's propensity to be innovative in the past as a predictor of adopting innovations in the future. As aforementioned, many scholars have considered community policing to be significant innovation; this constitutes further reason for including commitment to community policing as a positive predictor of intelligence-led policing adoption. Consistent with the diffusion of innovation would be to determine if state fusion centers had reached out to local agencies to educate them on the role of fusion centers and the resources they have to offer. It is not expected that many agencies will have had this experience as the case studies identified a significant need for this form of marketing; however the effects of fusion centersreaching out to local agencies are likely to be quite positive.

Peer emulation yielded one of the largest effects on intelligence-led policing adoption. While it is logical to assume agencies will reach out to peer agencies in an attempt to learn about intelligence-led policing or discuss intelligence-related problems, it is unclear as to which types of agencies are commonly contacted (cf. Chermak & Weiss, 2000). Do rural agencies tend to reach out to other rural agencies with similar demographics to get an idea of how they are adopting intelligence-led policing? Or do rural agencies instead tend to reach out to large metropolitan agencies because they assume these agencies are more likely to have a successful model for adopting intelligence-led policing? Moreover, which of the agencies that are commonly reached out to provide information that results in successful adoption? If so, why? Being able to identify types of agencies that are most helpful within peer circles will provide valuable insights as to agencies that may be engaged in best practices.

With respect to differences across agency size and responsibility, Schafer *et al.* (2009) examined homeland security innovation in local agencies and contrasted rural agencies with small agencies that are located in close proximity to metropolitan areas; this is an approach that would be beneficial to intelligence-led policing research as well. There is a significant difference between the roles a small rural agency has in the larger intelligence landscape as compared to an agency of the same size located on a metropolitan peripheral. Accounting for these differences would enhance attempts to identify common models of intelligence-led policing and benchmarks for successful practice.

Revisiting the notion of program fidelity, it has already been established that different agencies require somewhat different intelligence capabilities. Being able to sketch a model that could be generalized to agencies fitting certain demographics would be greatly beneficial to both academia and professionals. While program fidelity creates obstacles for refined research, it is necessary for scholars to continue examining intelligence-led policing fidelity across different organizations as these studies help the discipline maintain the pulse of adoption progression or regression. The key to fidelity is continued observation, and as studies increase so does the knowledge base from which refined concepts and measures can be derived. Perhaps if enough variance is observed to begin establishing commonalities across similar agencies, models of successful intelligence-led policing adoption and benchmarks to measure successful adoption can be identified. For example, if an agency with certain characteristics (e.g., municipal or sheriff, personnel, population served, proximity to metropolitan area, etc.) has adopted an intelligence-led philosophy successfully for their specific needs, it is possible to translate this model to an agency with a similar characteristic makeup. The present study serves as a starting point for such research as well.

Lastly, building on the idea of creating evaluations of success for intelligence-led policing, future research should account for agencies which indicate receiving external funding for intelligence-related initiatives, such as the Targeting Violent Crime Imative (TVCI) funded by the Bureau of Justice Assistance. Beyond examining the theory that agencies label themselves as intelligence-led to receive external funds, such grants provide an environment to evaluate the impact of intelligence-led practices. Once again focusing on the TVCI, these funds stipulated local law enforcement must employ an intelligence-led policing approach to reducing violent crime. Preliminary results indicate violent crime has been reduced in many of the grantee cities. As criminal justice scholars are trained to do, these effects should be questioned and rigorously evaluated. The difficulty of such an undertaking at the current time is not only due owing to the lack of understanding and unified acceptance as to the definition and purpose of intelligence-led policing, but also due to the fact that the intelligence-led policing approach incorporates a variety of analytical strategies ranging from the preparation of analytic reports and doing crime mapping to initiating and maintaining community and private partnerships. As such, it becomes difficult to determine which levers are being pulled and to which levers the effects should be attributed. A great deal of further exploration and continued conceptualization is required before such a comprehensive study could be carried out.

RESEARCH LIMITATIONS
The current study has some noteworthy limitations that should be addressed explicitly. In general, as an exploratory study the current study has no quantitative basis for comparison and thus is limited to drawing conclusions based on logically related theories and professional experience. Compounding this obstacle, examining program adoption through a cross-sectional survey design relies on a number of assumptions to provide context and causal order. These assumptions could be remedied by utilizing a more longitudinal panel design. More specific to the limitations of the current study, refined variable measures in the future will help to alleviate the need to draw assumptions from the literature and professional experience. These refined measures would assist in distinguishing more defined differences between some of the predictor measures of intelligence-led policing and the dependent variable of intelligence-led policing adoption. For example, functional differentiation and task scope are similar to indicators of intelligence-led policing. As discussed, agencies that have an intelligence unit and are engaged in creating intelligence outputs could be interpreted as already having adopted intelligence-led policing.

A further example would be the risk mediation construct. As the diffusion literature explains, risk mediation is an organization's method of assessing their potential for civil liability based on their engagement in certain practices. Typically, the practices thought to increase the potential for civil liability are mediated by the organization adopting the innovation. With respect to intelligence-led policing, risk mediation could occur in this "traditional theoretical" sense wherein agencies are collecting and sharing information, but without legal policies guiding these practices. As a result, agencies recognize the need to adopt formal intelligence-led policing practices rather than simply informally passing along all forms of information from one agency to another. Conversely, it is plausible that in order for agencies to become familiar enough with intelligence-led policing practices and the legal intricacies involved, that they must already be engaged in formal practices and are enhancing an existing intelligence-led capability by mediating civil liability. Again, such conceptual entanglement could be parceled out in the future by employing not only more refined measures, but additional constructs as well which could target issues of causal order. Despite such possible conceptual entanglements, the correlations and multicollinearity diagnostics presented indicate this is not a significant issue in the study presented in this book.

Furthermore, as a result of the targeted survey population being participants from an intelligence training course, the true effects of training are somewhat difficult to discern. Training is an important predictor of successful adoption, and as such effects from training must be parceled out. Future studies could greatly benefit from including agencies with no such training disposition. Also due to the sampling method, caution should be taken for generalizing findings to the greater law enforcement population even though it is believed these findings translate well to the varied law enforcement agency population due to the fidelity issues discussed.

Related to the sampling method employed, it should be noted specifically that the current study is not a test of the two predominant models of intelligence-led policing – namely, the Carter and Carter (2009a) model and the Ratcliffe (2008a) model. The intent of the current study is to advance our academic knowledge of intelligence-led policing in general as a means to create a foundation upon which future research can be built. Moreover, the persons included in the sample have received educational training on intelligence-led policing as it is conceptualized by the Carter and Carter (2009a) model, and therefore are not an appropriate representation of the population upon which a test of the models could be carried out. Furthermore, the current study is not a test of any of the theoretical concepts discussed throughout;

instead it draws from the organizational and policing literatures to guide an exploration of intelligence-led policing adoption. In no manner does the current study seek to reaffirm prior research in these areas. Once again, the intent is to contribute to the base of knowledge of the policing literature in general, and intelligence-led policing specifically.

Given the nature and sudden emergence of contemporary law enforcement intelligence practices, it is reasonable to assume that a significant portion of the persons that did not respond to the survey were likely re-assigned and no longer responsible for the intelligence function in their agency or were newly appointed and had scant knowledge of such practices. Given such circumstances, the responses that comprise the present study are thought to be problematic on the one hand, but nonetheless represent good data from the available population of key informants. Missing data presented another challenge for the current study. Given the adjusted response rate's impact on statistical power, further decreasing the sample size would be detrimental to the current study. Furthermore, since the study seeks to explore predictive relationships of intelligence-led policing adoption, it serves the purpose to err on the side of caution by coding missing values as minimal values of predictor variables.

Lastly, the Florida Fusion Center and Southern Nevada Counter-Terrorism Center case studies provided environments where developed intelligence practices could be observed to provide valid contexts for the issues discussed in the current study. While these environments were greatly beneficial for the current study, examining an environment specifically at the local level where intelligence practices are still being developed would have also benefited the current study. By not including a more representative environment of intelligence practices, the current study lacks specific insight as to how certain relationships are evolving and would also give credence to some causal order assumptions required by the current study. For example, it would have been beneficial to examine local agencies to determine "how" and "why" they determined to adopt intelligence-led policing and learn which characteristics of the agency were in place prior to others throughout the process of adoption.

CONCLUSIONS

The current study has yielded significant organizational factors relating to the facilitation of intelligence-led policing among state, local, and tribal law enforcement agencies in the U.S. These factors establish an empirical foundation for future research as well as document the struggle many local police departments face as they attempt to adopt this innovative philosophy of police operations. Diffusion types are perhaps most important, as indicated by theory and reinforced by empirical findings. Regardless of the type of diffusion, it is imperative for law enforcement to identify the reason their agency should adopt intelligence-led policing and the means by which they will educate themselves on the concept. Knowing how to get somewhere is just as important as deciding where you are going.

Differences between an agency's self-reported adoption and measured adoption mark an important starting position for future research. Implementation fidelity should not be interpreted as an explanation for why agencies are adopting intelligence-led policing differently; instead, it is a forewarning of expected differences. How intelligence-led policing fits specifically into the different types of police agencies in the U.S. is a formidable (and unrealistic) task for the time being. However, identifying common characteristics for purposes of developing an intelligence-led policing "profile" is certainly not out of the question. While police agencies differ across geographic location, size, proximity to metropolitan areas, level of jurisdiction, and available resources, they are still all policing agencies with common missions and shared practices on which consistency can be established. For state and local law enforcement, intelligence-led policing is not a matter of "should we or shouldn't we?", but rather a matter of "when should we and how will we?" get to this way of doing police business. Continued conceptualization and exploration will provide the answers.

References

Adama, N., Kozanoglua, A., Paliwala, A. & Shafiq, B. (2007). Secure information sharing in a virtual multi-agency team environment. *Electronic Notes in Theoretical Computer Science*, 179, 97-109.

Ahire1, S. L., Golhar, D. Y., & Waller, M. A. (1996). Development and validation of TQM implementation constructs. *Decision Sciences*, 27(1), 23-56.

Aiken, M., & Alford, R. (1970). Community structure and innovation: The case of urban renewal. *American Sociological Review*, 35, 660-665.

Aldrich, H. E. & Pfeffer, J. (1976). Environments of organizations. *Annual Review of Sociology*, 2, 79-105.

Aldrich, H. E. & Ruef, M. (2006). *Organizations Evolving, Second Edition.* Sage. Thousand Oaks, CA.

Allen, M. P. (1997). *Understanding Regression Analysis.* Plenum. New York, NY.

American Friends Service Committee, et al. v. City and County of Denver, 2004 U.S. Dist. LEXIS 18474.

Archbold, C. A. & Maguire, E. R. (2002). Studying civil suits against the police: A serendipitous finding of sample selection bias. *Police Quarterly*, 5(2), 222-49.

Armenakis, A. A. & Bedeian, A. G. (1995). Organizational change: A review of theory and research in the 1990s. *Journal of Management*, 25(3), 293-315.

Auten, J. H. (1981). The paramilitary organization of police and police professionalism. *Police Studies: International Review of Police Development*, 4, 67-72.

Association of Chief Police Officers [ACPO]. (2005). *Guidance on the National Intelligence Model.* Retrieved from http://www.acpo.police.uk/asp/policies/Data/nim2005.pdf.

Bachman, R. & Paternoster, R. (2004). *Statistics for Criminology and Criminal Justice.* Second Edition. McGraw-Hill. New York.

Baldridge, V. & Burnham, R. (1975). Organizational innovation: Individual, organizational, and environmental impacts. *Administrative Science Quarterly*, 20, 165-176.

Barnett, W., & Carroll, G. (1995). Modeling internal organizational change. *Annual Review of Sociology*, 21(3), 217–236.

Bayley, D. H. (1992). Comparative organization of the police in English-speaking countries. *Crime and Justice*, 15, 509-545.

Beck, K. & Wilson, C. (1997). Police officers' views on cultivating organizational commitment: Implications for police managers. *Policing: An International Journal of Police Strategies & Management*, 20(1), 175-195.

Berk, R. A. (2004). *Regression Analysis: A Constructive Critique.* Sage. Thousand Oaks, CA.

Bernard, H. R. (2002). *Research Methods in Anthropology: Qualitative and Quantitative Approaches, Third Edition.* Alta Mira. New York, NY.

Bittner, E. (1970). *The Functions of Police in Modern Society.* National Institute of Mental Health. Washington, DC.

Blakely, C. H., Mayer, J. P., Gottschalk, R. G., Schmitt, N., Davidson, W. S., Roitman, D. B., & Emshoff, J. G. (1987). The fidelity-adaptation debate: Implications for the implementation of public sector social programs. *American Journal of Community Psychology*, 15, 253-268.

Blau, P. M. (1970). A formal theory of differentiation in organizations. *American Sociological Review,* 35(19), 201-218.

Boland, R. J. & Tenkasi, R. V. (1995). Making and perspective taking in communities of knowing. *Organization Science*, 6(4), 350-372.

Bommer, W. H., Johnson, J. L., Rich, G. A., Podsakoff, P. M., & Mackenzie, S. B. (1995). On the interchangeability of objective and subjective measures of employee performance: A meta-analysis. *Personnel Psychology*, 48(3), 587-605.

Borum, R., Deane, M. W., Steadman, H. J. & Morrissey, J. (1998). Police perspectives on responding to mentally ill people in crisis: Perceptions of program effectiveness. *Behavioral Sciences & the Law*, 16(4), 393-405.

Bresser, R. K. & Bishop, R. C. (1983). Dysfunctional effects of formal planning: Two theoretical explanations. *The Academy of Management Review*, 8(4), 588-599.

Brown, B. (2007). Community policing in post–September 11 America: A comment on the concept of community-oriented counterterrorism. *Police Practice and Research*, 8, 239-251.

Brown, L. P. (1989). Community policing: A practical guide for police officials. *Perspectives on Policing*, 12(1). National Institute of Justice. Washington, DC.

Brown, M. M. & Brudney, J. L. (2003). Learning organizations in the public sector? A study of police agencies employing information and technology to advance knowledge. *Public Administration Review*, 63(1), 30-43.

Bryman, A. E. (2003). Imputation. In M. S. Lewis-Beck, A. E. Bryman, & T. F. Liao, (Eds.). *The SAGE Encyclopedia of Social Science Research Methods*, 477-483. Sage. Thousand Oaks, CA.

Bureau of Justice Assistance [BJA]. (2005). *Intelligence-Led Policing: The New Intelligence Architecture*. U.S. Department of Justice, Office of Justice Programs. Washington, DC.

Bureau of Justice Assistance [BJA]. (2009). *Navigating Your Agency Path to Intelligence-Led Policing*. U.S. Department of Justice, Office of Justice Programs. Washington, DC.

Bureau of Justice Statistics [BJS]. (2011). Law Enforcement Management and Administrative Statistics [LEMAS] 2003 Report. U.S. Department of Justice, Office of Justice Programs. Washington, DC. Retrieved from http://www.ojp.usdoj.gov/bjs/lawenf.htm

Burress, G. W., Giblin, M. J. & Schafer, J. A. (2010). Threatened globally, acting locally: Modeling law enforcement homeland security preparedness. *Justice Quarterly*, 21(1), 77-101.

Carmines, E. G. & Zeller, R. A. (1979). *Reliability and Validity Assessment*. Sage. Newbury Park, CA.

Carter, D. L. (2002). *The Police and the Community*. Seventh Edition. Prentice Hall. Upper Saddle River, NJ.

Carter, D. L. & Martinelli, T. J. (2007). Civil Rights and Law Enforcement Intelligence. *Police Chief Magazine*. June. Retrieved from http://www.policechiefmagazine.org/magazine/index.cfm?fuseaction=display_arch&article_id=1206&issue_id=62007

Carter, D. L. (2009). *Law Enforcement Intelligence: A Guide for State, Local and Tribal Law Enforcement Agencies, Second Edition*. U.S. Department of Justice, Office of Community Oriented Policing Services. Washington, DC.

Carter, D. L. & Carter, J. G. (2009a). Intelligence-led policing: Conceptual considerations for public policy. *Criminal Justice Policy Review*, 20(3), 310-325.

Carter, D. L. & Carter, J. G. (2009b). The intelligence fusion process for state, local and tribal law enforcement. *Criminal Justice and Behavior*, 36(12), 1323-1339

Chappell, A. T. (2009). The philosophical versus actual adoption of community policing. *Criminal Justice Review*, 34(1), 5-28.

Chappell, A. T. & Gibson, S. (2009). Community policing and homeland security policing: Friend or foe? *Criminal Justice Policy Review*, 20(3), 326-343.

Charmaz, K. (2003). Qualitative interviewing and grounded theory analysis. In J. A. Holstein & J. F. Gubrium (Eds.), *Inside Interviewing: New Lenses, New Concerns*, 311-329. Sage. London, UK.

Charmaz, K. (2006). *Constructing Grounded Theory*. Sage. London, UK.

Chermak, S. & Weiss, A. J. (2000). *Identifying Strategies to Market the Police in the News*. Final Report. US Department of Justice. National Institute of Justice. Washington, DC.

Child, J. & McGrath, R. G. (2001).Organizations unfettered: Organizational form in an information-intensive economy. *The Academy of Management Journal*, 44(6), 1135-1148.

Cole, R. (1974). *Citizen Participation and the Urban Policy Process*. Lexington Books. Lexington, MA.

Collins, J. & Porras, J. I. (2002). *Built to Last: Successful Habits of Visionary Companies*. Harper Business. New York.

Cope, N. (2004). Intelligence led policing or policing led intelligence? Integrating volume crime analysis into policing. *British Journal of Criminology*, 44, 188-203.

Corbin, J., & Strauss, A. (1990). Grounded theory research: Procedures, canons, and evaluative criteria. *Qualitative Sociology*, 13, 3-21.

Cordner, G. (1978). Open and closed models of police organizations: Traditions, dilemmas, and practical considerations. *Journal of Police Science and Administration*, 6(1), 22-34.

Crank, J. P. (1989). Civilianization in small and medium police departments in Illinois, 1973-1986. *Journal of Criminal Justice*, 17(3), 167-177.

Crank, J. P. (1990). The influence of environmental and organizational factors on police style in urban and rural environments. *Journal of Research in Crime and Delinquency*, 27, 166-189.

Crank, J. P. (1994). Watchmen and the community: Myth and institutionalization in policing. *Law and Society Review*, 28, 325-351.

Crank, J. P. (2003). Institutional theory of police: a review of the state of the art. *Policing: An International Journal of Police Strategies & Management*, 26(2), 186-207.

Crescenzo, L. D. (2007). *Application of the United Kingdom's National Intelligence Model to United States Law Enforcement.* Maters Thesis. Mercyhurst College. May.

Creswell, J. W. (2007). *Qualitative Inquiry and Research Design: Choosing Among Five Approaches.* Second Edition. Sage. Thousand Oaks, CA.

Culnan, M. J. (2007). Environmental scanning: the effects of task complexity and source accessibility on information gathering behavior. *Decision Sciences*, 14(2), 194-206.

Daft, R. L. (1982). Bureaucratic Versus Non-bureaucratic Structure and the Process of Innovation and Change. In S. B. Bacharach (Ed.), *Research in the Sociology of Organizations*, 129-166. JAI Press. Greenwich, CT.

Daft, R.L. (2001). *Organizational Theory and Design.* Seventh Edition. South Western Publishing. Cincinnati, OH.

Damanpour, F. (1991). Organizational innovation: A meta-analysis of effects of determinants and moderators. *The Academy of Management Journal*, 34(3), 555-590.

Damanpour, F., & Evan, W. M. (1984). Organizational innovation and performance: The problem of organizational lag. *Administrative Science Quarterly*, 29, 392-409.

de Lancer Julnes, P. & Holzer, M. (2001). Promoting the utilization of performance measures in public organizations: An empirical study of factors affecting adoption and implementation. *Public Administration Review*, 61(6), 693-708.

Denzin, N. (1970). Strategies of Multiple Triangulation. In N. Denzin, (Ed.). *The Research Act in Sociology: A Theoretical Introduction to Sociological Method*, 297-313. McGraw-Hill. New York.

Department of Homeland Security [DHS]. (2008). *Baseline Capabilities for State and Major Urban Area Fusion Centers.* Global Justice Information Sharing Initiative. US Department of Justice. Retrieved from http://www.it.ojp.gov/documents/baselinecapabilitiesa.pdf

de Vaus, D. (2001). *Research Design in Social Research.* Sage. Thousand Oaks, CA.

Dewar, R., & Dutton, J. (1986). The adoption of radical and incremental innovations: An empirical analysis. *Management Science*, 32, 1422-1322.

Dey, E. L. (1997). Working with low survey response rates: The efficacy of weighting adjustments. *Journal Research in Higher Education*, 38(2), 215-227.

Dodgson, M. (1993). Organizational learning: A review of some literatures. *Organization Studies*, 14(3), 375-394.

Downs, G. W. (1976). *Bureaucracy, Innovation and Public Policy*. DC Health. Lexington, MA.

Downs, G. W. & Mohr, L. B. (1976). Conceptual issues in the study of innovation. *Administrative Science Quarterly*, 21(4), 700-714.

DuBrin, A. (1978). *Fundamentals of Organizational Behavior*. Pergamon Press. New York.

Dunning, T., & Freedman, D. A. (2008). Modeling section effects. In W. Outhwaite & S. Turner (Eds.). *Handbook of Social Science Methodology*, 232-245. Sage, London.

Durlak, J. A. (1998). Why program implementation is important. *Journal of Prevention and Intervention in the Community*, 17, 5-18.

Eck, J. E. (1983). *Solving Crimes: The Investigation of Burglary and Robbery*. Police Executive Research Forum. Washington, D.C.

Edwards, J. R. & Parry, M. E. (1993). On the use of polynomial regression equations as an alternative to difference scores in organizational research. *The Academy of Management Journal*, 36(6), 1577-1613.

Eisenhardt, K. M. (1989). Building theories from case study research. *Academy of Management Review*, 14(4), 532-550.

Eisinger, P. (2004). The American city in the age of terror: A preliminary assessment of the effects of September 11. *Urban Affairs Review*, 40, 115-130.

Eltinge, J. L. & Sribney, W. M. (1997). Some basic concepts for design-based analysis of complex survey data. *Stata Technical Bulletin*, 6(31).

Erez, P. M., Earley, C. & Hulin, C. L. (1985). The impact of participation on goal acceptance and performance: A two-step model. *The Academy of Management Journal*, 28(1), 50-66.

Ericson, R. V. & Haggerty, K. D. (1997). *Policing the Risk Society*. Clarendon Press. Oxford.

Etzioni, A. (1960). Two approaches to organizational analysis: A critique and a suggestion. *Administrative Science Quarterly*, 5(2), 257-278.

Feagin, J., Orum, A. & Sjoberg, G. (1991). *A Case for Case Study*. Chapel Hill, NC. University of North Carolina Press.

Federal Bureau of Investigation [FBI]. (2011). Uniform Crime Report for 2009. Police Employee Data. Retrieved from http://www2.fbi.gov/ucr/cius2009/police/index.html

Fitzpatrick, J. L. & Sanders, J. R. (2003). *Program Evaluation: Alternative Approaches and Practical Guidelines*. Allyn & Bacon. Upper Saddle River, NJ.

Florida Department of Law Enforcement [FDLE]. (2010). http://www.fdle.state.fl.us/content/getdoc/595aab23-67a2-4dd8-9bdb-e0dac2f25559/OSI-Home.aspx

Florida Fusion Center [FFC]. (2010a). Interview with Florida Fusion Center Executive. Personal Communication. February 3, 2010. Tallahassee, FL.

Florida Fusion Center [FFC]. (2010b). *Florida Fusion Center Privacy Policy*. Version 3.0. Retrieved from http://www.fdle.state.fl.us/Content/Florida-Fusion-Center/Menu/Privacy-Policy.aspx

Ford, J. K., Weissbein, D. A. & Plamondon, K. E. (2003). Distinguishing organizational from strategy commitment: Linking officers' commitment to community policing to job behaviors and satisfaction. *Justice Quarterly*, 20(1), 159-186.

Forsyth, W. A. (2005). *State and Local Intelligence Fusion Centers: An Evaluative Approach in Modeling a State Fusion Center*. Thesis. Naval Post-Graduate School. Monterey, CA.

Foster, C., & Cordner, G. (2005). *The Impact of Terrorism on State Law Enforcement: Adjusting to New Roles and Changing Conditions*. Council of State Governments & Eastern Kentucky University.

Fox, J. (1997). *Applied Regression Analysis, Linear Models, and Related Methods*. Sage. Thousand Oaks, CA.

Franklin, R. A. (2004). *Criminal Intelligence Training for Law Enforcement: A Survey of Current Programs, Mandates and Instructional Materials Available to POST Agencies*. International Association of Directors of Law Enforcement Standards and Training. Retrieved from http://www.iadlest.org/crimtrain.pdf.

Friedmann, J. (1987). *Planning in the Public Domain*. Princeton University Press. Princeton, NJ.

Friedmann, R. R., & Cannon, W. J. (2007). Homeland security and community policing: Competing or complementing public safety policies. *Journal of Homeland Security and Emergency Management*, 4(4), 1-20.

Fuentes, J. R. (2006). *New Jersey State Police Practical Guide to Intelligence-led Policing*. New Jersey State Police. September. Retrieved from http://www.state.nj.us/njsp/divorg/invest/pdf/ njsp_ilpguide_010907.pdf

Georgiou, P. (1973). The goal paradigm and notes towards a counter paradigm. *Administrative Science Quarterly*, 18(3), 291-310.

Georgopoulos, B.S. & Tannenbaum, A. S. (1957). A study of organizational effectiveness. *American Sociological Review*, 22(5), 534-540.

Gerber, B. J., Cohen, D. B., Cannon, B., Patterson, D., & Steward, K. (2005). On the front line: American cities and the challenge of homeland security preparedness. *Urban Affairs Review*, 41, 182-210.

Giblin, M. J., Schafer, J. A., & Burruss, G. W. (2009). Homeland security in the heartland: Risk, preparedness, and organizational capacity. *Criminal Justice Policy Review*, 20(3), 274-289.

Global Intelligence Working Group [GIWG]. (2003). *National Criminal Intelligence Sharing Plan*. Retrieved from http://www.it.ojp.gov/documents/National_Criminal_Intelligence_ Sharing_Plan.pdf.

Global Intelligence Working Group [GIWG]. (2005). *Guidelines for establishing and operating fusion centers at the local, state, tribal and federal level*. Washington, DC: U.S. Department of Homeland Security. Retrieved from http://it.ojp.gov/documents/fusion_center _guidelines_law_enforcement.pdf.

Gorad, S. & Taylor, C. (2004). *Combining Methods in Educational and Social Research*. Open University Press. New York, NY.

Grant, R. M. (1996). Prospering in dynamically-competitive environments: Organizational capability as knowledge integration. *Organization Science*, 7(4), 375-387.

Graphia-Joyal, Renee. (2010). Are fusion centers achieving their intended purposes? Findings from a qualitative study on the internal efficacy of state fusion centers. *International Association of Law Enforcement Intelligence Analysts Journal*, 19(1), 54-76.

Greene, J. R. (1989). Police and community relations: Where have we been and where are we going?. In R. Dumham & R. Alpert (Eds.), *Critical Issues in Policing: Contemporary Readings*, 349-368. Waveland Press. Prospect Heights, IL.

Greene, J. R. (2000). *Community Policing in America: Changing the Nature, Structure, and Function of the Police.* Washington, DC. National Criminal Justice Resource Service. Retrieved from http://www.ncjrs.gov/criminal_justice2000/vol_3/03g.pdf.

Greenberg, M., Domitrovich, C., Graczyk, P., & Zins, J. (2001). *The study of implementation in school-based preventive interventions: Theory, research, and practice.* Center for Mental Health Services, Substance Abuse and Mental Health Administration, U. S. Department of Health and Human Services. Washington, DC.

Griffin, R. W., Welsh, A., & Moorhead, G. (1981). Perceived task characteristics and employee performance: A literature review. *The Academy of Management Review*, 6(4), 655-664.

Guidetti, R. A. & Martinelli, T. J. (2009). Intelligence-led policing - A strategic framework. *Police Chief Magazine.* October. Retrieved from http://www.policechiefmagazine.org/magazine/index.cfm?fuseaction=display_arch&article_id=1918&issue_id=102009

Guyot, D. (1979). Bending granite: Attempts to change the rank structure of American police departments. *Journal of Police Science and Administration*, 7(3), 253-287.

Hagan, F. E. (2003). *Research Methods in Criminal Justice and Criminology, Sixth Edition.* Pearson Education. Boston, MA.

Hall, R. H., Haas, J. E., & Johnson, N. J. (1967). Organizational size, complexity, and formalization. *Administrative Science Quarterly*, 32, 903-912.

Hamel, J., Dufour, S. & Fortin, D. (1993). *Case Study Methods.* Sage. Newbury Park, CA

Hammersley, M. & Atkinson, P. (1995). *Ethnography: Principles in Practice.* Second Edition. Routledge. London, UK.

Hanna, M. T. & Freeman, J. (1984). Structural inertia and organizational change. *American Sociological Review*, 49(2), 149-164.

Hardy, M. A. & Bryman, A. (2009). *Handbook of Data Analysis.* Sage. Thousand Oaks, CA.

Heaton, R. (2000). The prospects for intelligence-led policing: Some historical and quantitative considerations. *Policing and Society*, 9(4), 337-356.

Helms, R., & Gutierrez, R. S. (2007). Federal subsidies and evidence of progressive change: A quantitative assessment of the effects of targeted grants on manpower and innovation in large U.S. police agencies. *Police Quarterly*, 10, 87-107.

Henry, V. E. & Bratton, W. J. (2003). *Compstat Paradigm: Management Accountability in Policing, Business and the Public Sector*. Looseleaf Law Publications. Flushing, NY.

Her Majesty's Inspectorate of Constabulary [HMIC]. (1997). *Policing with Intelligence*. London, UK.

Higgins, O. (2004). Rising to the collection challenge. In, J. H. Ratcliffe (Ed.), *Strategic Thinking in Criminal Intelligence*, 99-118. Federation Press. Sydney, Australia.

Holder, H. (1987). *Control Issues in Alcohol Abuse Prevention: Strategies for States and Communities*. JAI Press. Greenwich, CT.

Home Office. (2004). *National Policing Plan 2005-08: Safer, Stronger Communities*. London. UK.

Homeland Security Council [HSC]. (2007). *National Strategy for Homeland Security*. Office of Homeland Security. U.S. White House. Washington, DC. Retrieved from http://www.dhs.gov/xlibrary/assets/nat_strat_homelandsecurity_2007.pdf

House Committee on Homeland Security [HCHS]. (2009). *Homeland Security Intelligence: Its Relevance and Limitations*. U.S. House of Representatives. Subcommittee on Intelligence, Information Sharing, and Terrorism Risk Assessment. Retrieved from http://homeland.house.gov/SiteDocuments/20090318101140-59912.pdf

Howe, K. R. (1988). Against the quantitative-qualitative incompatibility thesis or dogmas die hard. *Educational Researcher*, 17, 10–16.

Hsu, C. K., Marsh, R. M., & Mannari, H. (1983). An examination of the structural determinants of organizational structure. *American Journal of Sociology*, 88, 975-996.

Ingraham, P. W., Thompson, J. R., & Sanders, R. P. (1998). *Transforming Government: Lessons from the Reinvention Laboratories*. Jossey-Bass. San Francisco, CA.

International Association of Chiefs of Police [IACP]. (2002). *Criminal intelligence sharing: A national plan for intelligence-led policing at the local, state and federal levels.* Recommendations from the Intelligence Summit. Retrieved from http://epic.org/privacy/fusion/intelsharerpt.pdf.

International Association of Law Enforcement Intelligence Analysts [IALEIA]. (1997). *Intelligence-Led Policing: International Perspectives on Policing in the 21st Century.* Lawrenceville, NJ.

International Association of Law Enforcement Intelligence Analysts [IALEIA]. (2004). *Law Enforcement Analytic Standards.* Washington, DC. Global Justice Information Sharing Initiative. US Department of Justice, Office of Justice Programs.

Jenkins, C. R. & Dillman, D. A. (1995). Toward a theory of self-administered survey design. In, L. Lyberg, P. Biemer, M. Collins, E. DeLeeuw, C. Dippo, N. Schwarz, & D. Trewin, *Survey Measurement and Process Quality.* Wiley-Interscience. New York.

Jick, T. D. (1983). Mixing qualitative and quantitative research methods: Triangulation in action. In J. van Maanen, (Ed.). *Qualitative Methodology,* 135-148. Sage. Beverley Hills, CA.

Johnson, R. B. & Onwuegbuzie, A. J. (2004). Mixed methods research: A research paradigm whose time has come. *Educational Researcher,* 33(7), 14–26.

Johnson, R. B & Onwuegbuzie, A. J. (2007). Toward a definition of mixed methods research. *Journal of Mixed Methods Research,* 1(2), 112-133.

Johnson, W. J., Leach, M. P. & Liu, A. H. (1999). Theory testing using case studies in business-to-business research. *Industrial Marketing Management,* 28(3), 201-213.

Jorgenson, D. O. & Papciak, A. S. (1981). The effects of communication, resource feedback, and identifiability on behavior in a simulated commons. *Journal of Experimental Social Psychology,* 1 17(4), 373-385.

Justice Information Exchange Model [JIEM]. (2006). *Conceptual Framework.* The National Consortium for Justice Information and Statistics. Retrieved from http://www.jiem.search.org/JIEMConcepts.pdf

Kappelman, L. & Prybutok, V. (1995). Empowerment, motivation, training, and TQM program implementation success. *Industrial Management*, 37(3), 12-15.

Katz, C. (2001). The establishment of a police gang unit: An examination of organizational and environmental factors. *Criminology*, 39(1), 37-73.

Katz, C., Maguire, E. & Roncek, D. (2002). The creation of specialized police gang units. *Policing: An International Journal of Police Strategy and Management*, 25(3), 472-506.

Kennedy, M. M. (1979). Generalizing from single case studies. *Evaluation Review*, 3(4), 661-678.

Kim, J. & Mueller, C. W. (1978). *Factor Analysis: Statistical Methods and Practical Issues: Quantitative Applications in the Social Sciences*. Sage. Thousand Oaks, CA.

Kimberly, J. R. (1981). Managerial innovation. In P. C. Nystrom and W. H. Starbuck (Eds.) *Handbook of Organizational Design*, 84-104. Volume 1. Oxford University Press. New York, NY.

Kimberly, J. R. & Evanisko, M. J. (1981). Organizational innovation: The influence of individual, organizational, and contextual factors on hospital adoption of technological and administrative innovations. *The Academy of Management Journal*, 24(4), 689-713.

King, N. (1994). The Qualitative Research Interview. In C. Cassell & G. Symon (Eds.), *Qualitative Methods in Organizational Research*, 14-36). Sage. London, UK.

King, W. R. (2000). Measuring police innovation: Issues and measurement. *Policing: An International Journal of Police Strategy and Management*, 23(3), 303-317.

King, W. R. (1999). Time, constancy, and change in American municipal police organizations. *Police Quarterly*, 2(3), 338-364.

King, W. R. (1998). *Innovativeness in American Municipal Police Organizations. Doctoral dissertation*. University of Cincinnati. Cincinnati, OH.

Klinger, D. (2003). Spreading diffusion in criminology. *Criminology and Public Policy*, 2(3), 461-468.

Klug, D., Peterson, J. & Stoney, D. (1992). *Automated Fingerprint Identification Systems: Their Acquisition, Management, Performance and Organizational Impact*. Report to the National Institute of Justice. NIJ Grant 89-IJCX0051. Washington, DC.

Kuykendall, J & Roberg, R. (1982). Mapping police organizational change: From a mechanistic toward an organic model. *Criminology*, 20(2), 241-256.

Lan, Z. & Rainey, H. G. (1992). Goals, rules, and effectiveness in public, private, and hybrid organizations: More evidence on frequent assertions about differences. *Journal of Public Administration Research and Theory*, 2(1), 5-28.

Langworthy, R. H. (1986). *The Structure of Police Organizations*. Praeger. New York.

Latham, G. P. & Yukl, G. A. (1975). A review of research on the application of goal setting in organizations. *The Academy of Management Journal*, 18(4), 824-845.

Lee, E. S., Forthofer, R. N., & Lorimor, R. J. (1986). Analysis of complex sample survey data: Problems and strategies. *Sociological Methods Research*, 15(1-2), 69-100.

Lee, J. V. (2010). Policing after 9/11: Community policing in the age of homeland security. *Police Quarterly,* 13(4), 347-366.

Lewis, S., Rosenberg, H., & Sigler, R. T. (1999). Acceptance of community policing among police officers and police administrators. *Policing: An International Journal of Police Strategies & Management*, 22(4), 567-588.

Licate, D. A. (2010). *Innovations and Organizational Change in Ohio Police Departments.* Doctoral dissertation, Kent State University.

Lingamneni, J. R. (1979). Resistance to change in police organizations: The diffusion paradigm. *Criminal Justice Review*, 4(2), 17-26.

Little, R. J. & Rubin, D. B. (1989). The analysis of social science data with missing values. *Sociological Methods Research*, 18(2-3), 292-326.

London, M. & Smither, J. W. (1995). Can multi-source feedback change perceptions of goal accomplishment, self-evaluations, and performance-related outcomes? Theory-based applications and directions for research. *Personnel Psychology*, 48(4), 803-839.

Lumley, T. (2004). Analysis of complex survey samples. *Journal of Statistical Software*, 9(1), 1-19.

Maguire, E. R. (2003). *Organizational Structure in American Police Agencies: Context, Complexity and Control*. State University of New York Press. Albany, NY.

Maguire, E. (1997). Structural change in large municipal police organizations during the community policing era. *Justice Quarterly*, 14(3), 547-576.

Maguire, E. R., Kuhns, J. B., Uchida, C. D. & Cox, S. M. (1997). Patterns of community policing in nonurban America. *Journal of Research in Crime and Delinquency*, 34(3), 368-394.

Maguire, E. R., Shin, Y., Zhao, J., & Hassell, K. D. (2003). Structural change in large police agencies during the 1990s. *Policing: An International Journal of Police Strategies & Management*, 26(2), 251-275.

Maloney, M. M., Johnson, S. G., & Zellmer-Bruhn, M. E. (2010). Assessing group-level constructs under missing data conditions: A Monte Carlo simulation. *Small Group Research*, 41(3), 281–307.

Manhattan Institute for Policy Research. (2006). *Hard Won Lessons: The New Paradigm - Merging Law Enforcement and Counterterrorism Strategies*. January. Safe Cities Project.

Manning, P. K. (2001). Technology's ways: Information technology, crime analysis, and the rationalization of policing. *Criminal Justice: The International Journal of Policy and Practice*, 1, 83-103.

Mansfield, E. R. & Helms, B. P. (1982). Detecting multicollinearity. *The American Statistician*, 36(3), 158-160.

Martin, S. E. (1986). Policing career criminals: An examination of an innovative crime control program. *Journal of Criminal Law and Criminology*, 77(4), 1159-1182.

Martin, S. E. & Sherman, L. W. (1986). Selective apprehension: A police strategy for repeat offenders. *Criminology*, 24(1), 155-172.

Martinelli, T. J. (2009). ILP abbreviations for the ISE and NCISP can spell trouble. *Police Chief Magazine*. October.

Martinez, R. A. (1997). *High Intensity Drug Trafficking Areas Intelligence Program*. In, A. Smith (Ed.), *Intelligence-Led Policing: International Perspectives on in the 21st Century*. International Association of Law Enforcement Intelligence Analysts. September.

Mastrofski, S. D. (1998). *Community policing and police organizational structure*. In J. P. Brodeur (Ed.) How to Recognize Good Policing: Problems and Issues, 88-106. Sage. Thousand Oaks, CA.

Mastrofski, S. D., Worden, R. E & Snipes, J. B. (1995). Law enforcement in a time of community policing, *Criminology*, 33(4), 539-564.

Matland, R. E. (1995). Synthesizing the implementation literature: The ambiguity-conflict model of policy implementation. *Journal of Public Administration Research and Theory*, 5(2), 145-174.

Maton, K. I. & Salem, D. A. (1995). Organizational characteristics of empowering community settings: A multiple case study approach. *American Journal of Community Psychology*, 23(5), 631-656.

Maxfield, M. G. & Babbiee, E. (2006). *Research Methods for Criminal Justice and Criminology, Second Edition*. Wadsworth. Belmont, CA.

McElroy, M. W. (2000). Integrating complexity theory, knowledge management and organizational learning. *Journal of Knowledge Management*, 4(3), 195-203.

McGarrell, E. F., Freilich, J. D. & Chermak, S. (2007). Intelligence-led policing as a framework for responding to terrorism. *Journal of Contemporary Criminal Justice*, 23(2), 142-158.

Miles, M. & Huberman, M. (1984). *Qualitative Data Analysis*. Sage. Beverly Hills, CA.

Mohr, L. B. (1982). *Explaining Organizational Behavior*. Jossey-Bass. San Francisco, CA.

Monell v. Department of Social Services. 436 U.S. 658 (1978). U.S. Supreme Court

Moonen, M., Cattrysse, D. & Defoor, R. (2008). Quantitative support for COP and ILP implementations: Belgian case VLAS policing, 2(3), 375–385.

Moore, M. H. (1992). Problem-solving and community policing. *Crime and Justice*, 15, 99-158.

Moore, M. H. (2003). Sizing up CompStat: An important administrative innovation in policing. *Criminology and Public Policy*, 2(3), 469-494.

Moore, M., Sparrow, M. & Spelman, W. (1997). Innovations in Policing: From Production Lines to Job Shops. In A. Altshuler & R. Behn (Eds.), *Innovation in American Government*. Brookings Institute Press. Washington, DC.

Moore, M. H. & Stephens, D. W. (1991). *Beyond Command and Control: The Strategic Management of Police Departments*. Police Executive Research Forum. Washington, DC.

Morabito, M. S. (2008). The adoption of police innovation: The role of the political environment. *Policing: An International Journal of Police Strategies & Management*, 31(3), 466-484.

Morabito, M. S. (2010). Understanding community policing as an innovation: Patterns of adoption. *Crime & Delinquency*, 56(4), 564-587.

Morgan, D. L. (2007). Paradigms lost and pragmatism regained: Methodological implications of combining qualitative and quantitative methods. *Journal of Mixed Methods Research*, 1, 48-76.

Morreale, S. A. & Lambert, D. E. (2009). Homeland security and the police mission. *Journal of Homeland Security and Emergency Management*, 6(1), Article 68, 1-19.

Mullen, K. (1996). *The Computerization of Law Enforcement: A Diffusion of Innovation Study*. Doctoral dissertation, State University of New York at Albany.

National Commission on Terrorists Attacks Upon the United States [National Commission]. (2004). *9/11 Commission Report*. Retrieved from http://govinfo.library.unt.edu/911/report/index.htm

Nenneman, M. (2008). *An Examination of State and Local Fusion Centers and Data Collection Methods*. Thesis. Naval Post-Graduate School. Monterey, CA.

Nickels, E. (2008). Good guys wear black: Uniform color and citizen impressions of police. *Policing: An International Journal of Police Strategies & Management*, 31(1), 77-92.

Nunnally, J.C., & Bernstein, I.H. (1994). *Psychometric Theory, Third Edition*. McGraw-Hill. New York, NY.

O'brien, R. M. (2007). A caution regarding rules of thumb for variance inflation factors. *Quality & Quantity*, 41(5), 673-690.

Office of Community Oriented Policing Services. (2009). United States Department of Justice. Retrieved from http://www.cops.usdoj.gov/default.asp?item=36

Oliver, W. M. (2000). The third generation of community policing: Moving through innovation, diffusion, and institutionalization. *Police Quarterly*, 3(4), 367-388.

Oliver, W. M. (2006). The fourth era of policing: Homeland security. *International Review of Law, Computers & Technology*, 20(1 & 2), 49 - 62.

Oliver, W. M. (2009). Policing for homeland security: Policy and research. *Criminal Justice Policy Review*, 20(3), 253-260.

Osborne, D. (2006). *Out of Bounds: Innovation and Change in Law Enforcement Intelligence Analysis*. Joint Military Intelligence College. Thesis. Washington, DC.

Osborne, D. & Gaebler, T. (1992). *Reinventing Government*. Addison Wesley. Reading, MA.

O'Toole, L. J. (1997). Treating networks seriously: Practical and research-based agendas in public administration. *Public Administration Review*, 57(1), 45-52.

Ouchi, W. (1979). A conceptual framework for the design of organizational control mechanisms. *Management Science*, 25(9), 833-848.

Pate, T., Bowers, R. A. and Parks, R. (1976). *Three Approaches to Criminal Apprehension in Kansas City: An Evaluation Report*. Police Foundation. Washington DC.

Pett, M. A, Lackey, N. R. & Sullivan, J. J. (2003). *Making Sense of Factor Analysis: The Use of Factor Analysis for Instrument Development in Health Care Research*. Sage. Thousand Oaks, CA.

Pierce, J. L. & Delbecq, A. (1977). Organizational structure, individual attitudes, and innovation. *Academy of Management Review*, 2, 27-37.

Perrow, C. (1967). A framework for the comparative analysis of organizations. *American Sociological Review*, 32(2), 194-208.

Perrow, C. (1968). *Organizational goals*. In, The International Encyclopedia of the Social Sciences, II, 305-316. Macmillan. New York, NY.

Peterson, R, D. (1988). Youthful offender designations and sentencing in the New York criminal courts. *Social Problems*, 35(2), 111-130.

Pettigrew, A. M., Woodman, R. W. & Cameron, K. S. (2001). Studying organizational change and development: Challenges for future research. *The Academy of Management Journal*, 44(4), 697-713.

Pfeffer, J. & Sutton, R. I. (2000). *The Knowing-Doing Gap: How Smart Companies Turn Knowledge into Action*. Harvard Business School Press. Boston, MA.

Phllips, L. (1981). Assessing measurement error in key informant reports: A methodological note on organizational analysis in marketing. *Journal of Marketing Research*, 18(4), 395-415.

Hoover, L. T. (Ed.) (1998). *Police Program Evaluation*. Police Executive Research Forum. Washington, DC.

Quarmby, N. (2004). Futures work in strategic criminal intelligence. In, J. H. Ratcliffe (Ed.), *Strategic Thinking in Criminal Intelligence*, 129-147. Federation Press. Sydney, Australia.

Quinn, R. E. & Rohrbaugh, J. (1983). A spatial model of effectiveness criteria: Towards a competing values approach to organizational analysis. *Management Science*, 29(3), 363-377.

Radin, B. A. (2000). The government performance and results act and the tradition of federal management reform: Square pegs in round holes? *Journal of Public Administration Research and Theory*, 10(1), 111-135.

Ratcliffe, J. H. (2002). Intelligence-led policing and the problems of turning rhetoric into practice. *Policing & Society*, 12(1), 53-66.

Ratcliffe, J. H. (2003). Intelligence-led policing. *Trends and Issues in Crime and Criminal Justice*, 248.

Ratcliffe, J. H. (2005). The effectiveness of police intelligence management: A New Zealand case study. *Police Practice and Research*, 6(5), 434-445.

Ratcliffe, JH (2008a) *Intelligence-Led Policing*, Willan Publishing: Cullompton, UK.

Ratcliffe, J. H. (2008b). Intelligence-led policing. In R. Wortley & L. Mazerolle (Eds.), *Environmental Criminology and Crime Analysis* (pp. 263-282). Willan Publishing. Cullompton, UK.

Ratcliffe, J. H., & Guidetti, R. A. (2008). State police investigative structure and the adoption of intelligence-led policing. *Policing: An International Journal of Police Strategies and Management*, 31(1), 109-128.

Reisig, M. D. & Giacomazzi, A. L. (1998). Citizen perceptions of community policing: Are attitudes toward police important?. *Policing: An International Journal of Police Strategies & Management*, 21(3), 547 - 561.

Ratcliffe, J. H. & Walden, K. (2010). State police and the intelligence center: A study of intelligence flow to and from the street. *International Association of Law Enforcement Intelligence Analysts Journal*, 19(1), 1-19.

Reiss, A. J. (1971). *The police and the public*. Yale University Press. New Haven, CT.

Reiss, A. J. & Bordua, D. J. (1967). Environment and organization: A perspective on police. In D. J. Bordua (Ed.), *The Police: Six Sociological Essays*, 25-55. Wiley. New York.

Roberg, R. R., Kuykendall, J. (1990). *Police Organization and Management: Behavior, Theory and Processes*. Wadsworth Cole. Belmont, CA.

Roberg, R. R., Kuykendall, J. & Novak, K. (2002). *Police Management, Third Edition*. Roxbury. Los Angeles.

Roberts, G. E. (2003). Employee performance appraisal system participation: A technique that works. *Public Personnel Management*, 32(1), 89-98.

Rogelberg, S. G., Fisher, G. G., Maynard, D. C., Hakel, M. D. & Horvath, M. (2001). Attitudes toward surveys: Development of a measure and its relationship to respondent behavior. *Organizational Research Methods*, 4(1), 3-25.

Rogers, E. (2003). *Diffusion of Innovations*. 5th Edition. The Free Press. New York, NY.

Rogers, E. & Shoemaker, F. (1971). *Communication of Innovations: A Cross-Cultural Approach*. Second Edition. The Free Press. New York, NY.

Rojek, J., Kaminski, R. J., Smith, M. R., & Scheer, C. (2007). South Carolina law enforcement training survey: A national and state analysis. Unpublished manuscript. Department of Criminology and Criminal Justice. University of South Carolina.

Root, F. S. (2006). *Law Enforcement Intelligence Critical Elements*. Frank Root. Phoenix, AZ.

Ross, D. L. (2000). Emerging trends in police failure to train liability. *Policing: An International Journal of Police Strategies & Management*, 23(2), 169-93.

Ruscio, K. P. (1996). Trust, democracy, and public management: A theoretical argument. *Journal of Public Administration Research and Theory*, 6(3), 461-477.

Saari, S. C. (2010). *Fusion Centers: Securing America's Heartland from Threats*. Thesis. Naval Post-Graduate School. Monterey, CA.

Schafer, J. A., Burruss, G. W., & Giblin, M. J. (2009). Measuring homeland security innovation in small municipal agencies: Policing in a post-9/11 world. *Police Quarterly*, 12(3), 263-288.

Schafer, J. L. & Schenker, N. (2000). Inference with imputed conditional means. *Journal. Journal of the American Statistical Association,* 95, 144-154.

Scheider, M. C., Chapman, R. & Schapiro, A. (2009). Towards the unification of policing innovations under community policing. *Policing: An International Journal of Police Strategies & Management,* 32(4), 694-718.

Schofield, J. W. (2002). Increasing the generalizability of qualitative research. In, M. Huberman & M. B. Miles (Eds.), *The Qualitative Researcher's Companion: Classic and Contemporary Readings,* 171-203. Sage. Thousand Oaks, CA.

Schwandt, D. R. & Marquardt, M. J. (2000). *Organizational Learning: From World-Class Theories to Global Best Practices.* St. Lucie Press. Boca Raton, FL.

Shane, J. (2004). CompStat process. *FBI Law Enforcement Bulletin,* 73(2), 12-23.

Sheehan, K. (2001). E-mail survey response rates: a review. *Journal of Computer-Mediated Communication,* 6(2), 0.

Sheptycki, J. (2000). Editorial reflections on surveillance and intelligence-led policing. *Policing and Society,* 9(4), 311-314.

Silverman, E. (1999). *NYPD Battles Crime: Innovative Strategies in Policing.* Northeastern University Press. Boston.

Simeone, Jr., M. J. (2007). *The Integration of Virtual Public-Private Partnerships in Local Law Enforcement to Achieve Enhanced Intelligence-Led Policing.* Thesis. Naval Post-Graduate School. Monterey, CA.

Simic, M, Johnston, L. G., Platt, L., Baros, S., Andjelkovic, V, Novotny, T. & Rhodes, T. (2006). Exploring barriers to 'respondent driven sampling' in sex worker and drug-injecting sex worker populations in Eastern Europe. *Journal of Urban Health,* 83(1), 6-15.

Skogan, W. G. (2004). Community Policing: Common Impediments to Success. In L. Fridell & M. A. Wycoff (Eds.) *Community Policing: The Past, Present, and Future,* 159-167. Police Executive Research Forum. Washington, DC.

Skogan, W. G. & Hartnett, S. M. (1997). *Community Policing, Chicago Style.* Oxford University Press. New York.

Skogan, W. G. & Hartnett, S. M. (2005). The diffusion of information technology in policing. *Police Practice and Research,* 6(5), 401-417.

Skogan, W. G. (1998). *Community participation and community policing.* In J. P. Brodeur (Ed.) How to Recognize Good Policing: Problems and Issues, 88-106. Sage. Thousand Oaks, CA.

Skolnick, J. & Bayley, D. (1986). *The New Blue Line: Police Innovation in Six American Cities.* The Free Press. New York, NY.

Smith, A. (1997). *Towards Intelligence-Led Policing: The RCMP Experience.* In, A. Smith (Ed.), *Intelligence-Led Policing: International Perspectives on in the 21st Century.* International Association of Law Enforcement Intelligence Analysts. September.

Southern Nevada Counter-Terrorism Center [SNCTC]. (2010). Interview with Southern Nevada Counter-Terrorism Executive. Personal Communication. April 29, 2010. Las Vegas, NV.

Sparrow, M. (1988). Implementing community policing. National Institute of Justice. *Perspectives on Policing,* 9, 1-11. Washington, DC.

Spelman, W., Moore, M. & Young, R. (1992). *The Diffusion of Innovations and the Creation of Innovative Police Organizations.* Taubman Center for State and Local Government, Innovations Research Project. Working Papers. Kennedy School of Government. Cambridge, MA.

Stake, R. (1995). *The Art of Case Research.* Sage. Thousand Oaks, CA.

Stewart, D. M. & Morris, R. G. (2009). A new era of policing? An examination of Texas police chiefs' perceptions of homeland security. *Criminal Justice Policy Review,* 20(3), 290-309.

Strauss, A. L. & Corbin, J. M. (1990). *Basics of qualitative research: Techniques and procedures for developing grounded theory.* Sage. Newbury Park, CA.

Strauss, A. & Glaser, B. (1967). *The Discovery of Grounded Theory: Strategies for Qualitative Research.* Aldine . Chicago.

Sunshine, J. & Taylor, T. R. (2003). The role of procedural justice and legitimacy in shaping public support for policing. *Law & Society Review,* 37(3), 513-548.

Swiss, J. E. (1984). *Intergovernmental program delivery: Structuring incentives for efficiency.* In R. T. Golembiewski & A. Wildavsky (Eds.), The Cost of Federalism. Transaction Books. New Brunswick.

Tashakkori, A. & Creswell, J. W. (2008). Mixed methodology across disciplines. Editorial. *Journal of Mixed Methods Research*, 2, 3-6.

Tashakkori, A. & Teddlie, C. B. (1998). *Mixed Methodology: Combining Qualitative and Quantitative Approaches*. Sage. Thousand Oaks, CA.

Thompson, J. D. (1967). *Organizations in Action*. New Brunswick. Transaction Publishers.

Tipping, D. F. (1996). Effect of suspicion on personality ratings. In, M. Pagon (Ed.), *From Policing in Central and Eastern Europe: Comparing Firsthand Knowledge With Experience From the West*, 511-529. College of Police and Security Studies. Ljubljana, Slovenia.

Trojanowicz, R. & Bucqueroux, B. (1994). *Community Policing: How to Get Started*. Anderson. Cincinnati, OH.

Trojanowicz, R., & Bucqueroux, B. (1990). *Community Policing: A Contemporary Perspective*. Anderson. Cincinnati, OH.

Van de Ven, A. H., & Rogers, E. M. (1988). Innovation and organizations - critical perspectives. *Communication Research*, 15, 632-651.

Vaughn, M. S., Cooper, T. W. & del Carmen, R. V. (2001). Assessing legal liabilities in law enforcement: Police chiefs' views. *Crime and Delinquency*, 47(1), 3-27.

Walker, J. T. (1999). *Statistics in Criminal Justice: Analysis and Interpretation*. Aspen Publishing. Gaithersburg, MD.

Walsh, W. F. (2001). Compstat: An analysis of an emerging police managerial paradigm. *Policing: An International Journal of Police Strategies & Management*, 24(3), 347–362.

Warner, W. K., & Havens, A. E. (1968). Goal displacement and the intangibility of organizational goals. *Administrative Science Quarterly*, 12, 539-555.

Weisburd, D. & Braga, A. A. (2006). *Police Innovation: Contrasting Perspectives*. Cambridge University Press. New York, NY.

Weisburd, D. & Eck, J. E. (2004). What can police do to reduce crime, disorder, and fear? *The ANNALS of the American Academy of Political and Social Science*, 593(1), 42-65.

Weisburd, D. & Lum, C. (2005). The diffusion of computerize crime mapping in policing: Linking research and practice. *Police Practice and Research*, 6(5), 419-434.

Weisburd, D., Uchida, C. & Green, L. (Eds.) (1993). *Police Innovation and Control of the Police: Problems of Law, Order, and Community.* Springer-Verlag, New York, NY.

Weiss, A. (1998). *Informal Information Sharing Among Police Agencies.* National Institute of Justice. Washington, DC.

Weiss, A. (1997). The communication of innovation in American policing. *Policing: An International Journal of Police Strategies and Management,* 20(2), 292-310.

Weiss, A. (1992). *The Innovation Process in Public Organizations: Patterns of Diffusion and Adoption in American Policing.* Doctoral dissertation, Northwestern University.

Wejnert, B. (2002). Integrating models of diffusion of innovations: A conceptual framework. *Annual Review of Sociology,* 28, 297-326.

Whetten, D. A. (1989). What constitutes a theoretical contribution? *Academy of Management Review,* 14, 490-495.

Wilkinson, D., & Rosenbaum, D. P. (1994). The Effects of Organizational Structure on Community Policing. In D. P. Rosenbaum (Ed.) *The Challenge of Community Policing: Testing the Promises,* 110-126. Sage. Thousand Oaks, CA.

Wilson, J. M. (2006). *Community Policing in America.* Routledge. New York, NY.

Wilson, J. M. (2005). *Determinants of Community Policing: An Open Systems Model of Implementation.* Working Paper. RAND. Arlington, VA.

Wilson, J. Q. (1978). *Varieties of Police Behavior: The Management of Law & Order in Eight Communities.* Harvard University Press. Cambridge, MA.

Wilson, J. Q. (1968). *Varieties of Police Behavior: The Management of Law and Order in Eight Communities.* Harvard University Press. Cambridge, MA.

Wilson, J. Q. & Kelling, G. (1982). The police and neighborhood safety: Broken windows. *Atlantic Monthly,* 249, 29–38.

Wilson, J. Q. (1966). Innovation in Organizations: Notes Toward a Theory. In J. Thompson (Ed.). *Approaches to Organizational Design.* Pittsburgh Press. Pittsburgh, PA.

Wolfe, B. (1994). Organizational innovation: Review, critique and suggested research directions. *Journal of Management Studies,* 31(3), 405-431

Wood, J. & Shearing, C. (2007). *Imagining Security*. Willan Publishing. Cullompton. UK.

Worrall, J. L. & Gutierrez, R. S. (1999). Potential consequences of community-oriented policing for civil liability: Is there a dark side of employee empowerment?. *Review of Public Personnel Administration*, 19(2), 61-70.

Worrall, J. L. & Zhao, J. (2003). The role of the COPS Office in community policing. *Policing: An International Journal of Police Strategies & Management*, 26(1), 64-87.

Wycoff, M. A. (1994). *Community Policing Strategies*. Unpublished report. National Institute of Justice. Washington, DC.

Yates, D. L. & Pillai, V. K. (1996). Attitudes toward community policing: A causal analysis. *Social Science Journal*, 33(2), 193-210.

Yin, R. (1989). *Case Study Research: Design and Methods, Revised Edition*. Sage. Beverly Hills, CA.

Yin, R. (1994). *Case Study Research: Design and Methods*. Second Edition. Sage. Beverly Hills, CA.

Yu, J. & Cooper, H. (1983). A quantitative review of research design effects on response rates to questionnaires. *Journal of Marketing Research*, 20(1), 36-44.

Zhao, J. (1996). *Why Police Organizations Change: A Study of Community-Oriented Policing*. Police Executive Research Forum. Washington, DC.

Zhao, J., Thurman, Q. & Lovrich, N. (1995). Community oriented policing across the U.S.: Facilitators and impediments to implementation, *American Journal of Police*, 14, 11-28.

Index

CPSIA information can be obtained
at www.ICGtesting.com
Printed in the USA
LVHW091614130820
663092LV00008B/99